On Top of the World

1. Mont Collon, Switzerland   *H. N. Collinson*

On Top of the World

An Illustrated History of
Mountaineering and Mountaineers

BY

SHOWELL STYLES

WITH AN INTRODUCTION BY

FOSCO MARAINI

THE MACMILLAN COMPANY
NEW YORK

Published in the United States by The Macmillan Company, New York, 1967
Library of Congress Catalog Card Number: 67-16944

Copyright © by Showell Styles, 1967
First published 1967

Printed in the Netherlands by L. van Leer & Co., N.V.

Contents

List of Illustrations

Monochrome

viii

Colour Plates

xi

Diagrams

Acknowledgements

Acknowledgements are due to the following publishers for permission to quote copyright material: Messrs John Murray (NANGA PARBAT ADVENTURE by F. Bechtold); Messrs Paul Elek Ltd. (NANGA PARBAT by F. Herrligkofter); Messrs William Collins (K2, THE SAVAGE MOUNTAIN by C. Houston); Messrs Hodder & Stoughton (KANCHENJUNGA by Charles Evans).

Introduction

MAN'S ATTITUDE towards the sea appears to have changed very little with time. Open the Odyssey and you will find both enchantment for the "ample back of the sea" (Book V, 143) and dread of the "terrible roaring, cambering wave" (Book V, 36).

After thirty—or so—centuries, after Melville, Rimbaud, Conrad, the range of feelings does not appear substantially wider or different. Expressions of wonder and joy will still be heard when sailing the Mediterranean in full breeze, of disgust when crossing the Channel in full gale.

Man's attitude towards the mountains, on the contrary, has a curious history.

For centuries on end, at least in the West, mountains were hated and carefully avoided. Those who were obliged to cross them expressed a healthy disgust for such places. *Horridae frigoribus Alpes*, says Tacitus, while Polybius describes at length the "harsh and sterile" alpine regions, and Silius Italicus recounts their squalor: "The shadow of towering peaks hides the sky from our sight. There is no spring up there, no trace of summer's splendour. Hideous winter reigns supreme . . ." The same attitude prevails up to times not far from our own. Voltaire is quoted as cursing the Alps because they interfere with nations mingling naturally one with the other.

Exceptions can be found from time to time (Emperor Hadrian on Etna, Petrach on Mount Ventoux, Gessner on Pilatus, and so on) but the very fact that such excursions were given so much publicity shows how odd they appeared to most people. The normal attitude of fear and dislike, or utter lack of interest, was faithfully mirrored by ancient maps, in most of which coasts, islands, rivers, castles and cities were carefully delineated, while mountains were left out or vaguely shown by conventional rows of hills. Only certain passes—often dedicated to Jupiter in classical times, to St Bernard later on—were deemed worthy of notice. As for the higher peaks or the glaciers, these were anonymous features in a repugnant landscape. The Romans named only a handful of alpine peaks, and none of the highest. Even the name of Mont Blanc does not appear in maps of Savoy until quite late. In its place sometimes are found a Mount Mallet (*maledictus*, i.e. accursed), or a Mount Maudit, a fact which tells us, in six letter words, a whole story.

In more than one region mountains were thought to be a punishment from the gods for the sins of our human forefathers. Ghosts, monsters, goblins crowded the higher valleys. The city council of Lucerne is known to have forbidden access to a small lake on Mount Pilatus, where the spirit of the famous Roman administrator was said to dwell, lest it be disturbed and cause much damage. Peter III of Aragon saw "a horrible dragon of enormous size" on Mount Canigou. As late as 1723 J. J. Scheuchzer, in his *Itinera Alpina*, gave "a reasoned catalogue of Swiss dragons arranged according to Cantons."[1]

Then—sometime during the eighteenth century, say between 1740 and 1790—signs of a startling change became frequent and conspicuous. People took to visiting remote villages (such as Chamouni, also spelt Chamoigny) just for the pleasure of viewing lofty mountains, or "immense icicles" called glaciers. Places which had been shunned for centuries now turned into cherished goals for long and perilous journeys. Monsters and dragons disappeared. Points of view were turned upside down, nomenclature inside out. What before had been inhospitable, savage, repellent, terrifying, became splendid, august, majestic, sublime. The very word beauty took on its patient and spacious shoulders a host of new meanings.

Such change, an authentic conversion, is the crucial point in the fascinating story which Showell Styles sets out to tell us in this book. It is important to remember that all subsequent developments—the North faces, the Winter ascents, the Great Mountains of the World— are foreshadowed in that very first turn from fear and ignorance to familiarity and love.

* * * * * * * * *

As the nineteenth century unfolds, the centre of interest shifts from mountains, which have been fully accepted (the Alps have become "The Playground of Europe") to mountaineers. Quite rightly Styles avoids a heavy list of names, both topographical and biographical, concentrating his attention on a few outstanding personalities, on some memorable feats. The gallery contains portraits of the classics—Paccard, De Saussure, Whymper, Mummery, the Duke of the Abruzzi— and likenesses of many leaders of our days, from the Schmidt brothers to Shipton, from Merkl and Buhl to Lambert, Tenzing and Bonatti. An attentive eye also points out the colours in curious pictures tucked away in corridors, and worthy of being hung in better places. Here comes Miss Annie Peck ("The Lady of Huascaran"), or Tom Lloyd and sourdoughs who, totally ignorant of mountaineering as they were, managed to climb the highest peak of North America, Mount Denali (now McKinley).

The method is highly personal—I imagine many readers will think at once of this or that great episode, of this or that famous climber, not mentioned, or barely so. Personally I would question only one

[1] G. R. De Beer: *Early Travellers in the Alps* (London, 1930).

point; the assumption of a link between modern progress in rock climbing on the continent and Nazism. Georg Winkler, Paul Preuss, Hans Dülfer, Angelo Dibona (only the latter is named *en passant*), who were among the founding fathers of modern rock climbing, opened their breathtaking ways up limestone crags in the Eastern Alps long before the name of Hitler was ever heard.

Such details, however, are relatively unimportant. Showell Styles is not setting out to write a pedantic textbook of alpinism and its history, but to make those of us who climb, or have climbed, live again through some of the outstanding achievements in mountaineering as if we had taken part in them, be they the ascent of Mount Aiguille in 1492 or the conquest of Everest in 1953. As for readers who do not climb, or do not feel they have been infected by the microbe, I think this book is eminently designed to make them see the point.

* * * * * * * * *

This brings us to a question which is asked so often; why do people climb? The reader will find in this book a variety of answers. Some people will be seen climbing for money (Chamoniards after De Saussure's prize, Sherpas—15 of them needed to carry the coins to pay the other 500 in a gigantic Japanese expedition!), some climb for fame (Bourrit), some for advancement of science (De Saussure), others for home and country (Carrel), or because they "like that sort of thing" (Shipton), because mountains "are there" (Mallory), or to "knock off the bastards" (Hillary). It is also possible to climb mountains for the mystical experiences they seem to confer (Wills on the Wetterhorn, Tichy on Cho Oyu).

Styles himself does not let the question pass unanswered; he considers the "love of adventure" and the "subtler motive of domination" to be the chief driving forces behind all "voyages of discovery, desert journeys and mountain ascents". "The lords of the Earth," he adds, "cannot feel that they truly possess their estate while there remains some corner of the arctic waste, some lofty summit, still defying the tread of human feet. Man has to prove himself master of all the intricacies and rugosities on the surface of this world." I think this is perfectly true and very well put. It also explains the quest for the Moon, eventually for other planets and satellites of the solar system, now that the Earth has become a somewhat restricted estate.

Yet, it seems to me, the ultimate secret is not entirely unveiled. "Enumerate the parts of a carriage and you still have not explained what a carriage is", a Chinese saying goes. The motives of adventure and domination explain why mountains should be climbed once—the first time. Then again by all possible faces, ridges, couloirs and overhangs—the first time. Finally in all seasons, under all imaginable conditions—the first time. But when human feet have trod on every square inch of man's estate, why do it again? Clearly it is not only a question of adventure and domination, but a question of love; we are dealing with a sort of magnetic, irrational, irresistible attraction emanating from the mountains themselves, a secret and deeply rewarding link which unites man and crag, man and stone, man and sky, man and wind.

Such love is of a very special nature. Not only does it demand extremely hard work, but much risk, and—often—willingness to lose one's life. Danger is always there. The greatest masters have been known to make a fatal step in the silliest of places (Solleder, Comici, Lachenal, not to mention Rand Herron who was killed on the great Pyramid of Egypt on his return from Nanga Parbat). If one, two, ten people do something risky which is strictly speaking unnecessary, such as climbing, they may be considered aberrant or mad; but when these people become legion, belong to all ages, come from all classes and from many different countries, we are dealing with something that cannot be laughed or smiled away. An explanation is required setting bare the deepest roots of motivation.

The problem becomes easier to solve if we avoid stating it in the abstract (why does man climb?) and set it in a more circumscribed, historical, frame. We have observed that man's attitude towards mountains, at least in the West, has undergone a complete *volte-face*. At a given moment the hills ceased to appear repugnant and became admirable, even lovable. The question therefore should be: what brought about this change? Its causes must be related to the very essence of this new love. We should not ask "why does man climb?" but, "why did Western man start climbing?"

* * * * * * * * * *

The first fact which strikes me, in such a context, is that men belonging to civilisations other than the West seem gradually to have expressed love, not hatred, of mountains.

Even a superficial and indirect acquaintance with Indian literature shows us that the Himalayas have constantly been objects of wonder, worship, supreme inspiration. In the Mahabharata one finds repeated references to the "peaks of famed Kailasa" or to the "shining turrets of lofty Himalay". Sages speak from Himalayan recesses, Shiva's abode is among the most inaccessible snows. India, according to K. M. Panikkar, owes the very "continuity of its civilisation" to this cult of the Himalayas. And where did Pandit Nehru go in 1945, as soon as he was released from captivity? On a pilgrimage to the Himalayas and Kashmir, as he tells us in his *Discovery of India*. Many peaks of the greatest mountain range on earth are sacred to the Hindus, or to Buddhists, or to both, for instance Kailasa in the West, and Kangchenjunga in the East, of the chain.

In China, since earliest times, mountains have been not only objects of a somewhat animistic cult, but sources of poetic inspiration and philosophical meditation. It would be easy to quote Confucius ("Wise men find pleasure in water; the virtuous in mountains"), or the Book of Songs ("Mightiest of all heights is the Peak, Soaring up into the sky. . . ."), or poems from many ages of Chinese literature (Tao-Yun on "Climbing a Mountain", Po Chü-i on "Having climbed the topmost peak of the Incense-Burner Mountain")[2]. Though thirteen centuries have passed since Po Chü-i lived, climbed and wrote, the feelings of simultaneous wonder, excitement, pleasure and awe expressed in this last poem are perfectly modern, and are to be appreciated by any member of an Alpine Club or *Alpenverein*.

As for Japan, there we find an even deeper—and certainly more lyrical—feeling for nature, due in part to the influence of the ancient Shinto religion. Open the first Japanese anthology of poetry, the Manyoshu (eighth century), practically at random and your eye will fall on the ideogram for mountain, with its three prongs (peaks). Fuji, as is to be expected, is given a special place:

> Ever since Heaven and Earth were parted
> It has towered lofty, noble, divine,
> Mount Fuji in Suruga!   (Akahito)

But many other hills are mentioned with expressions of passionate love:

> From to-morrow ever
> Shall I regard as brother
> The twin-peaked mountain of Futagami . . .
>   (Princess Oku) [3]

Typical of Japan is also an ancient Mountain Religion (*Yama shukyo; Shugendo*), a compound of Buddhism and Shinto, whose devotees (yamabushi) climb mountains as part of their ritual.

If centuries of history testify in the West man's former hatred of mountains, in the East the evidence seems to point to his love for them. Which attitude is the more natural? I would say that such a question has really no meaning; so-called natural man is an academic abstraction; man has always and only lived in definite civilisations. Both attitudes, therefore, are legitimate; both depend on deeper and highly significant layers of conscious and subconscious motivation.

I propose here to say two words about the history of landscape painting, because it seems to give us a clue.

In the ancient West, in classical times, landscape painting may have been fairly important, as testified by a number of paintings in Pompeii, Herculaneum and the Vatican. Then, with the advent of Christianity, landscape painting practically disappears, or survives

---

[2] A. Waley: *A Hundred and Seventy Chinese Poems* (London, 1918).
[3] *The Manyoshu*, with English Translation: (The Nippen Gakujutsu Shinkokai, Tokyo, 1941)

only as a set of symbols. The blank lasts for over a thousand years. Giorgione's *Tempesta* is generally considered the first genuine Western landscape since the middle ages, but such paintings became important and generally accepted much later. It has been said that the *Encyclopédie* (1751–1772) contains one of the first positive valuations of landscape as a genre "*des plus riches, des plus agréables et des plus feconds de la peinture*".

These facts are explained by the nature of the religious and philosophical conceptions prevailing during late antiquity and the middle ages. I think it can be conceded that every civilisation must give its own interpretation of a fundamental triangle, man-God-nature. The West, with Christianity, had chosen an arrangement where the whole mystery of existence found its sense and explanation in a supreme God, intensely personal, conceived as creator, father and judge. Cosmology and history were seen as the drama of His dealings with man. Nature was something created, essentially passive, possibly delusive and suspiciously connected with a fall from spiritual perfection; a mere scene for the two main protagonists, manlike God and God-made man. It was understandable that the human figure should reign supreme in all the arts.

Only with the Renaissance, with a gradual change in the entire outlook on life, with a new statement of the relations binding man, God and nature, does landscape come again to be a subject worthy of the artist's attention. The fortunes of this form of art, as of all others, are not casual, but connected with the main currents of thought prevailing at different centuries.

If we turn to China we shall find that the tradition of landscape painting has been continuous since very ancient times. There "nothing occurred", we are told by Sherman Lee[4], "seriously to interrupt or reverse the steady growth of a generally accepted philosophy of nature that provided a perfect climate for great landscape painting." Both Confucianism and Taoism contributed their part to the Chinese *philosophia perennis*. The basic triangle, man-God-nature, was seen in a light quite different from that of the West. Nature ("vast, deep, high, intelligent, infinite and eternal", to mention a passage from the Chun Yung) practically absorbed God into its fold. His place was taken by the fundamental conceptions of *Li* (the natural order) and *Tao* (the Way). Nature was not conceived as something created, passive, purely "material", entirely dependent on ulterior principles for its existence, but as an immense living organism, *the* living organism. Wisdom was defined as a quest for harmony with nature. This applied both to the State (the Emperor as mediator between Heaven and Earth) and to the individual.

[4] Sherman Lee, *Chinese Landscape Painting* (Cleveland Museum of Art, n.d.)

It is hardly necessary to add that mountains—as one of nature's most conspicuous features—were considered, with water, noble and inspiring objects. A landscape painting was a *shan-sui*, a "mountain-water picture". The *Mustard Seed Garden Manual of Painting* (seventeenth century)[5] has a section on "Rendering the Ceremonial Aspects of Mountains", in which peaks are quite naturally conceived as living beings. If one lofty dome is like an emperor, the minor *aiguilles* round him should be treated as ministers, or friends, who share his company.

The foregoing observations remind us how all aspects of a given civilisation are bound together in one vast and definite structure. No important part is casual, and all have their roots in a few main intuitions about reality. If landscape painting—one example among many possible ones—is not taken up or abandoned at whim, but depends for its fortunes on the prevailing outlook on life, the same can be said for the love of mountains, and finally for the action of climbing them. The birth of mountaineering is therefore not to be considered a curious isolated episode, but the outcome of much vaster spiritual developments; a chapter in the history of ideas.

In particular, mountaineering is connected with a new interest in nature, detectable in the West since the time of Leonardo, with the birth and development of science, with the retreat of theology from a dominant position, with a general shift of emphasis from transcendental to human values, with the "return to nature" movement and with romanticism. It is also connected, for good and for bad, with the typical aspect of our times, competitive nationalism.

Someone might object that the West, with its traditional hatred of mountains, has finally given birth to climbing, while the East with its traditional love of mountains has not. This is true, but less paradoxical than might appear at first sight. Conversion, as everyone knows, produces high spiritual temperatures, and Western man is a recent convert to mountains. Most probably the very love of mountains, so prevalent in Asia, favoured contemplation and discouraged action. Apart from this, the general dynamic tension of Western civilisation—as opposed to a calmer East—should be kept in mind.

* * * * * * * * *

If mountaineering, as a social and historical event, can thus be situated and at least partly explained, what about the individual? How is an historical necessity to be translated into terms of emotions and personal experience? We have seen that many different motives can be culled from the fascinating story told in this book.

Many more can be imagined. I well remember ascending a minor virgin peak, some years ago, with only one thought in my mind, to get

[5] Mai-mai Sze: *The Way of Chinese Painting, etc.* (Paperback ed. Vintage Books, New York, 1959)

there before a rival party from a neighbouring city! And who has not climbed mountains to see the view, to get some exercise, to add a name to a list, to pass a day with a girl friend, to take photographs, to collect flowers, fossils or minerals? Yet there are some climbs—and I like to think of them as significant ones—which leave us with memories of a most special intimacy with trees and water, snow and rocks, sky, clouds or wind. Shall we speak of communion?

In his search for a new identity, for a new situation in the scheme of things, Western man, so far, has mainly taken active steps to dethrone God from his traditional place. Books about the death of God, some written by clerics, have become so commonplace that they cause no stir. On the other hand our relations with nature have undergone very little change. We still think in terms of spirit and matter. Our languages are stuffed with aristotelian dualisms. This creates a painful sense of unbalance, disorder, pointlessness. In the traditional view nature may have been material, passive and deceptive, but behind it stood God who vivified and explained everything. Now God has gone, or is going, and we are left with a heap of galactic junk, purely "material". We have let the keystone fall, without attempting to refashion the vault.

A new balance will surely be found some day. It is impossible to remain satisfied for long with mere matter, even if its marvels and intricacies seem to have no end. The very subtlety and complexity have a spiritual significance. The whole concept of nature must undergo the structural formations necessary to adapt it to a world without God, unless we be spiritually starved. Such a necessity has been seen very clearly—from a theistic and catholic point of view—by Teilhard de Chardin.

In this context a climber may be described as someone who has, at least partially, found himself a new and deeper statement of man's relationship with nature. Let me repeat Tichy's words on Cho Oyu: "Snow, sky, the wind and myself were an indivisible and divine whole." Or those of Rébuffat on a wall in the Alps: "the man who bivouacs becomes one with the mountain." The bliss felt in such moments is not something arbitrary or freakish, but the fulfilment of a deep urge born from our particular Western predicament.

One might also say that climbing is an act of religion—using this last word in a very wide sense, in senses, possibly, to be defined by future developments. Only a religious component transcending the individual, with its roots in the whole aspirations of an age, can explain why a climber may feel willing to risk so much, life included, and consider himself, be considered by others, perfectly sane.

FOSCO MARAINI

On Top of the World

1. The Jungfrau, Queen of the Bernese

Prologue

THE Lord of Dompjulian and Beaupré, Monseigneur Antoine de Ville, clutched the final rocks of Mont Aiguille's stupendous pinnacle with shaking fingers. Above him lusty *villeins* tugged at the hempen rope, others shoved from below to hoist the King's Chamberlain over the verge of the summit plateau. Monseigneur de Ville stood erect at last, heedful of the near-vertical precipices that fell from that lofty summit on every side. His feathered hat had blown away hours ago on the fearful ascent, but he made the motion of doffing it. "*Vive le Roi!*" cried Monseigneur de Ville hoarsely. He had accomplished the task set him by Charles VII of France and ascended the Mont Aiguille, believed by the inhabitants of Dauphiné to be totally inaccessible. This he knew. He did not know that he was the first Climber, the first man to plan and carry out the ascent of a really difficult mountain.

The year was 1492, and 6,000 miles away Christopher Columbus—another Royal Emissary—was nearing the coast of undiscovered America. Man was beginning his long quest for knowledge of his world, impelled by curiosity or avarice or the sheer love of adventure. The last, perhaps, has been the chief driving-force behind all voyages of discovery, desert journeys, and mountain ascents; and behind the love of adventure lies the subtler motive of domination. The lords of the Earth cannot feel that they truly possess their estate while there remains some corner of the arctic waste, some lofty summit, still defying the tread of human feet. Man has to prove himself master of all the intricacies and rugosities on the surface of his world. And this is the real clue to the reason why men climb mountains. George Leigh Mallory's famous reply to the question "Why do you want to climb Everest?" epitomises the reason: "Because it is there." Arnold Lunn has suggested that this was a rude answer designed to snub an importunate bore, but it is at least as likely that it was honestly given. The mountaintop is as much a part of Man's inheritance as the ocean, and the mere fact of its existence is sufficient reason for assuring himself that he is not debarred from possessing it. For a man does not "conquer" a mountain when he climbs it. He enlarges it, by a first ascent, from a remote wedge of upheaved rock and ice into a field for the adventure and pleasure of other men; he adds it to the accessible delights of the human heritage.

Today, nearly five centuries after De Beaupré's first ascent, Mont Aiguille is still regarded as a difficult climb. Those remarkable precipices, rising to a height of 6,880 feet above the sea, are draped with fixed ropes at the trickier passages to assist the climber who starts from Grenoble for the summit. The old chronicler writes that King Charles's Chamberlain scaled the peak "by subtle means and engines", so that De Beaupré would seem to have been the father of modern Artificial climbing. He also arranged for Mass to be said on the summit and had three crosses erected there. And his ascent was not repeated until a daring peasant climbed Mont Aiguille 342 years later.

Monarchs who wanted to assure themselves of their dominion over every part of their lands were responsible, at earlier dates, for the ascents of easier mountains. According to Livy, Philip of Macedon climbed Mount Haemus in the Balkans about 350 B.C. Peter III of Aragon climbed the highest mountain of his domain, the Canigou (9,135 feet) in the thirteenth century; and saw on the summit "a horrible dragon of enormous size, which flew about and darkened the air with its breath". A more notable ascent—the most astonishing of all, if the records are true—was achieved by Don Francisco Montano and others at the command of Cortez, when they climbed to the crater of Popocatepetl in 1521 to get sulphur for the making of gunpowder, setting a height record of 17,852 feet which endured for centuries. But other human forces were at work reducing the mountain strongholds. Trade between nations was obstructed by the barriers of the great ranges, and just as the dwellers in the far Himalayan lands pushed trade routes through the vast mountain-wall between India and Tibet so the commerce of Europe found passes whereby the long obstacle of the Alps could be crossed. Over the Great St Bernard, and the Théodule, and the Mont Cénis crawled the pack-trains of the traders, acquiring by bitter experience some knowledge of Alpine perils and their avoidance. By 1574 Josias Simler of Zurich was able to publish his book *Concerning the Difficulties of Alpine Travel*, which contains warnings against avalanches and hidden crevasses and reveals that travellers had discovered the usefulness of a rope and the necessity of dark glasses on the long snow traverses. Most of these Alpine travellers and traders had as much affection for mountains as a modern tourist has for the Channel crossing on a rough day. But their stories of soaring peaks glimpsed through the driving blizzard, of glaciers that gave forth eerie groans, of sudden breath-taking prospects, excited the interest of other and less commercially minded men: the scientists, curious to examine the reported phenomena of these lofty regions for themselves, and the priests, impelled by an inbred desire to know all God's mighty works.

The first of the greater peaks of the Alps to be climbed was the Vélan (12,251 feet) and the man who climbed it was Canon Murith of the St Bernard Hospice. It is the Benedictine monk Father Placidus à Spescha,

2 Mont Aiguille, Dauphiné

however, who has the best claim to be considered the father of mountaineering. This energetic religious was the first man, so far as we know, who made a practice of climbing mountains for the love of them, and from 1788 onwards his expeditions from the monastery of Disentis in the Grisons were devoted to solving the mysteries of unclimbed peaks. Eight Alpine summits over 10,000 feet high were among his first ascents. Yet his discovery of the delights that were one day to draw thousands of enthusiasts to the mountains made little stir at the time; eighteenth-century Europe was not interested in the exploits of mad priests, and there was no widespread net for the collection and dissemination of news. It took a distinguished scientist, a great mountain, and a dramatic story to start the pastime of mountaineering on its way to popularity.

Horace Bénédict de Saussure was not the first scientist to perceive that the untrodden high places of Europe offered a new field for research. Altmann and Gruner had published treatises on the glaciers of the Bernese Oberland and the Valais; though detailed descriptions and classifications of the dragons that dwelt in the High Alps were still being gravely considered in scientific circles. But De Saussure was the first man to aim really high and to have the means of achieving his aim. He was a scientist with a European reputation, and at the same time a man of wealth and social position. In the course of his study of glaciers he visited Chamonix, in 1760 already a recognised calling-place for rich travellers making the European tour, and there he saw Mont Blanc, the highest mountain in Europe apart from the Caucasus. To gain the summit and there set up, nearly 16,000 feet above the sea, a research station, was the project he conceived, and he at once set about seeking ways and means, only to find himself balked at the outset. The chamois-hunters and crystal-seekers of Chamonix knew the lower rocks and glaciers of the great mountain, but they were unanimous in declaring that there was no way of reaching its summit. Death, they assured him, awaited any man who should try the ascent.

De Saussure did not abandon his project. Almost alone of men, he believed that Mont Blanc could and must be climbed. After one of his many subsequent visits to Chamonix he wrote that his feeling for the Mont Blanc had become a kind of illness: "I could not even look upon the mountain, which is visible from so many points round about, without being seized with an aching of desire." This is a very unscientific confession. It is, in fact, the avowal of De Saussure's mountaineering passion.

He continued to hope and plan. Failing to arouse any disinterested enthusiasm, he offered a reward to the pioneer who should make the first ascent, and as a result several attempts were made on Mont Blanc between 1775 and 1785, in one of which he took part himself. All failed far below the summit. But the failures did produce one much-needed thing—an increased knowledge of, and confidence in, the snowslopes and glaciers that would have to be traversed. The hardy Chamonix men who had taken part in the attempts reported, perhaps a little boastfully, that only fatigue and doubt of the right way had turned them back. The legend of inaccessibility was fading in the light of hope and ambition.

There were many, now, who did not doubt that Mont Blanc would one day be climbed. Few of these, however, foresaw that a successful ascent would strip the terror of the unknown from hundreds of other great mountains, and that the Golden Age of a new recreation was at hand.

3 Mont Blanc, seen above the Chamonix Aiguilles. The usual ascent route goes up the snow shelf below the round white hump on the right, then follows the right-hand skyline to the summit

1 Mont Blanc and the Golden Age

A MAN may climb a mountain for many reasons—for personal aggrandisement, for money, for love of the mountain. All three of these motives were represented in the persons who figure in the first ascent of Mont Blanc.

Marc Théodore Bourrit was a Swiss writer who had made Alpine exploration his special subject and world-wide celebrity his aim in life. To his credit be it said that from the first he believed the ascent of Mont Blanc to be possible and had spent money in persuading the Chamonix men to search for a practicable route, accompanying the "guides" himself on several occasions. His attempts were all failures—sometimes quite ludicrous ones—but he was a trier, for whatever reason; and he watched with jealous eyes the rare essays of other candidates for the summit. One such candidate was Doctor Paccard.

Doctor Michel Gabriel Paccard was the physician of Chamonix, a man of quiet and cultured tastes who loved his valley and the huge mountain that brooded in white mystery above it. In 1775, as a young man of nineteen, he had begun exploring the wonders of the glacier mazes below the mountain, botanising and geologising and, incidentally, making many worthy mountain expeditions. He climbed the neighbouring peak of the Buet, and spent nights out in bivouac on the Géant glacier, thus gaining most valuable experience. Inevitably he was sought out by the indefatigable Bourrit, and these two—diverse in character and motive—agreed to try the ascent together in 1783.

Meanwhile, the reward offered by De Saussure twenty years earlier had induced a number of the Chamonix peasants, hunters of chamois and marketable crystals, to attack the higher slopes of Mont Blanc. One such attempt, made by four peasants in 1775, reached a height of about 11,000 feet, at a point a little above the rocks on which the Grands Mulets hut is now established. Their failures and discussions had led to the naming of the various parts of Mont Blanc's north-western flank, and since almost the whole of that flank, from base to summit, is in view from the valley of Chamonix all the landmarks and obstacles became known and recognisable. The stage—a vast, up-tilted white stage—was set for the final drama of triumph or disaster.

Seen from the north-west, Mont Blanc presents an aspect less complicated and more promising than from any other direction. The maze of glaciers east of the Aiguilles is hidden behind the long ridge that culminates in Mont Maudit, the Accursed Mountain, itself well over 14,000 feet high but a mere shoulder of Mont Blanc (see *Plate 4* and *Diagram* 1). A single glacier, falling 10,000 feet in its length of nearly five miles, descends from the plateaux below the summit-dome to the woods and pastures of the valley. This is the Glacier des Bossons. On the right of the glacier, as you look up the shattered lower icefall from the bottom, a steep and crested ridge of rock forms a natural ladder avoiding the ice. The top of this Montagne de la Côte ends below the *séracs*—jumbled ice-pinnacles—of the Jonction, but a 1,500-foot ascent through the *séracs* leads to the bottom of a smaller and narrower ridge of rock protruding from the middle of the broad white trench above. These are the rocks called the Grands Mulets, marking at 10,000 feet of height the "halfway house" of the ascent. But the major difficulties, as the explorers had already discovered, lay above the Grands Mulets. Here steep snowslopes, broken by enormous crevasses, rose in two mighty steps called the Petit Plateau and the Grand Plateau, and the second of these more level snowfields was cut off from

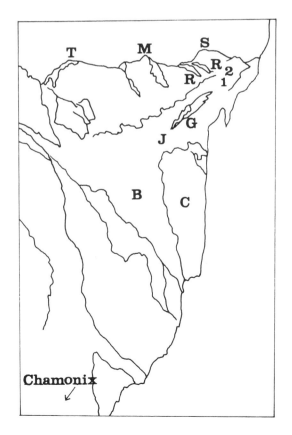

Diagram 1

Mont Blanc, showing route of first ascent

B. Bossons Glacier
C. Montagne de la Côte
J. The Jonction
G. The Grands Mulets
1. Petit Plateau
2. Grand Plateau
R. Rochers Rouges
T. Mont Blanc du Tacul
M. Mont Maudit
S. Summit of Mont Blanc

4 Mont Blanc from the Brévent, showing Dr Paccard's route (see Diagram 1

the summit 3,000 feet overhead by lofty walls of snow from which avalanches often fell. The dangers of these snow-walls (so it seemed to the pioneers) were too great altogether. They abandoned the Bossons route and made two attempts, both failures, to get at the summit over the Dôme du Gouter farther to the south. But Doctor Paccard believed he had discovered a practicable route to the summit from the Grand Plateau. Between two bands of reddish rock known as the Rochers Rouges, conspicuous from the valley, a steep shelf of snow and ice ran up to the left. By this, thought Paccard, he might gain the final easier snowslopes that led up the north side of the summit-dome. It was this route he had in mind when he started out with Bourrit in 1783.

The attempt was the first in which men other than the Chamonix peasants had taken part, and it failed. Bourrit proved to be a poor climber. He refused to leave the rocks of the Montagne de la Côte for the ice, and Paccard went on alone for some distance, turning back before he reached the Grands Mulets. The party came back disconsolate, but Paccard knew that with the right companion he could at least reach the Rochers Rouges. The man he needed would have to be bold, experienced, and above all resolute.

The second party to try the Dôme du Gouter route had been joined, without invitation, by a sturdy peasant crystal-hunter who greatly coveted De Saussure's reward. This man was of a stubborn and surly humour and disliked turning back with the others. He lingered and dawdled, was benighted among the high snows, and spent the hours of cold and darkness alone at a height of 12,000 feet without suffering any ill effect. When Paccard heard of this exploit he knew that his man was found. He sought out Jacques Balmat and made an agreement with him. Together they would attempt the route by the Rochers Rouges; if they succeeded in reaching the summit, the whole of De Saussure's reward would be Balmat's. On 7th August 1786, the two men set out from Chamonix, an oddly assorted couple. On the one hand the sturdy uneducated peasant with his hopes fixed on a fortune, on the other the gentle physician bent upon achieving the closest possible union with his beloved mountain. One may imagine the third of the *dramatis personae*, Marc Bourrit the journalist, biting his nails in the background and praying that they might fail.

From the valley the stages of the climb were anxiously watched. The two men were seen above the Montagne de la Côte by the evening of the first day, engaged with the difficult ice of the Jonction. Crouched among the rock pinnacles of the Grands Mulets they spent an uncomfortable night, and both were slightly frostbitten by morning. On they went at first light, safeguarding their steps with the long pointed staves they carried, and gained the Petit Plateau and then the Grand Plateau. The ramp of frozen snow and ice between the Rochers Rouges proved to be the hardest part of the ascent, but foot by foot they crept up it

2. The Wetterhorn from the Eiger *Picture-point*

to the broader final slopes and stood at last, breathless and exhausted, on the summit of Mont Blanc. They were the first to stand there, the highest men in Europe. The time was 6.30 in the evening of August 8th. Forty-eight hours later they were safely back in Chamonix, where they were given a hero's welcome.

Jacques Balmat duly received the full reward offered by De Saussure. Michel Paccard had sufficient reward in his achievement. But Balmat, his head turned by wealth and fame, began to boast of the ascent to all who would listen, and in his boasting his own part in the climb quickly assumed great and greater proportions. Soon he was implying, and then asserting, that Doctor Paccard had little or nothing to do with the final success; that he, Balmat, had planned the route—had forced the Doctor to climb the last steeps—had actually carried the Doctor up the slopes. It was not long before folk were whispering that Doctor Paccard had not reached the summit at all and that Balmat was the only man to do so. But for the envy and spite of Marc Bourrit the rumours would not have gained any credence among sensible folk. Bourrit, who would have conceded the right of a Chamonix peasant to climb better than himself, could not bear that a man of his own class and education should have succeeded where he had failed. He busied himself with pamphlets and articles supporting Balmat's claims and discrediting Paccard, and for years afterwards lost no chance of damaging the Doctor's Alpine reputation. Forty-six years after the first ascent, when Bourrit was seventy, he repeated his version of the story to Alexander Dumas the elder, who based his so-called history of the conquest of Mont Blanc upon it; and the wide circulation enjoyed by Dumas' book ensured the persistence of the false account for nearly a century. Modern historians of the mountains, however, found many of Balmat's statements to be suspect. Research into Doctor Paccard's diaries and papers confirmed the suspicion that he, and no one else, had planned and led the ascent, and further confirmation was gained through the dramatic discovery that a certain Baron von Gensdorff had not only watched the whole ascent through a telescope but had also made notes and sketches of what he witnessed. Those notes and sketches proved finally that Paccard had reached the summit and that he had taken a leading part in the climb throughout the ascent; Balmat's rôle had been that of a sturdy but docile follower.

So, years after his death, Michel Gabriel Paccard was vindicated. And meanwhile the ascent of Mont Blanc had become first a daring feat and then a mere 'snow grind" for experienced mountaineers.

De Saussure made his coveted expedition a year later, and the old prints and accounts of his ascent illustrate the primitive methods used for climbing mountains in the early nineteenth century. There were twenty men in the party: eighteen "guides" (Chamonix peasants), De Saussure himself, and—De Saussure's valet, who had never set foot

5 Horace Bénédict de Saussure

6 18th century drawing of Mont Blanc with de Saussure's route marked

7 An early ascent of Mont Blanc

on a mountain before! They carried enormous loads of scientific apparatus, and food, and ladders for crossing crevasses, and poles for conquering the snowslopes (*Plate* 7). On steep snow a peasant would hold each end of a pole while De Saussure used it as a handrail. Minor mishaps and near-mutinies were overcome by the resolute behaviour of the leader, and on the second day the party—all twenty of them, including the valet—stood on the summit. For more than four hours they remained there while De Saussure made his scientific observations on the temperature and density of the atmosphere and the boiling-point of water at 15,782 feet above the sea. Forty-eight hours later they were all down again in Chamonix.

De Saussure's was the ascent that gained world publicity; he was a great scientist, and his success was trumpeted across Europe, whereas the struggles of two natives of an obscure French village had received little notice. Men of action saw that here was a daring adventure. Less

15

8 On the Bossons Glacier in the early 18th century

9 Modern climbers on the ordinary way up Mont Blanc

than a week after De Saussure's climb Mont Blanc was ascended by an Englishman, Colonel Beaufoy. But though the ascents of the highest point in Europe multiplied, between 1786 and 1850, until they averaged one a year, the emergence of mountain-climbing as a sport or pastime had not yet begun. Mont Blanc attracted adventurers because its ascent gave an automatic *cachet* of daring or heroism. The hundreds of lesser peaks had not this *cachet* and were not attempted, though one or two enthusiasts in other districts of the Alps tackled and climbed the chosen peaks of their neighbourhood. The two sons of a wealthy Swiss merchant named Meyer, for example, made a hobby of exploring the valleys and glaciers above Grindelwald and in 1811 climbed to the summit of the Jungfrau. Seven years later Yeats Brown and Frederick Slade made a purely sporting attempt to climb the Jungfrau from the Rotthal saddle; they failed, but this was probably the earliest instance of British mountaineering endeavour in high mountains.

The scientists, fired by the publication of De Saussure's account of his Mont Blanc experiments, gave a new lead to mountain exploration. Agassiz and Desor, two well-known scientists from Neuchâtel, established themselves in a stone shelter high up on the moraine of the

10 Agassiz's party on the Jungfrau, from the cover drawing of his book

Unteraar Glacier to study glacial phenomena. At this "Hôtel des Neuchâtelois," as they called it, they were joined by a Scots scientist, J. D. Forbes, and there the devoted three spent weeks in glacier exploration and the evolution of theories. Both Agassiz and Forbes developed a passion for their strange environment and the peaks that rose above it, and both accepted the challenge of the summits. Ostensibly their objects in climbing a peak were scientific, and they always carried up with them a load of instruments such as thermometers, barometers, hair hygrometers, polariscopes, and chronometers. When Forbes reached the summit of the Jungfrau, however, all his four barometers were useless—three of them broken and the fourth out of order—and he seems to have been too interested in the climbing to bewail this sad loss unduly. Forbes, in fact, soon transferred his ruling passion from science to mountaineering. Between 1827 and 1844 he visited almost every district of the Alps, devising routes, crossing new passes, and making the first ascent of several high peaks. If Father Placidus is the father of mountaineering, Professor J. D. Forbes must rank as the father of British mountaineering.

Forbes was, as it were, the forerunner who spied out the Promised Land. The great British invasion of the mountains, known to later mountaineers as the Golden Age of Alpine climbing, was yet to come. Enthusiasts of other nations—isolated eccentrics of their day—climbed some notable peaks before the English Alpinist became a familiar figure in Swiss scenery. Dr Parrot, a Russian, reached one of Monte Rosa's ten summits as early as 1811; the Finsteraarhorn, monarch of the Bernese Oberland, was climbed by Rudolf Sulger of Basle in 1842; Edouard Desor, a German—the same who had inhabited the "Hôtel des Neuchâtelois" with Agassiz and Forbes—made the ascent of the Rosenhorn, third summit of the Wetterhorn, in 1844. A year after Desor's climb a young man named Stanhope Templeman Speer ascended the highest summit of the Wetterhorn and printed an account of his exploit in the *Athenaeum* and in *Chambers's Journal*. It was probably Speer's adventurous story that first brought home to the gentlemen of Early Victorian England that a new sport was here awaiting development and that the British might be the first in the field.

Then, as now, the Wetterhorn was a famous peak. Not because of its height, which is little more than 12,000 feet, but because of its bold shape and the snow-capped precipice that drops sheer to the valley of Grindelwald, most easily accessible of Swiss resorts to the northern tourist. The peak visible from Grindelwald is not the highest summit. The Wetterhörner are three: Rosenhorn, Mittelhorn, and Hasli Jungfrau. The last-named is the peak conspicuous from the valley, but the Mittelhorn is the highest. None of them are considered at all

11 The Wetterhörner. The highest summit, the Mittelhorn, is the centre peak   19
of the three on the left. On the right, farther away, is the Schreckhorn

difficult nowadays, though in the days when every unclimbed summit had its aura of mystery and terror the courage required for a resolute attempt was incalculably greater.

Young Speer was the son of a Scottish doctor living at Interlaken. He came to Grindelwald with the intention of making a first ascent of the Hasli Jungfrau, but learned there that it had been climbed by two Oberland men in the previous summer. The Mittelhorn, alone of the three peaks, remained virgin, and he determined to climb that. Meanwhile a certain Doctor Roth from Berne had heard of Speer's intention and, being an ardent Nationalist, resolved that the highest of the Wetterhörner should fall to a Swiss, and not to an intruding Britisher. Roth's party failed, and Speer, accompanied by three guides, achieved his ambition. The ascent was not very important, but the way Speer wrote about it was. He treated it as a great adventure, with no scientific excuse; and in Britain the tone of his story struck answering chords in the hearts of hundreds of young men.

Nevertheless, mountaineering tradition has always assigned to another Wetterhorn ascent the inaugural place in the history of true mountaineering.

On 17th September 1854 Mr Alfred Wills, later Sir Alfred Wills, climbed the Hasli Jungfrau from Grindelwald and recorded his impressions of the ascent in a book, *Wanderings among the High Alps*. Four guides, all Oberland men, did the hard work of route-finding and making steps in the snow, as was then the custom, and all the party carried *alpenstocks*, poles four feet long with an iron spike at one end and an axe-head at the other. Modern Alpine climbers may be surprised to hear that the Oberlanders used *crampons*, iron ice-claws which they strapped to their feet.

Wills's account is a splendidly vivid and dramatic one. His description of the arrival on the summit is familiar to most mountaineers:

> Suddenly, a startling cry of surprise and triumph rang through the air. A great block of ice bounded from the top of the parapet, and before it had well lighted on the glacier, Lauener exclaimed, "*Ich schaue den blauen Himmel!*" (I see blue sky.) . . . That wave above us, frozen, as it seemed, in the act of falling over, into a strange and motionless magnificence, was the very peak itself! Lauener's blows flew with redoubled energy. . . . As I took the last step, Balmat disappeared from my sight; my left shoulder grazed against the angle of the icy embrasure, while, on the right, the glacier fell abruptly away beneath me towards an unknown and awful abyss; a hand from an invisible person grasped mine; I stepped across, and had passed the ridge of the Wetterhorn!
>
> Alfred Wills's *Wanderings among the High Alps*, 1856.

The physical excitement so cleverly recorded had its balancing emotion in another famous passage; and it was perhaps this latter piece of writing that had the greater influence in drawing to mountaineering the cultured and God-fearing Victorians who were to be the pioneers of modern climbing.

> I am not ashamed to own that I experienced, as this sublime and wonderful prospect burst upon my view, a profound and almost irrepressible emotion— an emotion which, if I may judge from the low ejaculations of surprise, followed by a long pause of breathless silence, as each in turn stepped into the opening, was felt by the others as well as myself . . . We felt as in the more immediate presence of Him who had reared this tremendous pinnacle, and beneath the "majestical roof" of whose deep blue heaven we stood, poised, as it seemed, half-way between the earth and sky.
>
> Alfred Wills's *Wanderings among the High Alps*, 1856.

There must always be something mystical, semi-religious, in an Englishman's sport. Cricket would not have endured so long on its merits as a game if its almost devotional atmosphere had not been handed down from generation to generation of enthusiasts, nor would fox-hunting continue popular without its peculiar blend of *mystique* and tradition. The writings of the more sensitive Alpine pioneers, and especially Wills's book, showed the future climbers that there was more to "Alpinism" than mere exercise and dare-devilry. Clergymen like Llewellyn Davies and J. F. Hardy, great scientists like John Tyndall, essayists and philosophers like Sir Leslie Stephen, came to the Alps not merely to look at them, as did the growing influx of travellers made possible by improved European communications, but to climb them. Local men with experience of the higher mountain-sides were eagerly

13 John Tyndall

sought after as "guides", methods of safeguarding with ropes and dealing with the different conditions of snowslopes began to be devised—
the first postulations of a "technique" for the new sport. In the year
of Wills's Wetterhorn ascent a group of men, consisting mostly of those
who had encountered each other at Grindelwald or Chamonix or
Zermatt, formed the first of all mountaineering clubs—The Alpine
Club. And the Golden Age had begun.

The Golden Age of mountaineering in the Alps lasted for a decade—
from 1854 to 1865—and its terminal point is the ascent of the Matterhorn. In that decade the members of the Alpine Club climbed the
great majority of the more difficult peaks of the Alps and developed, as
they climbed, the tools, methods, and traditions of the sport. It is convenient to call mountaineering a sport; but from the day of Sir Alfred
Wills to modern times there have been mountaineers to maintain that
the term does scant justice to the real breadth of the pastime. Professor George Ingle Finch, of Everest fame, was once heard to say with
great severity: "Mountaineering is *not* a sport! It is a way of life."
Something of this theory grew into the manner in which the men of the
Golden Age regarded their mountains. It was a certain attitude of
mind that made a man a true mountaineer, not physical courage or
aptitude for high places. Good humour and comradeship formed the
basis of their association and any kind of competition for a peak was
frowned upon—though a climber was fully entitled to keep his own
counsel about his plans for ascending some virgin peak. Courage and a
certain amount of daring were desirable attributes, but recklessness on
a mountain brought down the wrath of the English Alpine hierarchy
upon the head of the offender.

"It'll go, Melchior," urged an early mountaineer, pointing out a
dubious route to Melchior Anderegg.

"Yes," returned the famous guide, "but *I* won't!"

And the party retreated—not because the passage was difficult but
because it was dangerous by reason of falling stones. The classic
exchange was typical of the union of courage and prudence which was
to become traditional in British mountaineering and cause it, in the next
century, to be accused of pigheaded conservatism.

The English-gentlemanly principle of caring for one's dependents
first and oneself last transferred itself to the icy slopes and perilous
rock-ridges of the European mountains. These leisured Victorian
scholars and aesthetes, choosing to spend their vacations in the most
uncomfortable and dangerous of pastimes, never climbed without
guides and porters. Often their acquired skill and better education
made them more competent than the men they employed, but it was in
accordance with an older tradition that a hired servant should do the

14 The Pennine Alps from the Aiguille du Chardonnet. The Matterhorn is unmistakable in the centre distance, with Monte Rosa on the horizon to its right

laborious tasks like load-carrying and hewing long ladders of snow-steps. But before long the relationship between the *Herr* and his guide began to change. The educated man learned that some at least of the rough peasants could feel towards mountains as they did themselves; the peasant learned that a rich foreigner with eccentric tastes could match him in skill and endurance on high places. Comradeship between Guide and Amateur grew into the tradition and sprouted the many famous "partnerships" that recur throughout mountaineering history: Mummery and Burgener, Whymper and Carrel, Ryan and the Loch-matters, Winthrop Young and Josef Knubel.

24

3. The Lauterbrunnen Valley *H. N. Collinson*

15 On the Rochefort Ridge in the Chain of Mont Blanc

The new sport was not accepted as a legitimate pastime by the general public. Never had any band of sportsmen to suffer the jeers, obloquy, and accusations of suicidal madness that were endured by the first mountaineers. Small wonder that they drew into close fraternity and guarded jealously the privilege of membership. Not without reason, they held that only a man with the right background of class and education could understand their attitude towards mountain-climbing; and the Alpine Club became an upper-class stronghold—though a stronghold which most of upper-class England had no desire to enter. And yet the members of the Club had a soft spot for any genuine enthusiast, especially when he turned up at an Alpine centre. When a young man of not very good education, son of a wood-engraver and inclined to drop his aitches, arrived at Zermatt in the summer of 1860 he was welcomed by Leslie Stephen and other Alpine Club members who were assembled there, and one of them, Hinchliff, took him for his first climb on the Riffelberg, in sight of the Matterhorn. His name was Edward Whymper.

Whymper was then twenty years old, strong and hardy for his age, a great walker. At the age of fourteen he had been apprenticed to his father's business of wood-engraving, and was already a master of his craft. William Longman, the publisher, wanting illustrations for a book about the Alps, commissioned him to travel among the mountains and make sketches for the engravings, and into this task he threw himself with characteristic enthusiasm. He had no previous knowledge of mountains or climbing, but he must have acquired what information he could before leaving for Europe; doubtless he was not ignorant of the Alpine Club and the feats of its members. He knew, probably, of the exploits of men like Stephen and the Kennedys and he may have heard of the Reverend Charles Hudson, the most skilful amateur of the day, who had written of the Matterhorn: "It has the appearance of a frowning Deity who would forbid the approach of mortal feet." And in the first weeks of his tour, when he visited Kandersteg and Saas and crossed the Gemmi Pass, his extraordinarily keen observation quickly brought appreciation of mountain structure. Then he tramped up to Zermatt.

Whymper—the Matterhorn: the two names are more closely linked than any others in mountain history. When this young man plodded round the corner a mile below Zermatt and had his first sight of the peak that was to dominate the rest of his life, what were his impressions? His diary of that time records them:

> Saw, of course, the Matterhorn repeatedly. What precious stuff Ruskin has written about this, as well as about many other things! When one has a fair view of the mountain as I had, it may be compared to a sugar loaf set up on a table; the sugar loaf should have its head knocked on one side. Grand it is, but beautiful I think it is not.
>
> Edward Whymper's diary (unpublished).

Something of Edward Whymper's character emerges from this extract, and more from his classic book *Scrambles amongst the Alps*. He was opinionated, intolerant; bold to the point of recklessness; one who must always be the leader, who preferred his own company, who never relinquished any project once he had resolved upon it. When he became a mountain-climber—and he rapidly gained the necessary

16 Edward Whymper: a photograph taken in the year he climbed the Matterhorn 27

skill once the idea had gripped him—it was the factor of domination, of "conquering" a new summit, that appealed most strongly to him. If his first feeling for the Matterhorn was one of contempt, the unique form and legendary inaccessibility of the great peak were bound, sooner or later, to challenge such a nature as his.

The character of the Matterhorn is well known. It is a great shaft of steep and crumbling rock, 14,782 feet high, with four mighty ridges soaring to its narrow summit. On the south the Italian ridge, giant rock steps ending under a final cliff; east and west (roughly speaking) the very steep Furggen and Zmutt ridges; northward the Hörnli ridge. It presents its most forbidding aspect to the Zermatt valley, and in 1860 the peasants of the valley had many tales of the evil spirits that haunted its impossible crags. Certainly the Matterhorn was a peak of storms; standing in splendid isolation on the high snow-plateau between Switzerland and Italy, it "made its own weather". Yet the English climbers did not consider it inaccessible. Before Whymper thought of attempting the mountain three Liverpool brothers—Alfred, Charles, and Sandbach Parker—had climbed to a height of 12,000 feet on the Hörnli ridge *without guides*, before turning back. And Professor John Tyndall was already planning an ascent from Breuil on the Italian side (*Plate 17, Diagram 2*).

Rising as it does upon the very frontier, the Matterhorn is half in Italy and half in Switzerland; indeed, its short and narrow crest is divided into a "Swiss summit" and an "Italian summit". This was at the root of the tragedy which was to attend its conquest.

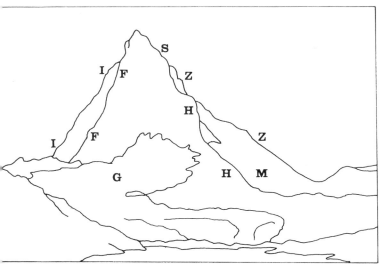

Diagram 2

The Matterhorn, showing Edward Whymper's route on the first ascent

I, I.   Italian Ridge
F, F.   Furggen Ridge
Z, Z.   Zmutt Ridge
H, H.   Hörnli Ridge (Whymper's route)
S.   The Shoulder
G.   Furggen Glacier
M.   Matterhorn Glacier

17 The Matterhorn from the Riffelsee (see Diagram 2)

During that first visit of 1860 the spell of the Alps, and especially of the unclimbed peaks, laid itself upon Edward Whymper. The following year, 1861, he was back again, this time taking part in the first ascent of Mont Pelvoux in the Dauphiné; a success which encouraged him to go on to Zermatt, whence the two finest Alpine peaks still unclimbed could be attempted—the Weisshorn and the Matterhorn. He arrived to find that Tyndall had been before him at Zermatt, had made the first ascent of the Weisshorn and was in Breuil for an attempt on the Matterhorn. Whymper hurried across the Théodule Pass to Breuil and learned to his relief that Tyndall had abandoned his intention. At once he set about looking for a guide or guides who would accompany him in the ascent from the Italian side, and so met for the first time the man whose name, next to Whymper's own, is most closely associated with the Matterhorn.

Jean-Antoine Carrel was an Italian patriot who had fought in the wars of liberation, a bold and hardy adventurer who loved his native mountains. In its own way his character was the counterpart of Whymper's; he was mightily independent, stubborn in resolve, single in purpose. He was determined that the Monte Cervino (to give the mountain its Italian name) must be climbed, and from the side of Italy, preferably by Italian climbers but in any case by Jean-Antoine Carrel. With his brother, a less skilful mountaineer, he had prowled up the beginning of the Italian ridge many times, reaching a height of 12,650 feet and discovering that the main difficulties of the route really began here. The advent of a determined young Englishman bent on climbing his mountain did not please Carrel. At first he refused to go with Whymper; but at last, concluding that it was better that an Italian should go with the young man than that he should have the chance of succeeding alone or with Swiss guides, Carrel and his brother joined him in his first attempt, though they held themselves free to climb on independently should Whymper turn back. This venture failed. So did the attempted partnership with Jean-Antoine Carrel. When Whymper returned to the attack in 1862 with two Zermatt guides who insisted on turning back when things became difficult, the news brought Carrel up from Breuil hot-foot, and again he joined the party, to lead boldly on where the Zermatt men had failed. At 13,000 feet he insisted on giving up the attempt, though it was perfectly possible to climb higher. It seems clear (though it was apparently not so to Whymper) that the "haughty chasseur" was determined to keep the coveted prize from falling into the hands of a foreigner.

Fifteen attempts were made on the Matterhorn before its final conquest, and seven of them were made by Edward Whymper, all from the Italian side. Characteristically, he held to the route he had first decided upon, though the bold Parker trio had again proved the Hörnli Ridge to be practicable for more than half of its height before a severe

18 The Matterhorn from the Col d'Hérens, showing
   the Italian Ridge on right of summit

storm forced them to retreat. He was convinced from what he had seen
of Carrel that the Italian was the one companion who would eventually
ensure his success. And when he came to Breuil in July 1865 he had a
kind of half-agreement with Carrel that they would join forces in this,
his eighth attempt. Carrel met him with a refusal. He had been
"engaged to travel with a family of distinction in the valley of Aosta".
Whymper grumbled, let him go, and looked round for some other
guide. There was not one to be found in Breuil. Moreover, he soon
discovered that Carrel's "family of distinction" was in fact a party of
Italian mountaineers, and that the party was already on its way to the
Matterhorn.

What had happened was this: Jean-Antoine Carrel's dream had come true. An Italian Alpine Club had been formed, and two of its founder-members, Felice Giordano and Quintino Sella, had engaged Carrel as chief guide for their attempt to climb the Matterhorn. While Whymper was actually in Breuil, Giordano was writing to Sella urging him to make haste, since the ascent might become a race for the top:

> I have tried to keep everything secret; but that fellow whose life seems to depend on the Matterhorn is here, suspiciously prying into everything. I have taken all the best men away from him; and yet he is so enamoured of the mountain that he may go with others and make a scene. He is here in the hotel and I try to avoid speaking to him.
>
> A letter from Giordano (unpublished).

Carrel had good reason, then, for his lie. But Whymper was furious. He had been "bamboozled and humbugged"—made a fool of—swindled out of his chance. Very well! He would beat the Italians in spite of all. Their caravan of guides and porters would take a day or two to establish the route for their masters. He could race back across the Théodule to Zermatt, find a guide somehow, and climb—against time and his rivals—by the Hörnli ridge.

The theme of the story has changed. Instead of the joyous conflict of man with mountain, here was the angry rivalry of man with man. Whymper's greatest ascent was undertaken not in the true spirit of mountaineering but in a spirit of wrath and revenge—and in haste.

"Mountains are no places for running silly races."

says a modern climbing jingle. Is it too fanciful to suggest that the Matterhorn resented this cavalier treatment?

In any case, luck seemed to be with Edward Whymper in his new and somewhat desperate resolution.

The Reverend Charles Hudson had just arrived at Zermatt with a young companion named Hadow and the best of the Chamonix guides, Michel Croz, intent on making the first ascent of the Matterhorn. Hudson was a better mountaineer than Whymper, and had seen from the first that the Hörnli ridge from Zermatt offered the best hope of success. It is significant that the Lonsdale *Mountaineering*, the British authority on mountain-climbing and its history, speaks of "*Hudson's* conquest of the Matterhorn". Hadow was a strong walker and had climbed Mont Blanc, but was not an experienced mountaineer. Almost at the same time Whymper fell in with Lord Francis Douglas, a young man who had achieved some difficult Alpine climbs and was now burning to try the Matterhorn. Douglas confided to Whymper that his guide, Peter Taugwalder, had been prospecting the Hörnli ridge and was confident that it could be climbed. Whymper, guideless and impatient, coveted Croz and Taugwalder but could not take them

from their employers, especially as Douglas and Hudson had the same ambition as himself. He could only suggest that they should form one party, including himself, and start immediately. This was agreed to.

Accordingly, they started together from Zermatt on the morning of 13th July 1865, in perfect weather, with the gigantic finger of the Matterhorn beckoning them on from high in a heaven of cloudless blue. That day they scrambled easily enough up the long ridge of shattered rock that looks so deceptively steep from Zermatt and halted to bivouac at a height of 11,000 feet. Next morning, mounting the hitherto unclimbed upper part of the ridge, they thought the climbing so simple that the rope could almost have been dispensed with. They numbered seven: Whymper, Hudson, Hadow, Lord Francis Douglas, Croz, "old" Peter Taugwalder and his son "young" Peter, who went with them as supplementary guide and porter.

To about 14,000 feet the ridge continued "like a huge natural stair-case". At the levelling-out of the arête called "the Shoulder" the difficulty became greater for a short distance, but beyond this there was only one awkward corner and 200 feet of easy snow. Throughout the ascent Whymper had been tormented by the thought that the Italians might have beaten him to the top. They had started out four days before. It was possible—indeed probable—that they had won the race. He records how Croz and he unroped from the others on that final snowslope and dashed together for the highest point. "Hurrah! Not a footstep could be seen!"

They had triumphed—and there, tiny black dots on the Italian ridge 1,200 feet below, were Whymper's rivals. He yelled himself hoarse, but it seemed that Carrel and his men had not seen him. He summoned Croz to help him lever great rocks from the summit and hurl them down until it was certain their victory was observed. "The Italians turned and fled." Whymper's account in *Scrambles amongst the Alps*, written years later, tells how the defeated men reported to their employers that the evil spirits on top of the Matterhorn hurled stones at them. In fact, Carrel knew at once who had stolen his coveted peak. "It was Whymper," he told Giordano. "I recognised him by his white trousers."

It was 1.40 in the afternoon when the British party reached the sum-mit. An hour later they began the descent.

There can be no doubt that excitement and the relaxed tension after the uncertainty of the climb made them careless, even Hudson and Whymper. Some started down before the others were ready; an old rope was used which had not been intended for climbing; the agreed proposal to fix a safeguarding rope at the difficult section was not carried out. In high spirits the first five men plodded down the sunlit snow—a white roof beneath which sheer rock-walls fell a vertical mile to the shadowed ice of the Matterhorn glacier. Whymper and the younger Taugwalder, who had lingered on the summit, caught them up as they were beginning the descent of the difficult rocks, and roped themselves to "old" Peter, who was descending last. All seven men now formed one rope of climbers.

Young Hadow, who was not properly shod and had little experience of steep rock, was having his feet placed in the holds for him by Croz when the fatal slip occurred. Hadow slid from his holds, fell against Croz, and knocked him over. Hudson and Lord Francis Douglas, on the rope above them, were dragged down instantly. The two Taugwalders and Whymper, higher up the rocks, braced themselves to resist the jerk. But the link between them and their companions was the old rope—the rope that should never have been used.

What followed is best described by Whymper himself:

> We held; but the rope broke midway between Taugwalder and Lord Francis Douglas. For a few seconds we saw our unfortunate companions sliding downwards on their backs, and spreading out their hands, endeavouring to save themselves. They passed from our sight uninjured, disappeared one by one, and fell from precipice to precipice on to the Matterhorn-gletscher below, a distance of nearly 4,000 feet in height. From the moment the rope broke it was impossible to help them . . . So perished our comrades!
>
> Whymper's *Scrambles Amongst the Alps*, 1900.

For half-an-hour the three survivors remained where they were, unable to move. When, at last, they recommenced the descent the two Taugwalders were suffering so severely from shock that they could scarcely move without support; and for Edward Whymper the most perilous part of that ill-fated expedition was the shepherding of two utterly unnerved men down the Hörnli ridge to safety. Not until the morning of the following day did they reach Zermatt, bringing with them the news of a catastrophe which was to shock Europe.

The Matterhorn disaster of 1865 did not, as is sometimes asserted, halt the progress of mountain exploration or of mountaineering as a pastime. It is true that the enormous publicity given in Britain to the accident (perhaps because one of the victims was a young nobleman) brought united denunciation from the Press, and that Queen Victoria asked her advisers if mountaineering could not be put down by law. But the slowing-up of notable ascents was due to the fact that by the end of 1865 all the greater Alpine peaks had been climbed. The Golden Age of first ascents was over.

For Edward Whymper, the result of the tragedy was that from a young climber known only to the small circle of Alpinists he became a world celebrity, able to live by his writings and lectures. He continued to climb, and nine years after his first ascent climbed the Matterhorn a

19 Gustave Doré's engraving of the Matterhorn disaster

20　The path to the Hörnli hut on the Matterhorn; Monte Rosa in the background

21　Looking up the Hörnli Ridge from the hut

23　The Swiss summit of the Matterhorn

second time. But most of his later ascents were made in ranges other than the Alps.

The Matterhorn has retained its fame and its dramatic reputation, though today it is a humbled mountain. Every year hundreds of tourists, many of them incapable of real climbing, are towed up and down the Hörnli ridge by guides who know every foot of the way; and not only have all its four great ridges been climbed but also the faces between them.

Of the other persons of that drama of a hundred years ago, Peter Taugwalder the elder suffered most severely. Though he had withstood the tremendous jerk of the fall like a man, it was soon rumoured that he had cut the rope to save himself from being dragged down—or, alternatively, that he had ensured that the weakest rope was below him, in case of an accident. These unfounded suspicions drove him to escape from his native valley to the United States, where he lived for several years.

A happier sequel is the subsequent history of Jean-Antoine Carrel. That bold chasseur, once defeated but never daunted, stood on the topmost point of his beloved mountain only three days after Whymper's ascent. He had climbed it by the Italian ridge, whose final cliff is far more difficult than anything on the Hörnli route, and his only companion for the last part of the ascent was a young potboy from the Breuil inn named Baptiste Bich. It is pleasant to record that fourteen years later, when Whymper went to climb in South America, Jean-Antoine Carrel was engaged as his leading guide; and the two old

22　Climbers on the Hörnli Ridge

antagonists made together the ascents of Chimborazo and Cotopaxi and climbed several virgin peaks much higher than the Matterhorn.

Far from discouraging mountain-climbing, the story of the Matterhorn attracted more and more adventurous spirits to the Alps. The routes followed by the pioneers were repeated again and again, and the lesser summits (some of them harder climbs than the Matterhorn or Mont Blanc) were ascended by parties who climbed purely for the sport of it. With the end of the Golden Age, mountaineering as we understand it today had begun.

No longer was it necessary to use scientific research as an excuse for the ascent of the splendid Weisshorn, as Professor Tyndall had done on his first ascent, in 1862, of that peak which is a finer and higher mountain than the Matterhorn. Ruskin might fulminate in print against the red-faced Alpinists who turned his quiet Alpine villages into climbing centres, but the adventure had come to stay. Nor was it only British-born enthusiasts who manned the front rank of the venturers. W. A. B. Coolidge, born near New York in 1850, made the first ascent of the Meije's central peak in the Dauphiné, with his aunt Miss Brevoort, and together they made the twenty-fifth ascent of the Matterhorn. Another American, Dr W. O. Moseley, was killed on the

24 Dauphiné: the Meije

25 On the East Ridge of the Weisshorn

26 Alpine Hut Réfuge du Réquin,
    in the Mont Blanc region

Matterhorn in 1871. Germans, Italians, Frenchmen—men of all European nations joined the growing band of mountaineers. Huts, some of them fine stone buildings like the Réquin Hut above the Mer de Glace, superseded the old bivouacs of the pioneers; and the scientists —at last achieving their high research-station—later built the observatory on the Jungfraujoch, where today a rack-railway carries the tourist to a height of 10,000 feet. In the Austrian Tyrol, where the Gross Glockner (12,461 feet) and the other chief peaks were first climbed by Austrian parties, large hut-hotels such as the Braunschweiger were soon being built to accommodate the many "moderate" climbers who visited this lovely region for the ascent of peaks in the Zillertal, Oetztal, and Stubai Alps. The snow-crest of the Ramolkogl and the harder Biancograt of Piz Bernina in the Engadine, the steep rocks of the Rimpfischhorn and the crags of the Bavarian mountains, could be tackled with confidence by ordinary mountaineers, for improved technique and increased knowledge of potential dangers gave a greater margin of safety.

5. The Gosausee, Austria   *H. N. Collinson*

27 The Observatory and Hotel on the Jungfraujoch, Bernese Oberland

28
Snow-covered séracs
below the Jungfrau

29 Gross Glockner (12,461 feet) in the Tyrolese Alps

30 The Schwarzsee, in the Zillertal Alps

31 Braunschweiger Hut and the Wildspitze, Oetztal Alps

32 The summit ridge of the Ramolkogl, Austrian A

34 Approaching the summit of the Rimpfischhorn, Pennine Alps

35 On the Bondo Glacier of Piz Badile, Bernina Alps

On the Biancograt, Bernina range

36 Crossing a crevassed glacier

37 Practice in crevasse rescue

38 Belaying for the leap across a crevasse

39 A bridged crevasse in the Oberland

The use of the climbing-rope now provided far more security than it did in Whymper's day; methods of "belaying"—anchoring the rope to sound rock-spikes or to a deep-driven ice-axe—arrested many a slip that would otherwise have been fatal. The ice-axe, developed from the unwieldy alpenstock, had emerged as a well-balanced implement 3 feet long, spiked at one end and equipped at the other with a steel head composed of pick and adze for efficient step-cutting in snow and ice. The hidden crevasses on snow-covered glaciers had lost much of their terror, for the linking rope could support a member of a strong party if he fell through. Ways of rescuing a man who had fallen into one of these bottle-necked chasms in the ice were devised. And the merits of ice-claws—crampons—were rediscovered. The Alps began to deserve the name that Leslie Stephen had bestowed on them: The Playground of Europe.

The stalwarts of the Alpine Club still yearned for unclimbed summits. A. F. Mummery, who had startled the mountaineering world with his climbs on the dizzy Aiguilles of Mont Blanc and had made first ascents in the Caucasus, wrote truly that the mountaineer is first and foremost an explorer, a wanderer into untrodden realms. Douglas Freshfield explored the Caucasus and in 1868 climbed Elbruz (18,480 feet) the

47

40 Crossing the upper couloir on the Schreckhorn, Oberland

6. The Fée Glacier *H. N. Collinson*

41 Aiguilles du Dru and Verte from Aiguille du Midi, French Alps

Top
42 Pinnacles above Romsdal, Norway

Centre
43 The Trolltind peaks, Norway

Bottom
44 Rock peaks in the Romsdal Mountains
    Norway

45 Kvandalstind, a Norwegian rock-pinnacle

highest summit, with Moore and Tucker—the first important climbing expedition outside the Alps. Sir Martin Conway led a Himalayan expedition in 1892 and reached the summit of Pioneer Peak, 22,600 feet. Aconcagua, 22,829 feet and the highest summit of the Andes, was climbed in 1897 by Edward Fitzgerald's Alpine guide Matthias Zurbriggen. Nearer at hand were the lower but innumerable peaks of the Norwegian ranges, and here William Cecil Slingsby, bearded and jocular and immensely strong, found a "playground" to rival the Alps themselves—a world where the glaciers reached almost to the blue-green fjords, and rock-pinnacles more fantastic than the Alpine *aiguilles* tottered on razor-sharp crests. Norman Collie of the Alpine

51

46 Mount Sir Donald (10,808 feet) British Columbia

Club was one of the first to climb in the Rocky Mountains of North America, where magnificent quartzite peaks like Mount Sir Donald and near-Matterhorns like Mount Assiniboine challenge the mountaineer.

Meanwhile, a new outlet for this exploratory urge had been found in the Alps: the ascending of the great peaks by routes different from those of the first ascents. A. W. Moore—the same who climbed Elbruz with Freshfield—showed the way with his famous ascent of the Brenva ice-ridge route to the top of Mont Blanc. This was as early as 1865, the year of the Matterhorn tragedy. It was the beginning of a siege of the unclimbed ridges and faces, an era when the new route, not the summit, was the objective. Mummery on the Zmutt and Furggen ridges of the Matterhorn foreshadowed such later sporting achievements as the climbing of the Brenva "triptych" by Professor Graham Brown—the ascent of all three of the immensely difficult ridges of ice and rock that plunge down the southern face of Mont Blanc.

But the most surprising development of this Silver Age of mountaineering was the incursion of women into a sport that had been considered the prerogative of men only.

52

7. Dent Perroc, Arolla   *H. N. Collinson*

47 The Brenva Face of Mont Blanc

48 Grosser Löffler, Zillertal Alps

49 The Karwendel peaks of Bavaria

50 Mont Mallet and Dent du Géant from the Mer de Glace

Mademoiselle Henriette d'Angeville had climbed (or been hauled) to the summit of Mont Blanc in 1838, and had scratched on the summit snows with her alpenstock these words: *Vouloir c'est pouvoir*. Other ladies followed her precept and example. Six years after the first ascent of the Matterhorn Miss Lucy Walker climbed it. Miss Brevoort, the American lady who climbed with her nephew from 1870 to 1876, has already been mentioned. At the turn of the century Mrs Aubrey le Blond (later to make pioneer ascents in Norway) was climbing in the Alps; and was on one occasion forced to make two ascents of the Zinal Rothorn summit in one day, having left there her detachable skirt— without which she would not have been received by any reputable inn in the valley.

In the first decade of the twentieth century a middle-aged American lady was to astonish the world with one of the most remarkable achievements in mountaineering history.

51 Huascaran, Peruvian Andes

2 The Schoolmarm from Providence

THE little schoolmistress from Providence, Rhode Island, squatted in the darkness of the tent tending a smoky kerosene stove. A foot or two from her lay the two Swiss guides, snoring in their sleeping-bags. Outside the tent the vast tilted snowslope plunged to the desolate valleys of Peru, invisible in the black night; and along the snowslope roared the wind, beating and tearing at the tiny canvas shelter until it seemed that this attempt to climb the loftiest peak of the Peruvian Andes must end in tragedy before it had well begun. Annie Peck patiently scooped more snow from the bucket beside her and let it slide into the steaming billy-can. Melting snow was the most tedious of tasks—three packed billy-cans of snow were needed to make one billycan of water—but the flasks had to be filled ready for the morning and she had set herself the job of doing it, dog-tired though she was. Resolution in small things, as well as courage and mountaineering skill, was needed for the conquest of Huascaran.

Miss Annie S. Peck, at fifty-eight, was in fact a little more than a schoolmistress. She had taught in the High Schools of Providence, Saginaw, and Cincinnati, but of late she had specialised in Greek and Roman Archaeology and gave lectures on these subjects. On her vacations (she told incredulous friends) she really *lived*. When she was forty-five she had visited the Alps and climbed the Matterhorn, and since then mountains had been her second life. In Mexico, in Bolivia—where, on Mount Sorata, she had climbed to 20,500 feet—and in Peru she had explored and climbed. And now her heart and soul were set on reaching the summit that rose far above the snowslope where this first camp was placed, a summit higher than any she had attempted before. Indeed, Miss Peck had hopes of proving it to be higher than Aconcagua itself, and therefore the utmost crest of the two American continents.

She had made a bold reconnaissance of the great mountain in 1904, accompanied by a party of ragged *peones* from the valley who had never stepped on ice before. That first visit had shown that the mighty precipices of Huascaran's east flank were impracticable; no one could climb difficult rock at so great a height above the sea. A year later she was back again to try the west face, where a gigantic glacier, much crevassed, soared to the saddle between the mountain's twin summits.

That attempt had failed because of the natural timorousness of her Peruvian porters and their lack of high-altitude equipment. It was evident now, if it hadn't been before, that she could only hope to succeed with the aid of Swiss guides accustomed to difficult snow and ice climbing. In 1908 Gabriel and Rudolf Taugwalder crossed the Atlantic to join her in New York and travel with her to Yungay in Peru. And here she was, encamped at 11,000 feet on Huascaran and ready for her third attempt.

At last the water-flasks were filled and the stove could be put out. Miss Peck crawled wearily into her sleeping-bag beside the guides and lay for a few minutes reflecting on the thorns that beset the path of a lady mountain-climber in the year 1908.

That she was considered eccentric, even mad, was only to be expected; and there was a certain comfort in the knowledge. The label of madness spared her the less bearable accusations that arose from her present position—a woman alone with two men, actually sleeping with them in the same small tent. And she had already discovered that her guides wore the traditional superiority of the male and would not yield to the decisions of a woman, however experienced on mountains. Her choice of a site for the first camp had been vetoed, and Gabriel and Rudolf had insisted on seeking this exposed position, which wasn't even on the route for the saddle. "One of the chief difficulties in a woman's undertaking an expedition of this nature," she wrote later, resignedly, "is that, whatever her experience, every man believes that he knows better what should be done than she. So it is not strange that, in common with my previous helpers, the Swiss guides should conclude that my experience counted for nothing in comparison with their own judgement." Rudolf Taugwalder especially, who was older than Gabriel and more temperamental, tended to regard himself as the real leader of the expedition and would need tactful handling. Miss Peck dismissed the problem from her mind and composed herself for sleep, with the sleeping-bag drawn tight round her ears to deaden the noise of the gale and the snoring of her companions. Her last waking thought was of the summit, night-hidden and remote a mile above her head. If Huascaran proved to be higher than Aconcagua—and if she could climb it—she would not only have ascended the highest mountain in the two Americas but also have climbed higher than anyone, man or woman, had climbed before.

Huascaran towers above the Cordillera Blanca, the granite-enclosed chain of ice-clad mountains in the Peruvian Andes, 200 miles north of Lima on the Pacific coast of South America. Fifteen hundred miles to the south is Aconcagua, 23,080 feet high and (so far as was known in 1908) the culminating point of the two American continents. Aconcagua presents no technical climbing problems for the mountaineer, being in its upper part a 1,000-foot slope of debris exposed to frequent storms and intense cold. It had been climbed in 1897 by Matthias Zurbriggen, the leading guide of Edward Fitzgerald's expedition, who reached the summit alone. Annie Peck knew very well that her own chosen peak was a far harder mountaineering proposition than Aconcagua and that she would probably have to face similar conditions of wind and cold, and the half-dozen hardy Indian *peones* who carried up her tent and stores were as warmly equipped as herself and her European guides. But little was known, at that time, about the special hazards of mountaineering above 20,000 feet, except that climbers were sometimes attacked by a mysterious illness, a kind of "mountain sickness," called *soroche* by the Peruvian hillmen. Against the untrodden ice of 24,000 feet Miss Peck opposed ordinary Alpine equipment, with a few items of extra clothing. For her own protection against the weather she relied on "an Eskimo suit borrowed from the Museum of Natural History"—the first recorded use in mountaineering of the now universal *anorak*.

That gale-swept camp was the second on the ascent, the first to be placed on the snow of the west face. Miss Peck's plan was to traverse into the giant trough down which a glacier plunged steeply from the saddle between the twin summits; to climb the glacier, camping as necessary on the way, to the saddle; and from a camp on the saddle, at about 20,000 feet, to attack one of the two summits. Her observations from the valleys had revealed no discernible difference in the heights of the two peaks of Huascaran. A metre or so could make no real difference to her achievement if she gained one of them.

Next morning the terrible wind died down. The Indian porters came up from the snowline camp with more stores, and Rudolf set off with one of them to reconnoitre the traverse to the glacier. He returned exhausted and unwell, obviously suffering from the dreaded *soroche*. On the following morning he was worse, and it was decided that he should go down with the *peones*. Gabriel volunteered to remain and continue the attempt.

With the two toughest Indians, the Swiss guide and the elderly American lady started for the summit. The corner was turned, and there before them rose the enormous glacier, its dully gleaming surface broken by blue chasms and vertical ice-walls. Far, far overhead the snow-rim of the saddle hung dazzling white against the pale blue sky of a clear day. Below it the glacier narrowed and steepened, guarded on either hand by a mighty pillar of rock. Roped together, the four began the long ice-climb, hindered by the deep soft snow that lay on the ice and masked the crevasses. Forced to zigzag by the steepness of the slope, sinking to knees and sometimes to waist in the powdery stuff, they struggled slowly upwards, while the wind rose once more to freeze their double-gloved fingers. Little by little the two great pillars of rock above—"the portals," as Miss Peck called them—drew nearer.

> We had now passed the faces of the mountain and were between the two peaks, surrounded on all sides by yawning crevasses, ice-falls, great hollows, perpendicular walls of snow, a heterogeneous collection of everything that could be fabricated out of ice and snow by the presiding genius of the upper world.
> *Harper's Magazine*, New York, 1910.

But the day was ending. They camped, still far below the saddle, in a snowy corner enclosed by vertical white walls. And Wednesday was a repetition of this day's slow and laborious work, with one incident which demonstrates the quality of the Lady of Huascaran. The party was stopped by a crevasse which stretched right across the icy slope and was bridged, in one place only, by a frail gangway of snow. Gabriel would not cross despite the protecting rope, fearing that if he fell in those above would not have strength enough to pull him out. Little Miss Peck—by far the lightest of the party—took over the lead and crossed first, securing the others with the rope passed round her deep-driven alpenstock.

That night they camped again among walls and chasms of ice. But "the portals" were below them and the final ice-wall of the saddle just above. Next morning Gabriel began work on the vast precipice of ice, whose lower reaches he estimated to have an angle of 80–85 degrees—an exaggerated estimate, but Miss Peck found it steep enough to be "terrifying", even to her. The hard, slow labour of step-cutting went on all morning and all afternoon, until at last the slope eased. Still they were not on the crest of the saddle, but Gabriel could do no more. They camped at the first opportunity. And next day, at 1 p.m., the whole party stood at last on a slanting field of hard snow, half a mile wide and 20,000 feet above the sea—the saddle. On one hand rose the south peak, so well defended at its base by high walls of glittering ice that they deemed it impossible. The north peak, at the other side of the saddle, was very steep and clad with ice but seemed to offer a possible route to its summit. There was still 3–4,000 feet of difficult climbing to do, so they made camp on the saddle, resolving to start for the final assault at 3.30 a.m. next morning.

There was a steady, freezing wind blowing across the saddle and the cold was intense at half-past three. Gabriel, who was suffering from the altitude, declared that the danger of serious frostbite was too great at that hour. They waited until half-past six and then Miss Peck and the guide set out into the wind and bitter cold. The labour of step-cutting began again, with Gabriel performing Herculean feats in spite of his *soroche*. A long oblique traverse on hard snow; then up, and up, and up, by shelf and wall and roof-top slant of ice, for hour after hour.

With every hundred feet—and it might take sixty minutes to gain so

8. Mountain Track, Arolla   *H. N. Collinson*

much—the wind grew stronger. Gabriel, who was doing all the skilled work of cutting the interminable ladder of ice-steps, was tiring fast, and showing unmistakable symptoms of illness. As for Annie Peck, she felt capable of climbing on indefinitely, though she feared frostbite. But it was two in the afternoon, the summit still far above, and the guide exhausted. If Gabriel slipped it would be impossible, on such a slope, to arrest the slip with her ice-axe. They would fall for 10,000 feet, unless the fatal slide ended in a crevasse. She called up to Gabriel to halt.

The big man, supporting himself with his long-shafted ice-axe, turned to look down at her. In spite of the intense cold his bearded face glistened with sweat, and Miss Peck saw that his knees were shaking.

"If you think it's dangerous to go on, Gabriel," she said clearly, "we must retreat."

It was, in effect, a command. But it tacitly left the decision to the man. The Swiss did not hesitate. In another minute they were descending, with infinite care, the icy staircase that had been carved so laboriously up the final tower of Huascaran.

The need for absolute sureness of foot, combined with the knowledge that Gabriel—on whom, as last man down, the safety of both depended if one of them slipped—was far from well, gave Annie Peck some bad moments. She found this descent, as she frankly confesses in her account of it, "alarming". Yet even on that perilous retreat she was planning a counter-attack. Apart from the wind, the weather was fair and settled, making possible a second—possibly a third—night in camp on the saddle. A day's rest might allow Gabriel to recover, and if the faithful porters would agree to stay with them they could make a second assault, using the steps they had cut that day.

They reached the little tent on the saddle completely exhausted. It was an hour before they could summon the strength to make tea and eat some *quinoa* meal. But that night Miss Peck went cheerfully to rest cheek by jowl with her three male followers, for all of them had agreed to try the ascent again after a day's rest.

Aptly enough, the rest-day was a Sunday. The Schoolmarm from Providence, however, was busy all day—melting snow on the kerosene stove to make drinks for her inert companions. And Gabriel did not improve. On Monday morning it was plain that he was incapable of making the effort of climbing that last 4,000 feet and down again in a day. There was not enough food left for a longer stay on the saddle and there was nothing for it but to abandon the climb—to go back down the ice-wall, and the glacier, and the lower rock-slopes, all the way down to Yungay in the Huailas Valley, whence they had started out nine days ago.

In clear, still weather they began the descent, with a last glance for the pyramidal summit of Huascaran's north peak glittering high above. Their heavy burdens could be lowered down the great ice-wall, and this was done; but one of the bales escaped from the rope and fell, to be lost for ever in a crevasse. It was the bundle containing the Eskimo suit borrowed from the Museum of Natural History. This was the only casualty of the hazardous downward climb. When they were off the snow and were stumbling wearily down the mountainside above Yungay they were met by Rudolf Taugwalder and three *peones*, who had come up to begin the search for them. News of their long disappearance had been telegraphed to Lima, and the Peruvian Government had ordered search-parties to be organised immediately.

Nine gruelling days on the high snows, and a very gallant failure, would have been more than enough to satisfy any other woman. But not Annie S. Peck. As soon as she was safely down in Yungay she busied herself with the preliminaries for a return match with Huascaran—"consultation with the guides, telegrams and messages to neighbouring towns and mines to procure heavy shoes, woollen stockings, and flannel shirts for the porters . . . making two more pairs of unmentionables, as these could not be purchased". An alcohol stove was obtained to replace the kerosene snow-melter. It took ten days to get what she wanted, and then—on August 28th—she was off again.

A completely recovered Rudolf Taugwalder found his employer in resolute mood. This time Miss Peck insisted on making direct for the camp-site she had chosen, thus saving a day, and the following day the party was once again on the great glacier falling from the saddle. There had been a change of weather during the ten days at Yungay, and the snowslopes had been softened by sun and then frozen hard, so that they made very fast progress where they had previously floundered through deep snow at the rate of a few feet a minute. On the afternoon of the second day they reached the site of their fourth camp on the first attempt, and pitched the tent there. Now began the hard ice-climbing. For the final load-carrying to the saddle camp they kept with them three well-tried Indian porters—Lucas, Adrian, and Anacreo—and the party of six climbed on two ropes, Rudolf leading one and Gabriel the other. The steps cut previously had disappeared and the formation of the glacier itself had altered, but they went on without hindrance, passing the intricacies of the lower ice and then attacking the great ice-wall that same morning. By early afternoon they were above the wall and on the easier slopes leading to the saddle. And here an unexpected obstacle confronted them—a *bergschrund*, or giant crevasse, had opened right across the brow of snow.

Rudolf found a snow-bridge, the only way of crossing, but it was so rickety in appearance that he wormed his way across on hands and knees to distribute his weight, and belayed the rope carefully to his driven ice-axe on the other side. It was as well that he did so. Miss Peck, confiding in her much lighter weight, walked across safely. But the Indian Lucas, who was third on the rope, tried to follow in the same way—and fell through the unstable snow into the crevasse. The axe-belay held. Gabriel swiftly untied the other rope from his men and lowered the end into the crevasse. Lucas was dangling head-downwards in the bottle-necked chasm, but he retained enough presence of mind to tie this second rope to his waist, and so was drawn up unhurt by those above. Somewhat shaken by this incident, the party climbed on up the lessening slant of hard snow and gained the saddle between the twin peaks.

Once more the little tent was pitched—this time with difficulty, for a fierce wind was blowing across the saddle. And the wind was bitterly cold. It was getting late in the season and they were 4,000 feet higher than the summit of Mont Blanc. To expose a bare hand to such a wind for more than a few seconds was to risk frostbite and the subsequent loss of a limb. All night the wind screamed past the tent, and in the morning Annie Peck told the guides that it would be safer to wait until the wind abated; but once again the men knew better. Rudolf and Gabriel argued that their route up the North Peak might well give them a little shelter from the wind, and if it didn't—well, they could always turn back. At eight o'clock the lady and her two guides set out for the assault, leaving the Indian porters in the tent.

Miss Peck records her outfit on this occasion:

> For this cold ascent I was wearing all the clothing I had brought—three suits of light-weight woollen underwear, tights, sweaters, four pairs of woollen stockings ... My hands were made comfortable by a pair of vicuña mittens made with two thicknesses of fur. As the sun rose higher these became too warm, and were exchanged for two pairs of wool mittens.
>
> *Harper's Magazine*, New York, 1910.

For the first half-hour of plodding up easy snowslopes they carried with them the precious can of alcohol, fuel for the stove on which they depended for warm drinks and food on their return; if they left it in the tent the porters were sure to drink it. When the slopes steepened the guides deposited the can in the snow.

"Are you sure we can find it when we come back?" asked Miss Peck.

Somewhat impatiently the men replied that they were perfectly sure.

The three held roughly to the course she had taken on her first attempt with Gabriel, and the long traverse to the left across the icy slopes took them out of the wind. Then they climbed more directly upward, their zigzag route forced upon them by gaping crevasses and toppling *séracs*—great ice-splinters pushed out by the slow-moving glacier underfoot—that continually barred their path. For most of the way steps had to be hewn in the ice, but they climbed at the rate of 500 feet an hour, fast progress at this altitude. At last they were forced on to a snow ridge, the backbone of the peak; and at once the freezing wind gripped them. Miss Peck's vicuña mittens had been put in

Rudolf's rucksack, and in getting them out for her the guide let one of them slip from his fingers. It blew away at once and vanished down the walls of ice below them.

It could have been a warning of what was to follow.

Miss Peck hastily put the remaining fur mitten on her right hand, which had to grasp the cold iron of the ice-axe, and used both woollen gloves for the left. On they went up the broad crest of ice, the guides alternating in bouts of step-cutting which became shorter and shorter as the effects of altitude and cold made themselves felt. Behind them the long ladder of steps stretched away down white slopes of appalling steepness. Annie Peck dreaded the thought of descending that perilous ladder. She set her mind resolutely on the summit, that still invisible height which she hoped to prove the highest in the Americas; the hypsometer—the most efficient instrument then known for measuring height above sea-level—was in Gabriel's rucksack.

"Twenty-four thousand," said Miss Peck to herself, balancing up her icy ladder. "It *must* be twenty-four thousand."

It was now almost unbearably cold. Anchoring themselves with their axes, they tried to eat some food. But the meat they had brought was frozen iron-hard and they could only nibble a little chocolate. On again, with grey space on three sides and the white spine of Huascaran still rising ahead. At two o'clock Rudolf halted.

"It is too much, *fraülein*," he panted. "I can do no more."

Miss Peck looked at Gabriel. The second guide bent and began to carve a hole in the ice with his axe.

"Leave your sack here, Rudolf," he grunted. "You'll manage better without it."

Rudolf obeyed without a word. Gabriel, taking over the lead, worked on at the endless ladder, stopping every few minutes to recover his waning strength. The ridge was steepening, the wind seemed to chill the inner core of their exhausted bodies. Rudolf was obviously nearing the end of his strength and even the indomitable Miss Peck knew she could not climb much farther. And then the narrow slope broadened and the angle suddenly eased. Beyond the stinging cloud of powder-snow that whipped into their faces they saw the summit—a hundred paces of easy walking.

Miss Peck realised that there was no feeling in her left hand. She pulled off the wool mittens and saw that her fingers were black. Frantically she beat the hand against her thigh until painful sensation returned, and they stumbled on, up to the top of Huascaran.

Grey cloud and flying snow hid most of the tremendous view, and the intense cold and her dread of that long and dangerous descent spoiled the moment of victory for Annie Peck. "There was no pleasure here," she wrote afterwards, "hardly a feeling of triumph." But at least she could take back the scientific proof she had set her heart on—proof

9. Descent from the Breitlehner jochl *Showell Styles*

that Huascaran was higher than Aconcagua. Somehow they got out the hypsometer. The thing depended on ascertaining the boiling-point of water on the summit, from which the altitude could be determined. Match after match was struck behind the cover of a flapping *poncho*, but the tearing wind defeated their united efforts to light the hypsometer stove. Rudolf refused to help them. Unless they descended at once, he said, they would be too cold to move. In spite of her overwhelming disappointment Miss Peck had to agree.

They packed away the hypsometer and began the descent, leaning sideways against the terrible wind. They had not reached the steepest part of the ice-steps when Miss Peck saw something black fly past her— it was one of Rudolf's gloves. Turning, she saw that both his hands were bare. He had already lost the other. "Such carelessness," she wrote in her account of the climb, "was inexcusable, and brought terrible consequences." The sentence was to bring accusations of callousness against her, but it was a fair criticism.

There was nothing that could be done in the circumstances, with time racing against them and their strength fast waning. Step by step they climbed back down the exposed ridge, and the shadow of Night rose from the invisible valleys to meet them. Hour after hour, rope's-length by rope's-length, the three crawled downward, numbed and stiffened by the increasing cold that came with darkness. The moon rose above Huascaran to light their way, but it was behind them, throwing a black shadow on the next tiny ice-step below. Annie Peck was utterly exhausted now, hardly able to stand. Again and again she slipped and went sliding down, but always the guides stood firm and the rope checked her. In the maze of *séracs* and crevasses she told them that she could no longer stand, that they must carve a shelter for her in the ice. Rudolf and Gabriel urged her on—warmth and hot drinks, they said, were vitally necessary if they were to survive—and somehow she contrived to go on. And at last they reached easier slopes, the first place for nearly six hours where there was no danger of a slip proving fatal. Soon the guides were searching for the can of alcohol; they could not find it. At 10.30 p.m. they reached the tent and collapsed in its welcome shelter, too tired to eat and lacking the means of making hot drinks. All three were beyond thought or movement and the Indian porters could only gape at their inert condition. Rudolf, recovering a little, tried weakly to rub his frozen hands with snow; but Miss Peck, watching him, knew that nothing short of medical attention could help him now.

The terrible wind did not abate that night or next day, and they remained in the tent until the following morning, glad enough to rest and recuperate but longing for better food than the mixture of snow and *quinoa* meal which was their only sustenance. In calmer weather they began the descent from the saddle, and two days later they were safely back in Yungay.

The news of Annie S. Peck's victory was cabled round the world. "The conquering of Mount Huascaran will stand as one of the most remarkable feats in the history of mountain-climbing," wrote one journalist. "That this first ascent has been accomplished by a woman renders it still more wonderful." Today, sixty years afterwards, the assertion remains true. The little ex-schoolmistress from Providence and her two guides had no high-altitude equipment, no ice-claws, no efficient windproofs—none of the aids and safeguards that would be used by a modern party of experts tackling a 24,000-foot peak. The theory of acclimatisation and the causes of high-altitude sickness were unknown to them. Yet they achieved their objective.

> A deplorable sequel to the ascent of Mt Huascaran was the necessary amputation of the left hand at the wrist, and outer joints of the fingers of the other, and a portion of a foot, as the result of frostbite suffered by the guide Rudolf Taugwalder of Zermatt.

So reported an American newspaper, adding that the American Alpine Club and the Appalachian Mountain Club had opened a subscription list to aid the crippled man. Critics were not lacking (chiefly of the male sex) to declare that this was what came of letting a woman organise a climbing expedition. But it was another woman mountaineer who took the last of the gilt off Annie Peck's gingerbread.

In her account of the climb Miss Peck gave an estimate, approved by her guides and based on her observations of the height of the saddle, of the altitude of Huascaran's north peak. "It may therefore be regarded as certain," she concluded, "that Huascaran is above 23,000 feet, hence higher than Aconcagua (altitude 22,800 feet) and the loftiest mountain known on this hemisphere. . . . I have the honor of breaking the world's record for men as well as women." Now in 1906 Dr and Mrs Bullock Workman, Americans exploring and climbing in the Nun Kun massif of the Punjab Himalaya, had reached a height of 22,810 feet. Fanny Bullock Workman was thus the holder of the height record for women climbers and naturally jealous of her title. She sent two French surveyors to Peru in 1909 to ascertain the exact height of Huascaran. The surveyors found the north peak of Huascaran to be only 21,812 feet above the sea; the south peak was 230 feet higher.

Poor Miss Peck! Both her hopes had crumbled at a single blow. She held no record, and her peak was not "the loftiest mountain known on this hemisphere." Worst of all, the summit she had gained was the lower top of Huascaran. Such a discrediting of her claims was bound to relegate her to a very minor place in the records of mountain achievement; and so, for a time, it did. To a world that values only the highest summit and the latest record she was no longer memorable.

Half a century later, however, the steep ice-walls and paralysing winds of Huascaran are no less formidable, though crampons and modern high-camping equipment have lessened its difficulties. The rare climbing-parties mostly follow the route pioneered by Annie S. Peck to the 19,000-foot saddle between the peaks, now called the Garganta. In 1964 four young American climbers, described as "a uniquely strong group," made the ascent and encountered the same severe ice and the same snow-filled wind at their two high camps; they thought the achievement worthy of description in *Summit*, the chief American mountaineering journal. The two peaks, now accurately measured (Huascaran South 22,208 feet, Huascaran North 21,837 feet) had lost nothing of their impressiveness. To the climbers of today it seems pedantry of the worst order to deny the Schoolmarm from Providence the real, and first, conquest of Huascaran.

52 The Tasman Glacier, New Zealand Alps

3 Mount Cook

WHEN, on 29th May 1953, two men stood together on the highest point of the earth's surface, they were both natives of countries whose mountains are difficult snow and ice peaks. Their success owed something at least to this fact. One was a Sherpa of the Himalaya, the other a New Zealander.

New Zealand is not one of the places that spring first to mind when we think of great mountains. The names of its remote white summits are less familiar to British and American climbers than those of a hundred minor Alpine peaks, though today mountaineering is as much a national sport in New Zealand as Rugby football, producing the exceptionally hardy and skilful ice-climbers of whom Sir Edmund Hillary is the famous example. Young mountaineers in New Zealand today are apt to think a little scornfully of the Alpine climbers of the past, with their comfortable bases in Swiss villages and their leisurely rhapsodies on the loveliness of valley and peak. Not for the New Zealander the preliminary afternoon walk up to hut or bivouac with a sturdy porter carrying the baggage, or the ascent next day behind a professional guide who cuts the steps in the ice-slope. The mountain ranges of South Island are a hard school for climbers. Even today, the young men who set off for a weekend's climbing among the white peaks of the Great Divide must carry loads of fifty or sixty pounds—a full Sherpa load—to their camp-site on rock ledge or barren moraine; they will probably have to ford or swim a glacial river to get there, and it is an even chance that on their return the stream will have risen and become impassable. Those days and weeks of brilliant weather with the snow in grand climbing condition, never absent for long in the Alps of Europe, are rare indeed in the New Zealand Alps, where bad weather is the rule and the sudden clearing of the skies may last only for a few hours before the storms of snow or rain return to make the climbers' work doubly hazardous. Such conditions have bred a species of mountaineer for whom the sport is a grimmer and less light-hearted matter than it was for the Alpine pioneers; a type of climber admirably fitted to tackle the treacherous snow and unpredictable weather of the Himalayan giants.

It is worth remembering that the British, pioneers of mountain-climbing in many parts of the world, have no mountains in their home country comparable with those they set out to climb. Snowdon, the highest in England and Wales, may have no snow on its 3,561 feet of height even in midwinter; Ben Nevis (4,406 feet) the highest in the United Kingdom, offers some short snow-climbing in early spring but cannot be called Alpine. Glaciers, crevasses, ice-slopes, the extra hazard of altitude—these were things which the British mountaineers had to cross the sea and travel many hundreds of miles to experience. Though some of them had money and leisure many others scraped and sacrificed to obtain the means of adventure on greater mountains, as indeed they do to this day. Young climbers in France, Germany, Italy, Austria, and Switzerland could perfect themselves in every branch of mountain craft by weekend visits to the icy giants of their own lands, but the young adventurers from Britain had only the short rock-climbs of Wales or Cumberland on which to learn one part of the manifold science of mountaineering. Equipped with this, and acquiring from Alpine mountain guides some skill in icecraft, they sought out un-climbed peaks four times as high as any in Britain and as far away as Mount Cook.

Mountain-climbing began late in New Zealand. One day in 1868 Sir Julius von Haast, the explorer, was leading a party of young men over the lower snows of the Mount Cook range in a mist. They were very tired, and Sir Julius prepared to retreat. "At least, gentlemen," he said impressively, "we are now standing nearer the summit of Mount Cook than man has ever stood before." As he finished speaking a figure loomed out of the mist above them. "I say," it shouted. "Have you chaps seen any of my sheep?" The story—let us hope it is true—points the fact that in those days no one climbed higher than the sheep-farmers in the course of their day's work. At a period when all the major summits of the European Alps had been climbed no attempt had been made to ascend a single one of the New Zealand Alps.

The North Island of New Zealand has no mountains over 10,000 feet high, though Ruapehu (9,175 feet) and two other great volcanoes come within a thousand feet of this height. It is in South Island, in the Southern Alps, that real mountaineering is found—ice-climbing of a length and difficulty comparable only with Himalayan climbing. The peaks are not very high by Swiss Alpine standards. Only sixteen sum-mits exceed 10,000 feet, and Mount Cook, the highest, is 12,350 feet, more than 3,000 feet lower than Mont Blanc. Yet the easiest way up Mount Cook is far more difficult than the easiest way up Mont Blanc, and its dangers far greater. Moreover, if mountain heights were measured from snowline to summit instead of from sea-level, Mount Cook would have the same height as Mont Blanc—about 10,000 feet. For the Southern Alps enjoy (if that is the right word) a tremendously heavy snowfall, combined with almost perpetual cloud which prevents the sun from melting and dispersing the snow. Sliding from the precipices, the vast volume of snow is compacted into glaciers of more than Alpine size, like the Tasman Glacier of Mount Cook, which is nineteen miles long, or the Franz Josef Glacier which ends only 700 feet above the sea. The rarity of clear weather and the likelihood of sudden dangerous storms were two of the many problems to be faced when a member of the British Alpine Club, the Reverend W. S. Green, turned his attention to the highest New Zealand peak in 1882. The others included difficulty of access and lack of accurate maps. But the chief problem was posed by the formidable defences of the peak itself.

53 Ruapehu (9,175 feet) in eruption

Mount Cook rises less than sixty miles from the north-west coast of South Island, fronting the north-westerly winds that race in across the 1,000-mile expanse of the Tasman Sea. The average annual rainfall in this Westland district is well over 200 inches, and on the high mountains this is, of course, snow. The great Tasman Glacier, dead straight for ten miles of its length, runs along the western bases of Mount Cook and its neighbours, Silberhorn and Mount Tasman; on the east side smaller glaciers push down from summit-slopes of fearful steepness between the tangled ridges of snow and ice mountains. Mount Cook stands at the northern extremity of a lofty range, some seven miles long, running south-to-north. Northward again, beyond a glacier and snow col (seen just right of centre in *Plate 52*) rises Mount Tasman (11,475 feet) a peak of snows and glaciers with very little rock outcropping. The crest of Mount Cook is a long ridge, a knife-edge of snow slanting up from the lowest of three summits to the highest point one and a half miles beyond it, with the flanks on either side sloping like the sides of a bivouac tent. The nature of the east flank, which offers the best hope of access to the crest, can be seen from the illustration. A 10,000-foot precipice hung with ice and ribbed with crumbling rock sweeps down

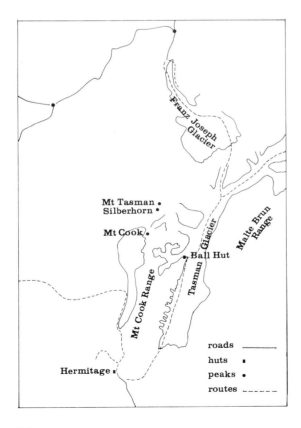

Diagram 3
Mount Cook and vicinity

to the inaccessible buttresses that tower above the Tasman Glacier, out of sight in the clouds at the bottom of the picture. Between these buttresses huge broken icefalls carve their slow way, splintering into towers and chasms as they discharge their thousands of tons of ice into the main glacier. All this enormous mountainside is continually changing. One day the ridges and rock-faces may be bare, the snows between them ice-hard; the next, one of the fierce north-westerly storms may have turned the lower snowslopes to a morass and plastered the crags with white, while avalanches of snow and ice roar down every face and couloir. At either end of the east flank steep glaciers run up westward towards the main ridge. The glacier at the northern end—now called the Hochstetter Glacier—can be seen in *Plate 54*, below and to the left of Mount Tasman, with the gigantic ice-blocks of its impassable ice-fall visible.

The map of Mount Cook and vicinity shows the position of the mountain and its glaciers. But it must be noted that this map was drawn in 1947. None of the roads, tracks, huts or routes shown on it existed in 1882, when for the first time a man set out to climb Mount Cook.

54 The Hochstetter Icefall and Mount Tasman

William Spotswood Green was a clergyman from Dublin, an athletic, jovial, muscular Christian of the type of Charles Kingsley, delighting in "the great inanimate giants of Nature" and rejoicing in the skill that enabled him to use them for his physical and spiritual recreation. Little is known of his Alpine record, and the Alpine Club, of which he was a member, printed no obituary of him when he died; but he had climbed some of the big Alpine routes with two good Oberland guides, Ulrich Kaufmann and Emil Boss, and was not immune to the exploratory itch which every true mountaineer feels. When the Governor of New Zealand offered Government help to any Alpinist who would come over and tackle the unknown peaks of his incompletely explored country the Reverend W. S. Green jumped at the chance. The New Zealand summer being during the British winter, he sailed from England with Kaufmann and Boss on 12th November 1881 and landed at Christchurch on 5th February 1882. This reminder of the lengthiness of travel eighty years ago is paralleled by the rest of his journey to Mount Cook. There was a railway as far as Albury and after that a wagon trail. The trail crossed the gravelly bed of the Tasman River at a place where it is two miles wide and the stream flows in several branches. In one of the streams the wagon wheels sank in the gravel bottom and the water poured through the wagon, drenching all their stores; the climbers ran along the pole between the plunging horses, jumped into the river, and hauled them up the other bank. They were able to dry and sort out their equipment at a remote sheep station called Birch Hill, where the trail ended.

From now on the Irish clergyman and his two Swiss companions were on their own. Flogging their way through the bush, they pushed up the wild valley of the Tasman River, camping each night. They lived like hunters, shooting blue duck for the pot and finding the thieving *keas*, or New Zealand parrots, good to eat. Plagues of blowflies harrassed them at every camp, laying eggs (which became maggots) in their tents, stores, and clothing. "A coat full of maggots," commented Green philosophically, "does you no harm. After all, they don't eat the material." It must have seemed an odd beginning for a nineteenth-century mountain climb. In another half-century the long and arduous journey on foot with its attendant insect nuisances was to be a common-place of all Himalayan expeditions.

Eight days after leaving the coast the three men pitched their tent about two miles south of the snout of the Tasman Glacier. On this spot now stands the Hermitage, a large mountaineering hotel with a motor-road running to it; but in 1882 the area and the wilderness of ice and snow beyond it was *terra incognita*. A day's reconnaissance took them up the moraine beside the glacier and revealed the immensity of their problem. It was clear at once that Mount Cook, if it could be climbed at all, would not be climbed from this camp, so they moved their single

55 East Flank of Mount Cook

tent higher up the glacier; but at once the rain-bearing wind from the north-west descended upon them and drowned them out, forcing a return to the earlier camp. They were still only 2,500 feet above the sea. Several days passed before the weather lifted and they moved tent and baggage up the Tasman Glacier again. And now they could see their mountain and scan it for routes to the top; something no one had ever done before them.

There was a side glacier, they saw, thrusting far up round the southern end of the peak and running up to its south ridge at a point where it fell to about 8,000 feet. The south ridge looked hard, and if they succeeded in climbing it to the south summit of Mount Cook there would still be the very long crest to traverse to the highest top, and that might prove impossible. Nevertheless, it was a route to try. And there was another possibility. From the right-hand side of the glacier, looking up it, another ridge—a rock ridge—ran straight up to the south summit, snow-crested in its upper part and very narrow. (Both these ridges may be seen, uniting at the south summit, at the extreme left of *Plate 55*.) Green named the glacier after the first President of the Alpine Club, John Ball; and from it they resolved to make their first attempts on Mount Cook.

Incidentally, Green was a sufficiently staunch adherent of the old tradition of British mountaineering to pay the customary tribute to science: he and his men planted a line of stakes across the Tasman Glacier, intending thereby to measure its rate of flow.

They made their first essay on February 25th, carrying up sleeping-bags and food for a bivouac. On the rocks above the Ball Glacier they found a suitable ledge at 7,000 feet, and here Green stayed to level the site while the Oberland men went ahead to prospect the south ridge. They were quickly back with bad news. There was much rock to be climbed and all of it was unsafe. Green went up with them to see for himself. When he found himself on a shaky tower of loose slate poised on the exposed crest he knew for certain that this was no route for them; the only uncertainty was whether they would fall down to the Tasman Glacier or hurtle down the opposite slope on to a big glacier under the west flank. They retreated. Two days later they were off again with their bivouac equipment, this time heading for the east ridge rising from the Ball Glacier. The weather was fine. The sun was dislodging avalanches of stones, previously held in place by the frost higher up, and the hum and crash of these filled the air as they sought a line up the steep rocks to the ridge. By snow gully and rock rib they climbed; the gullies, natural channels for the debris coming down from high over-head, were only less dangerous than the rib crests, for on the latter the rock was so unstable that the two men below the leader were in con-tinual peril from pieces of the crest unavoidably dislodged. But they climbed on—for seventeen hours. Before nightfall they had learned that the east ridge held insuperable difficulties ahead and climbed cautiously down again. Fortunately there was clear moonlight that night, enabling them to descend between the crevasses of the Ball Glacier without mishap. One useful thing they had seen from high on the ridge: beyond the flank of the mountain, under its northern end and directly below the summit, was an upper plateau of snow. The big ice-fall descending from this inviting shelf was obviously unclimbable, but if they could get up the bold spur to the right of it, coming down from snowy Mount Tasman, they could gain the plateau. And then the north end of Mount Cook, never before seen, would be right above them and might—just possibly—offer a route to the summit.

They passed one day of rest in camp. Then they started off up the drab, stony moraine of the Tasman Glacier, a pigmy Expeditionary Force marching beneath the walls of a giant's fortress. In their tweed suits and heavy nailed boots, carrying no crampons (ice-claws) and grasping their long unwieldly ice-axes, they would have been laughed at by the young men who today climb Mount Cook in warm duvets and windproofs, with vibram-soled boots to ward off frostbite and a lightweight nylon shelter in case of a forced bivouac, "cramponning" in half an hour up frozen slopes that took the pioneers many hours of

10. Mount Cook *Aerofilms*

step-cutting. But Green was a sound and skilled mountaineer for all that, and the one mistake he made was a venial one, for there was no one to tell him the sort of weather he might expect in the next twenty-four hours.

Ten hours of climbing brought them high on the rocks of the Tasman spur, and here they bivouacked just below the edge of the snow plateau, "Kauffmann making for us," says Green, "a nice bed of material somewhat like road-metal." They had had several fine days, and though mist hid the Tasman Glacier far below them, the weather seemed set fair. When, in the morning, the clearing sky in the north-west showed a strange pea-green hue, they found nothing sinister in that. The sun was warm on the snow-plateau when they gained it—and they saw above them what they had hardly dared to hope for: another steep snow-covered glacier mounting behind the long north-east ridge of Mount Cook which had hidden it from view. This glacier, though at a very high angle and by no means safe from avalanches, ran up to the north ridge below an impossible precipice; that way was barred. But by climbing it almost to the top and then—if they were lucky—finding a way up to the left on to the upper part of the north-east ridge they would place themselves on the final ice-cap of the pointed summit.

In *Plate 56* the north-east ridge is seen coming down to the right from the summit of Mount Cook, across the upper centre of the picture. Green's route went up the narrow glacier on the far side of this ridge (which hides it) and emerged on the ridge itself just below the top, at the point where a rocky cliff appears to overhang the sunlit snow on the ridge-crest. In fact, the snow ridge continues behind the rocky cliff, straight to the summit.

Big crevasses defended the lower part of the glacier. Roped together, they trod the tightrope edges of ice between the green chasms and gained the tilted snow of the glacier's upper section. It was ten o'clock and the sun blazed down on them, though across the far-sunken Tasman Glacier clouds were gathering round the peaks of the Malte Brun range. Kaufmann and Boss were so confident of success that they wanted to leave their coats here, but Green would not allow it. In this he was wise, but less wise in dumping the heavier gear—food, flask, camera—so that they could climb more speedily. All the same, they were glad of light loads on the exhausting climb up the snow, which was of that peculiarly trying sort with a breakable crust overlying deep incoherent powder. At one o'clock in the afternoon they reached a snow shelf of the narrowing glacier. Here they were in a sloping white trench between huge rock walls. The upper end of the trench was a snowy gap on the skyline overhead—on the impassable south ridge. A little to the left and much higher, the dazzling cone of the summit seemed to hang in the zenith, with a veritable chute of snow-covered ice falling straight

56 Mount Cook from the Tasman Glacier

from it to where they stood; apart from the impossibility of the 100-foot wall of blue ice halfway up the chute, it was only too plainly a route taken by avalanches coming down and therefore not to be taken by climbers going up. There remained a steeply slanting shelf of snow running out across the wall of the cliffs on their left, the cliffs of the north-east ridge. Not having crampons, however, they would have to spend precious hours cutting steps across the hard snow of the shelf, and the afternoon was wearing on. Still, they started along it. And then they saw, cleaving the precipitous rocks overhead, a long and narrow ice-gully. It would take them to the higher shoulder of the north-east ridge; but down it, every minute or two, small ice-avalanches fell in hissing white waves to the glacier. They would have to keep close under the rock-wall that enclosed the gully on its right if they were to avoid being swept away.

They hacked and clung their way up the gully, thankful for the occasional handhold on the wall. One bad slip here, and all three would have fallen several thousand feet. Before long they reached a place where the gully had to be crossed if they were to go on. Kaufmann cut the traversing steps at top speed and one by one they sped across to the safety of the other side. Difficult rocks almost barred their exit, and beyond these was an ice-slope. But at last they toiled up to emerge on the narrow crest of the north-east ridge—and into a savage gale.

While they laboured in the gully the threatened north-wester had swept across the sky at their backs and now broke in its full fury on Mount Cook. The wind tore fragments of ice from the crest overhead and sent them whirling down past the upward-toiling men. For they went on, driving in the picks of their axes at every step to prevent themselves from being blown off the ridge. There, not far above them, was the summit itself. Through the spray of blown ice and the rain which now began to drive across (for the north-wester is a thawing wind) they could see plainly that the narrow edge of snow, though corniced with white scallops that overhung the 10,000-foot wall below on their left, would lead them straight to that coveted pinnacle.

But the pinnacle was a cone of ice. It might take them half an hour or more to cut steps up it to the highest point, and the storm was growing worse every moment. Green looked at his watch, and made out with difficulty in the fading light that it was twenty past six. *Twenty past six!* It had taken them fourteen hours to climb this far. They should have turned back hours before if they were to reach a place where they could hope to live out the night in such weather. Hanging on with his axe, he peered up once more at the storm-lashed summit so close overhead. It could not, he thought, be more than fifty feet above him. But every second counted now, and the men with him—staunch companions, but paid servants none the less—had wives and children in far-off Grindelwald. He gave the order to turn back.

It was an order easier to give than to fulfil. Already the tilted ridge of snow was softening into wet slush and the steps, in which each man had trodden in turn as they climbed, broke beneath their hurried descent. They crept downward, like ants crawling down a lofty flying-buttress of some great cathedral. To complete the analogy one would need to imagine the spray from an ultra-powerful fire-hose streaming in their faces, for the rain—strange opponent at that height of 12,000 feet—drove across the crest unceasingly. The depths below their sliding feet were hidden now by swirling dark-grey mist. When they reached the highest rocks, where they must turn down on the left into the glacier-trench, Green remembered that they had left nothing as proof of their achievement. He wrapped Kaufmann's tin match-box in his handkerchief and they piled fragments of rock on this impromptu evidence to prevent it from being blown away. Then they turned down the ice-slope.

The steps they had hewn were filled with water and difficult to discern in the growing gloom. On the very steep descent into the gully Green lowered Boss, and Kaufmann lowered Green. It was dark in the gully and ice and water were sliding down it continuously. They made the necessary crossing safely and started to grope their way down the ice-floored groove, feeling for handholds on the vertical rock-wall on the left and half-expecting every moment the slip and the sudden cry, the irresistible drag of the rope, the swift downward slide to death on the glacier hundreds of feet below the bottom of the chute. It was now too dark to see their footing. Finding a small ledge on the rock-wall beside the ice, Green called a halt and they prepared to stay there for the night. All three were drenched and chilled to the bone, and though it was rain and not snow that blew up the ice-chute they were in danger of getting frostbitten feet. They took off their sodden boots and wrung out socks and stockings. Hardly had they done so when an ice-avalanche came leaping and crashing down the chute, its flying fragments thudding on heads and shoulders. Had it been only a little larger they would have been swept from their perch on the gully wall. Another "bedroom" would have to be found.

Down they went again through the turbulent blackness, and found another ledge. It was very narrow and sloped outwards, so that they could not stand securely without holding on to the wall of rock above it, but it was out of range of the ice bombardment. It was not out of range of the water, though. All through that long night they clung there with an icy stream pouring off the rock-wall to keep their soaked clothing perpetually wet and cold. How they longed for the food they had left behind them on the glacier that morning! But the indomitable Green had his jest ready. "We shall dine three times this night," he told his companions solemnly. In his pocket was a tin containing nine meat lozenges. At intervals of two hours each man sucked one.

To keep themselves alive they had to move continuously, stamping their feet, thumping themselves with one hand while they hung on with the other. There was no likelihood of their dropping off to sleep and falling off the ledge, for in addition to the crash and slither of ice hurtling down the chute a few feet away there was the more distant but louder thunder of huge snow-avalanches plunging down the flanks of Cook and Tasman. Boss and Kaufmann got some comfort from sucking their empty pipes, in true Swiss fashion, and to keep their minds off the agonising cold and ever-present danger the three discussed European politics and criticised the system of Poor Law administration in Switzerland.

And the darkness passed into a murky twilight of dawn. Through the mists three men, barely alive, urged stiff and shaky limbs on the descent to the glacier. An avalanche had fallen down the glacier in the night, but to their unspeakable joy the food they had left there was intact, and fortified by this they were able to continue the long route down to safety and reach their tent at seven o'clock that night. They had been on their feet for thirty-nine hours of gruelling toil. And they had conquered Mount Cook.

Later parties confirmed that only easy climbing lay between the point where Green turned back and the summit of Mount Cook. They considered, however, that the distance he had still to climb was nearer 200 feet than 50. The fact remained that no one had stood on the very summit of the great mountain; and another British Alpinist, Edward Fitzgerald, travelled out to New Zealand with that virgin ice-cone as one of his objectives. Hearing of his intention, a New Zealander named George Graham resolved to be first on the top, and with T. C. Fyfe and Jack Clark, two other New Zealanders, succeeded in reaching the summit by the difficult west ridge on Christmas Day 1894. Fitzgerald had to content himself with making the first ascent of Mount Tasman, following it with the first ascent of Mount Sefton by a very difficult and dangerous rock ridge.

Mountaineering in New Zealand had had its gates pushed open. It remained for an attractive young Australian girl to throw them wide for the influx of men and women climbers of the twentieth century.

Freda du Faur had to battle with prejudice and convention before she could wage war on the snows of the New Zealand Alps. There was no other woman for her to climb with; she must climb with men as her guides. "Don't spoil your life for so small a thing as climbing a mountain, my dear!" an old lady begged with tears, when she heard that Freda had engaged Peter Graham, a guide, to take her up Mount Sealy in 1909. Miss du Faur considered it less reprehensible to be a "fallen woman" in the Victorian sense than a literally fallen woman at

57 Mount Sefton, seen from the Ball Pass

58 Mount Aspiring

the bottom of an ice-slope, and made her ascent with the blameless
Graham. Next year she climbed Mount Cook in record time, and in
1913 made the first traverse of all three summits of the great mountain,
of which an English climber wrote: "Nowhere in the Alps is there such
a ridge . . . that endless stretch of knife-edge snow perched above
everything else in the world."

Freda du Faur was no sexless man-hater intent only on usurping the
male prerogatives of sport. Here is how she describes herself at the
Hermitage (by 1913 a large mountain hotel) on the evening after her
greatest mountaineering feat:

84

11. Mount Kenya from the south   *R. A. Caukwell*

Being perfectly well aware that the average person's idea of a woman capable of real mountaineering or any sport demanding physical fitness and good staying power, is a masculine-looking female with short hair, a loud voice and large feet, it always gives me particular pleasure to upset this preconceived picture. Consequently, I strolled out to dinner immaculate in my prettiest frock.

The Conquest of Mount Cook by Freda du Faur, 1914.

She was a pioneer not only of New Zealand climbing but also of the New Age of mountaineering soon to dawn, when the grandest sport in the world would be available to all adventurous spirits irrespective of sex or wealth or social position.

59 Mount Kenya, 17,040 feet – "Snow on the Equator"

4 To the Highest Peaks

GREEN's nearly successful ascent of Mount Cook came at the end of an epoch in mountaineering history. The traditional need for a scientific approach to mountain-climbing vanished with the coming of the twentieth century, and the men who felt the call of the great peaks set forth openly to climb them in a spirit of adventure. But the true mountaineer is always an explorer with a special kink; he explores vertically instead of horizontally on the earth's surface. And the mountainous part of the earth's surface was still largely unexplored.

As recently as 1848 Dr Rebmann's report that he had seen great snow mountains on the Equator, in Central Africa, was ridiculed by all European geographers. Thirty-four years later the first description of Mount Kenya was published, confirming Rebmann's story, and in 1899 Sir Howard Mackinder with two Alpine guides reached the 17,000-foot top of Batian, the higher of Mount Kenya's two summits. The second summit, Nelion (16,950 feet) remained inviolate until 1929, when Eric Shipton—later to go three times to Everest—climbed it with Wyn Harris. In Alaska a great Italian mountaineer, the Duke of the Abruzzi, was exploring and surveying unknown territory before 1900 and climbed Mount St Elias (18,024 feet) the second highest Alaskan peak. There was a special significance about the ascent of Mount St Elias: it was the first big mountain climb to be recorded by the camera. Vittorio Sella, pioneer of mountain photography and one of the greatest photographers of all time, went with the Duke's party and brought back pictures which stirred the imagination of many a future mountaineer. He climbed and photographed in the Caucasus with Douglas Freshfield, and in 1909 was with the Duke of the Abruzzi again, this time in the Karakoram, whence he brought back superb pictures of the second highest mountain in the world, K2. And a British scientist, J. Norman Collie, led expeditions to the Canadian Rockies and the great Columbian icefield, climbing four of the high peaks. Collie was one of the first explorer-mountaineers to discover that British mountains, as well as the Alps and other overseas ranges, could offer adventure and excitement to the climber.

These mountaineers of the early 1900's were men of wealth and leisure. Though a few less privileged enthusiasts were beginning to find sport on the crags of North Wales and Skye and the Lake District, time and money—and the social position which gave a man *laissez passer* abroad—were as essential to high mountain-climbing as skill and courage. In one quarter of the world, however, this rule was somewhat abated. The British were the rulers of India, and on the northern frontiers of India were the highest peaks to be found anywhere on the globe.

One day in 1852 (so the story goes) an Indian clerk in the offices of the Indian Trigonometrical Survey rushed into the room of Sir Andrew Waugh, the Surveyor General. "Sir!" he cried excitedly. "I have discovered the highest mountain in the world!" His calculations were checked and found faultless. "Peak XV" was 29,002 feet high—nearly 800 feet higher than Peak K2 in the Karakoram, its nearest rival. Later, the Surveyor General renamed Peak XV "Mount Everest", after Sir George Everest who had originated the greatest trigonometrical survey ever made. The tale of that survey is a record of adventure as exciting as any in fiction. The British are inveterate map-makers, and one of their first actions when they became masters of India was to survey and explore. The northern frontier—a barrier of rock and snow and ice 2,200 miles long—presented an almost insuperable problem, for here warlike tribes and embattled native states opposed the entry of white men. Route surveys were essential, and they were the equivalent of raids into unknown enemy territory. Sometimes it was a small band of fighting-men headed by a daring young subaltern of the Indian Army that brought back the coveted figures and angles, sometimes it was one of the famous Pundits—Indian natives in the service of Government—who took their lives in their hands and penetrated the forbidden mountains with sextant and compass. On more than one occasion young adventurers like Alexander Gardner made perilous explorations in disguise. Little by little, year by year, the mapping of the Great Himalayan Range proceeded, until the highest of its thousands of gigantic mountains were measured and placed on the map and some of the valleys that approached them were comparatively open to bold travellers. Though the difficulties and dangers of travel in the Himalaya still remained very great, the almost illimitable prospect of further exploration attracted mountaineering explorers like the Americans, Dr and Mrs Bullock Workman; like Martin Conway (afterwards Lord Conway of Allington) who took an expedition to the Karakoram in 1891 and climbed Pioneer Peak (22,600 feet) the highest summit then ascended; like the botanist Sir Joseph Hooker, whose search for new discoveries in the plant world took him into the heart of the wild valleys beneath Kangchenjunga. The great names in the early history of the Himalaya were still, at this period, those of people privileged by wealth or position to spend their time in this kind of adventuring. But a humbler but no less venturesome brand of mountain enthusiast was being produced among the many thousands of young soldiers maintained in India by the British Government. Only a few of the men who spent their youth campaigning on the Frontier felt the urge to climb, but those few were splendidly placed for indulging their passion. There was Lieutenant Francis Younghusband of the King's Dragoon Guards, who in 1887 made a daring crossing of the Great Karakoram by the 18,000-foot Muztagh Pass; as Sir Francis Younghusband, he was to become, forty years later, the first Chairman of the Mount Everest Committee. There was Captain Noel, the young man who travelled in disguise through forbidden Tibet to Everest and found the route by which the first attempts on the great mountain were made. And there was Lieutenant Charles G. Bruce of the 5th Gurkhas, who devoted himself to training his men in load-carrying at high altitudes for his mountain expeditions.

60 The Himalayan challenge: Ama Dablam

Charlie Bruce, huge and exuberant, wrestling with giant Sikhs and beating them, idolised by his tough little Gurkhas, is a recurrent figure in the early part of the Everest saga. He spoke the Nepalese tongue like a native and had an enormous fund of Rabelaisian stories which, with his reputation as a great warrior, made him free of every village on the approaches to the Nepal Himalaya. In 1895 Bruce joined A. F. Mummery, Geoffrey Hastings, and J. Norman Collie in the first attempt ever made on Nanga Parbat; but a recall to his duties pre-prevented him from taking part in the abortive assault, in which Mummery and two Gurkhas perished. His life ambition was to climb Everest, in those days a mountain unknown and unapproached. And when the Alpine Club, celebrating its fiftieth anniversary in 1907, decided to mark the occasion by sending two noted mountaineers to make the first reconnaissance of Everest, Bruce gained a place on the expedition by undertaking the job of organiser in India.

The two chosen members of the Alpine Club were Arnold Mumm and Dr Tom Longstaff. Dr Longstaff had already climbed in the Kumaon district of the Himalaya and had been the first mountaineer to look into the great "sanctuary" that surrounds Nanda Devi, most romantic of all Himalayan peaks. Mumm was a very experienced Alpine climber. They brought with them to India three Alpine guides. Bruce contributed a party of trained Gurkhas. Then, when all pre-parations were made, the plan was flattened into dust by pressure from above. Mount Everest rises on the frontiers of Tibet and Nepal, two independent countries at that time; and Lord Morley, the Secretary of State for India, decided that such a reconnaissance would jeopardise the treaty he was trying to conclude with Russia. "It is known," said *The Times*, supporting the decision, "that Russian susceptibilities are easily awakened by reports of movements, however innocent, in the heart of Asia." It is interesting, in passing, to note how little Soviet susceptibilities today differ from those of Russia under the Tsars.

So Everest was ruled out. As a consolation-prize, Longstaff persuaded his companions to join him in another probe at the defences of the apparently inaccessible Nanda Devi and perhaps make an attempt on Trisul, the second highest peak in this group. They agreed. And in the result Longstaff was to perform one of the greatest feats of mountaineering ever recorded.

If ever an Elizabethan adventurer was born four centuries too late it was Tom Longstaff. A small man, with an eagle-beak nose and a fiery moustache, he was a climber and explorer from early youth. Alps and Caucasus, Tibet and Nepal, the Rockies and Spitzbergen and Green-land—the record of his many adventures (in his book *This My Voyage*) is so condensed that one feels it should have been expanded into four

61 Trisul from Nanda Devi

volumes. Mumm, a modest and retiring man to whom the discomforts of Himalayan travel were a burden, was a contrast to the lively and indefatigable Longstaff. And the gigantic Charlie Bruce, who cared for neither man nor devil so long as he had "bloody chops" to eat, was a contrast to both the others. The party spent four weeks in exploring the immensely difficult and fatiguing terrain round Nanda Devi, but failed to find any way through the terrific wall of mountain—nowhere less than 18,000 feet high—which surrounds the great peak. On the last day of this exploration Bruce injured his knee so severely that he could no longer hope to climb. The date when the monsoon could be expected to break in dense cloud and snowstorm was not far off. Leaving the unfortunate Bruce to rejoin them when he could walk, Longstaff and Mumm set off to make an attempt on Trisul. They had with them Inderbinnen, Mumm's guide; Alexis and Henri Brocherel, the hardy Piedmont men that Longstaff had brought with him; four of Bruce's Gurkhas under their *sirdar* Karbir; and twenty-three coolies carrying their tents and stores.

It was a four-day march to get into position for the assault, and it took them from the gorgeous Himalayan forests over a difficult snow-pass and across the nearly impassable Rishi torrent. At the river the coolies at first refused to attempt the crossing, whereat Karbir the Gurkha became angry and laid a hand on his *kukri*, the razor-keen Gurkha weapon. Longstaff remonstrated with him for threatening the men. Karbir was hurt.

"I did not threaten, *sahib*," said he. "I only said I would cut off the head of the *first* man who refuses to cross. Now they will all cross—you will see."

The coolies crossed. Two days later they were paid off and dismissed, and the climbing-party, having got past a 100-foot ice-wall at the end of a side glacier, were encamped below the snout of the Trisuli Glacier. On the following day they began the ascent.

Trisul, the great Trident of Shiva, lifts its triple peak fifteen miles to westward of Nanda Devi, which is the only higher summit in the group of a dozen huge mountains. Its height, 23,406 feet according to the Indian Survey, was almost the only certain fact Longstaff knew about it, for there were no detailed maps of its surroundings. Indeed, he was only guessing that the glacier above them would lead to the northern base of the mountain. But he had seen the southern side of Trisul when he was returning from a journey in Tibet two years earlier and had concluded that no ascent could be made on that flank. What lay above the northern glacier was a complete mystery; he knew only that the northernmost of the three peaks was the highest and for that peak he must aim. For him the next day's work was intensely exciting, easy though it proved, for the great ice-river twisted and curved as they climbed slowly up its lateral moraine and the dark cliffs above hid the mountain. At last they turned a corner. "Glory be! We were on the right track." Overhead and straight in front of them soared the vast north-east face of Trisul, draped in snow and ice.

They camped at 16,500 feet, on the last patch of moraine that was free from snow, and at 5.30 next morning were away on the first stretch of hard climbing. A steep and narrow snowslope led up between the glittering icefall of the glacier and the black cliffs on its right. The snow was hard and they made good progress, for they were as physically fit as men can be; but the altitude—that mysterious factor for which no remedy had yet been found—took no account of

12. Sunset on Rakaposhi in the Himalayas   *M. Banks*

physical fitness and soon set them gasping and halting to get their breath. Moreover, the wind increased as they climbed higher, driving loose powder-snow across the slope. The climbers were wearing the traditional Alpine clothing of warm tweeds, for windproof cloth had still to be invented, and the thin snow penetrated to their skins. Chilled and exhausted, they gained a place where the snowslope eased its angle and there pitched the two bivouac tents, which were of the pattern designed by Mummery before he died on Nanga Parbat.

In the night the wind increased its violence. No one had any sleep, for the tents "clapped and banged like rifle-shots" and threatened every moment to blow away. The morning brought no relief. It was impossible to continue the climb through a howling blizzard, and they stayed where they were. Three of the four Gurkhas were suffering intensely from the cold induced by the powder-snow that almost filled their tent, so when a lull in the storm came at noon they were sent down to the lower camp. The second night was worse than the first, and the next morning the storm had not abated. All were weakened by the ordeal and had barely strength enough to uproot the tents and climb down the long and perilous slope—down past their first high camp to the camp below the glacier snout. The first attempt had failed.

A day's rest below the terrors of the storm revived the hardy little doctor but revealed the sad state of his companions. Mumm was ill, with severe diarrhoea; Inderbinnen was suffering from blinding headache; the three Gurkhas would not face the intense cold again. Only Karbir the *sirdar* and the two Brocherels were fit to make a second assault, and Karbir—though he made little of it—had a frostbitten toe. Longstaff spent the rest-day planning that second assault.

He knew that lack of oxygen above 20,000 feet had weakened his own resolution, and he feared what it might do at greater heights— heights never before reached by man. The cells of the brain, of all the body's tissues, are the most sensitive to deprivation of oxygen. If that high camp could be avoided, if the peak could be climbed in one day from a lower camp, might he not cheat the Demon Altitude of its prey? Could "rush tactics" succeed on a virgin Himalayan peak? It would mean ascending 6,000 feet from the highest camp to the summit, and that implied a descent in the dark. But he had had a glimpse of the upper snowslopes and thought they were not too difficult for a night descent.

A modern Himalayan climber would have told him the thing was impossible. Longstaff knew it would be difficult to bring off but trusted in his own resolution and the loyalty of the three men who would go with him. His great fear was lest he, the leader, should have his mind so affected by altitude that he would order a retreat from those upper slopes. So—"I exacted a promise from Alexis and Henri that they would not allow me to turn back whatever I might say." There is an element of real greatness in this, the greatness of the old Greek and Roman heroes; but one wonders what those unimaginative Piedmontese peasants, the two Brocherels, thought of it.

One day's rest was enough for Tom Longstaff. He was away next morning with Karbir and the two guides, and that first day climbed no higher than 17,450 feet, where they camped and at once set about making hot drinks for the great effort of the morrow. The doctor had proposed to start at 4 a.m. for the summit, but at that hour the cold was so intense that it numbed their hands completely before they could put on their frozen boots. It was half past five when they left the two Mummery tents on their ledge in the snowslope and started on the long final climb. The day was clear and intensely cold, the wind less violent but still strong enough to drive powder-snow through their clothing. Five hours very hard work, roped together, saw them above the place where they had camped for two wretched nights. The hard snow steepened, but Alexis Brocherel, who was leading, scarcely slackened the fast pace he was setting. It was indeed too fast for Longstaff. "Henri cheerfully offered to pull on my rope; an offer I gratefully accepted without the least qualm." One o'clock. They had been climbing for seven hours, with half an hour for rest and food, and had reached a height of 21,000 feet by the barometer. The bitter wind strengthened, rattling the icicles that had formed on the climbers' beards and moustaches. Longstaff sucked his icicle-moustache—"a most convenient method of assuaging thirst without calling a halt", is his comment. For there could be no halt now if they were to succeed; the afternoon was fast advancing and they did not know what difficulties were yet to be encountered. There were crevasses about them—an extra big one across the narrowing slope could mean defeat.

And now the slope was getting even narrower—it was a defined ridge. Up it they shuffled, very slowly by sea-level standards but at racing speed for such an altitude. Longstaff's mind began to wander; he thought himself confined in an endless chicken-run with wire-netting on each side of him. The hallucination passed. The four rose higher, forced now to halt briefly at every few steps to gasp for breath, their strained lungs seeking the rare oxygen in that thin and freezing air. The great grim peaks that had stood distantly beside their airy ridge sank below their level—all were gone except Nanda Devi alone. The slope levelled out. Alexis Brocherel turned and shouted "The top!" It was four o'clock and Trisul was won.

Longstaff could hardly believe it. Just beyond them across a dip in the summit ridge was another snow-point, from which a snow cornice drooped over the tremendous precipice on the south. To the doctor it looked slightly higher than the crest where they stood. The Brocherels insisted that it was lower than their summit, but Longstaff had to make sure. Taking over the lead, he fought his way through the violent wind, down and up again, and cut a few steps in the ice of the cornice. He looked over. Incredibly far below him the Himalayan foothills crept like little brown waves to the feet of the snow-clad giants. He saw the whole scarp of the western Himalaya—"so vast that I expected to see the earth rotating before my eyes". His extra climb—a remarkable effort in the circumstances—had been needless; the guides were right and their first summit had been the highest point of Trisul. But for Tom Longstaff the reward was not so much in the achievement of the loftiest peak ever climbed as in the revelation of the earth's immensity he had been granted. That much of the Elizabethan, the adventuring visionary, he had in him besides the faith and daring that can accomplish the impossible.

The suffocation and headache of altitude fell upon the four men again as they began the descent. But when they were below 20,000 feet they could move and breathe and think normally once more, and quickened their pace. By 7 p.m. they were back at the tents. Daylight lingered at this height on the snowslope, and they bundled up the two tents and went on down to their old camp-site on the snow-free moraine. They had descended nearly 7,000 feet in a little over three hours.

This extraordinary climb, made with traditional Alpine equipment on a Himalayan giant 8,000 feet higher than the highest of the Alps, had established the possibility of ascending even higher peaks and brought the dream of Everest a little nearer reality. Longstaff rightly counted it a triumph for his "rush tactics", but he was the last man to rest on his laurels—or, indeed, on anything else. The very next day after the ascent of Trisul he was off again, climbing high up the glacier to fix the position of an unmapped ridge. On the day after that he started with two Gurkhas for another probe at the Nanda Devi defences. And when, four days later, the approaching monsoon ended that venture he journeyed north away from the bad weather into the unexplored maze of peak and glacier round Kamet, there to survey and map and travel for another six weeks.

Someone once called Tom Longstaff "a mini-superman". He would never have agreed to the "superman". He was an ordinary man, he would say, living as a man was intended to live. He died in 1964, aged 89.

It is not strictly true to say that luck gave the British the chance to make their seven assaults on Mount Everest and excluded the climbers of other nations. For a century the British Raj in India had toiled to establish friendly relations with the independent states of Tibet and Nepal, on whose frontiers Everest stands, and had respected their desire to exclude all foreigners. From time to time permission for special missions to Lhasa or Katmandu had been granted, however, and little by little the Dalai Lama—ruler of a nation which puts things spiritual far above things material—had been brought to see that the climbing of Everest was something to be done not for material gain but for the triumph of the human spirit. The rulers of Nepal still resolutely opposed any approach to Everest through their country. To reach the mountain it would be necessary first to obtain the Dalai Lama's permission to enter Tibet; and, second, to make a very difficult journey on foot, lasting more than a month, over the high passes east of the Nepal Himalaya and then westward across the desert plateau of Tibet until the northern valleys descending from the glaciers of Everest could be entered. All the food and paraphernalia for this and the return journey, as well as the climbing equipment for the ascent, would have to be carried by coolies from Darjeeling. It was a tremendous and expensive undertaking, quite impossible for a small private party of mountaineers such as Longstaff's expedition. But when the grim interlude of the 1914–1918 war was past and men could look again towards the high peaks, Captain Noel—the first explorer to reconnoitre the Everest approaches from Tibet—proposed a second reconnaissance. Sir Francis Younghusband was President of the Royal Geographical Society at that time, and he formed an Everest Committee composed of members of the R.G.S. and the Alpine Club to further the project. Funds for the first expedition were raised by private subscription. Application was made to Lhasa. And in 1921 a vital document was received from the Dalai Lama—"Despatched on the Seventeenth day of the Eleventh month of the Iron Bird Year, under the Great Red Seal of the Holy Rulers of Tibet". It enjoined all officers and headmen in Tibet to allow a party of Sahibs to approach the Sacred Mountain Chomolungma, the Goddess-Mother of the Snows.

The 1921 Expedition was officially a reconnaissance expedition. But all its members nourished a hope that the mountain might not prove as formidable as most people thought; that there might be a chance of launching an actual assault. The team of mountaineers included George Leigh Mallory, considered the finest climber of the day, whose name was afterwards to be inseparable from that of Everest as Edward Whymper's is from the Matterhorn.

Mallory was then thirty-three years old, a master at Charterhouse. There was nothing at all of the hearty, bulldog mountain-climber about him. Slim and lightly built, good-looking in a way that suggested the poet rather than the man of action, his withdrawn and sometimes difficult manner concealed an inner fire of resolution that never burned low. On that first expedition he proved his mettle, for it was he who pioneered the route over the difficult Hlakpa La, 22,350 feet high, into the basin of the East Rongbuk Glacier, after twelve

62 Members of the 1921 Everest Expedition:
  Standing, L to R: A. F. R. Wollaston, Lt.-Col. Howard-Bury, Dr A. M. Heron,
    Harold Raeburn
  Seated, L to R: G. H. L. Mallory, E. O. Wheeler, G. H. Bullock,
    Major H. T. Morshead

weeks of exploration and hard climbing had shown that the only feasible way of attacking Everest was from this glacier. It was Mallory who led the way to the top of the North Col, Mallory who still hoped—in spite of the terrible wind against which no human being could stand—to make an attempt on the summit. From the moment he first saw the great mountain it became for him an irresistible magnet. That year the final assault could not be made; it was late in September and the weather was utterly prohibitive. But Mallory had found—or believed he had found—the way to the top.

63 Everest from 22,000-foot peak above Base Camp, 1933

64 Everest (behind on left) Lhotse, and Ama Dablam

A simplified diagram of Everest shows the main mountain as a great ridge more than a mile long, slanting up to the summit at its southern end. From the summit a south ridge falls and rises again to the lower peak of Lhotse, and another ridge sweeps down to the west to form the northern wall of the upper Khumbu Glacier, now called the Western Cwm. From the other, northern, end of the main peak (called by the first expedition the North-East Shoulder) two ridges fork; one north-westward, forming a long saddle between the Shoulder and the North Peak, the other north-eastward along the head of the East Rongbuk Glacier. The news brought back to England by the expedition of 1921 was that a practicable way up the mountain did exist: via the East Rongbuk Glacier, the North Col between the Shoulder and the North Peak, up to the Shoulder and along the main north-east ridge to the summit. The chief climbing problem, they reported, was to reach the North Col, which was inaccessible from the west side and presented on the east a mighty wall, 1,800 feet high, consisting entirely of snow-covered ice. This problem they had solved, though with great difficulty. Above it the climbing route to the North-East Shoulder and the summit-ridge did not look difficult. And if the next expedition attacked earlier in the year they might escape the fearful winds and arctic weather that had turned back the reconnaissance party. Six high camps might be needed before the climbers were high enough to launch a final assault.

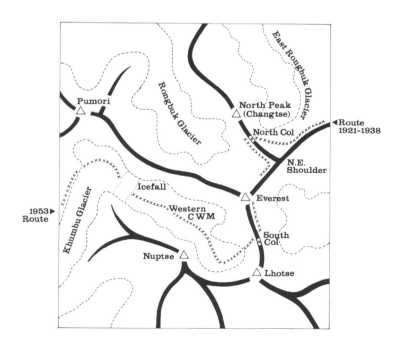

Diagram 4
Mount Everest

In fact, Mallory and his companions had underestimated their mountain, as it is all too easy to do in the Himalaya. Moreover, they had no solution to offer for what might prove to be the greatest problem of all. What happened to a man's body and mind when he climbed beyond 24,000 feet was still a matter for grim speculation.

Mallory was with the expedition that went out again in 1922. The great caravan of thirteen British, fifty Nepalese, 100 Tibetans and 300 yaks reached Base Camp on the Rongbuk Glacier in early May. By May 18th the North Col—now a wall of blue ice—had been gained after difficult step-cutting and the fixing of ropes and the attack on the unknown upper ridges began. This expedition was led by "Charlie" (now General) Bruce, and among its members was Doctor Tom Longstaff, fulfilling at last a great ambition (*Plate 65*). Poor Longstaff was ill from the first, and never reached the North Col. Another newcomer was Captain George Ingle Finch. Finch had always been quite certain that Everest would never be climbed without the use of oxygen apparatus to assist breathing, and backed up by Howard Somervell he had persuaded the party to take out oxygen with them. The apparatus was so extremely heavy and cumbrous that Mallory and the rest would only agree to use it if the first assault without oxygen failed.

The first assault did fail. Mallory and three companions climbed to nearly 25,500 feet from the North Col, and they found that at that height they had to pause and take two or three breaths between each upward step. Mounting at 200–300 feet in an hour they could not hope to reach the summit still 4,000 feet above them. Not only that, but their mental and physical co-ordination was seriously affected. On the descent there was a bad slip by the third man on the rope, which would have been fatal to all of them if Mallory had not retained sufficient alertness to thrust in his axe and belay the rope round it, thus saving the three others.

George Finch and Geoffrey Bruce (son of the famous Charlie) now tried an assault with oxygen. The apparatus was unsatisfactory, but it helped them to reach a height of 27,230 feet—only half a mile from the summit and 1,700 feet below it. They found that the route up the crest of the ridge was far more difficult than had been thought, while the alternative they chose, across the steep face of the mountain, led over outward-shelving slabs like roof-tiles, thinly covered with powder snow. It was the terrible Everest wind, numbing limbs and senses, that drove them down again, utterly exhausted. Some days later that expedition came to an end in tragedy. Seven Nepalese porters climbing to the North Col were swept down and killed by an avalanche.

1924 saw a third expedition on the mountain, this time led by Colonel Norton, who had been on the previous attempt. Mallory was there, of course. The youngest member was twenty-two-year-old Andrew Irvine, fresh from Oxford.

13. Kangchenjunga   *John Jackson*

65 Members of the 1922 Everest Expedition:
   Back row, L to R: Major H. T. Morshead, Capt. J. G. Bruce, Capt. J. B. Noel,
      Dr A. W. Wakefield, Dr T. H. Somervell, Capt. C. J. Morris, Major E. F. Norton
   Front row, L to R: G. H. L. Mallory, Capt. G. I. Finch, Dr T. G. Longstaff,
      General Bruce, Col. E. L. Strutt, C. G. Crawford

66 Members of the 1924 Everest Expedition:
   Standing, L to R: J. de V. Hazard, R. W. G. Hingston, Dr T. H. Somervell,
      Bentley Beetham, E. O. Shebbeare
   Seated, L to R: Capt. J. G. Bruce, Col. E. F. Norton, Capt. J. B. Noel, N. E. Odell

The mountaineers had some inkling, now, of the obstacles arrayed against them by the highest mountain in the world. Everest could not be treated like an extra-big Alpine peak. In all respects it was different —the paralysing effects of its altitude, the unpredictable difficulties of its ridges, the treacherous quality of its snow. The snowslopes that had avalanched and killed seven men would not have avalanched had it been in the Alps. They realised that the North Col route was dangerous, but there was no other way. The old prejudice against the use of oxygen, as being "unsporting", was fast dying, for it was plain that against such an antagonist Man must use every means at his disposal. Even Mallory was willing to use oxygen, for he was (in Younghusband's words) "absolutely possessed with the idea of climbing Everest".

Another theory, that of acclimatisation, had gained some ground. It had been found that a climber in top physical condition could accustom his mind and body to increasingly rarefied air if he mounted slowly, at intervals of some days or even weeks, to higher and higher altitudes. Norton had elaborated a plan based on both theories: the difficult climbing should be done by teams of two, the best-acclimatised doing without oxygen and other pairs using it. He himself wished to climb without oxygen. Gurkhas were to be used as porters, and a few tough little men of the Sherpa tribe for carrying to the higher camps. He got his big party to Base Camp on the Rongbuk Glacier on April 29th. And now Everest got in the first paralysing blow.

Bad weather smote the party before if had reached the base of the North Col ice-wall. Tremendous gales and heavy snowstorms, coupled with 53 degrees of frost, flung them back from Camp III with heavy casualties. Two Gurkhas died, another was ill with pneumonia, the climbers themselves were laid low with half a dozen different ailments. And the North Col itself was sheathed in a thick covering of new snow that would make it unsafe for days. "It is a terrible mountain," Mallory wrote in a letter home; and added that climbing it was more like war than sport.

And the war was on. Five days later the attack began again. The 1,800-foot wall of the North Col was completely changed, a precipice of hanging snow-wreaths and gaping crevasses, but Mallory forced a way up it, nearly losing his life in a crevasse on the way. Ladders and ropes for the porters were fixed at the critical places and Camp IV, on the North Col, was established—but not for long. Down came the blinding snow again, and the temperature dropped to $-24°$ Fahrenheit. Hazard, one of the climbers, was marooned on the snowswept Col with twelve porters. In a lull on the third day he managed to bring eight of them down safely—but the other four refused to make the perilous descent. The snow was still falling and the condition of the great wall was more dangerous than it had ever been. But the four men had to be rescued at once or die of cold and starvation. Norton,

Mallory, and Somervell—the best and fittest climbers just then—climbed up the great ice-cliffs, traversing slopes that were ready to avalanche at any moment, and brought the frozen, panic-stricken men down to safety. The effort, made at 23,000 feet in shocking conditions, cost them their physical fitness. Snowblind, coughing and choking with "high-altitude throat", they limped down through the relentless snowstorms to Camp I. Everest had won the first two rounds.

At Camp I Norton held a council of war. In 1922 the climbing had been done after the monsoon; and in that year the monsoon weather, in which no human being can exist on the high Himalayan peaks, had arrived on May 31st. It was now May 25th. If a third assault was to be mounted it must be very swift and as simple as possible. Seven climbers might be considered fit enough to go up again to the North Col—if the weather improved and if Mallory, Norton, and Somervell made a good recovery from the troubles contracted on the North Col rescue. They would climb in pairs. Two more high camps would have to be placed above the North Col, and from the highest camp the fittest pair would make a final assault. If they failed, it would be the turn of the second fittest pair, while the third pair waited at Camp IV in support and Hazard, the seventh man, at Camp III. On May 30th, in clear weather, the final move forward began.

Mallory and Bruce had been chosen to make the first attempt, and nine porters volunteered to carry up Camp V. The North Col was safely reached—Irvine and Odell, the third pair, remained there—and Mallory's party went on up the great windswept backbone of Everest. The sky was clear blue; but clear sky on Everest means *wind*. The wind lashed and tore at them, penetrating to their very bones, hurling them from their footing on the snowy rocks. At 25,000 feet the porters flung down their loads and themselves and refused—it was natural enough—to go any higher. The two little tents were pitched, and Bruce managed to persuade three of the men to remain there to carry up the sixth camp next morning to 27,200 feet. But during the long and sleepless night, in tents ceaselessly battered by the ravening wind, the last of the porters' courage ebbed away, and in the morning they demanded to go down again. Geoffrey Bruce was suffering from a strained heart. There was nothing Mallory could do but retreat.

Norton and Somervell, the second assault pair, succeeded in persuading three porters to carry beyond Camp V. Napboo Yishay, Lhakpa Chedi, and Semchumbi were the names of these gallant men, and on June 3rd they carried up Camp VI, one tiny tent, to 26,800 feet—1,000 feet higher than any man had climbed before. From that tent, next morning, Norton and Somervell launched their assault on the actual summit.

They were without oxygen, for it had been decided that the heavy apparatus was more handicap than help. Somervell was suffering badly with throat trouble; an ailment from which, later, he nearly died. It was impossible to face the wind on the crest of the ridge, so they kept below it, moving very slowly across the vast shelving face and gaining height almost imperceptibly. A wide band of yellowish rock crossed the face to a great couloir falling from below the final pyramid of Everest, which was now in full view ahead, and Norton led along this. They were not roped together; there was no means of safeguarding themselves on those easy but treacherously sloping slabs, and if one fell the rope would have dragged the other down the 8,000-foot precipice below them. At midday they had reached 28,000 feet, not far short of the great couloir, and here Somervell's breathing became so bad that he could no longer walk. Leaving him resting on a safe ledge, Colonel Norton went on.

For every step he took, Norton needed eight or ten complete respirations. After every twenty steps, he had to rest for a minute or two. Yet he went on, and slowly the great couloir drew nearer. The agonies of partial snow-blindness hindered him and he had difficulty in seeing the ground at his feet, but he went on. He gained the couloir. It was full of loose powdery snow and unclimbable. He crept slowly across it and out on to the rooftop slant of the farther side—tilted rocks thinly covered with snow like granulated sugar. The footing was most dangerous, he could make very little height, and he was half blind. He turned back, in doing so making the decision between living and dying. Accurate theodolite observations afterwards established the point at which Norton turned back was 28,126 feet—876 feet below the summit of Mount Everest.

Norton and Somervell came safely down to Camp IV. And now—if the weather held—it was the turn of the third pair of climbers, Odell and Irvine, to make a last attempt. Noel Odell, an experienced Alpine climber, had shown signs of acclimatising too slowly; and Mallory, fighting fit and eager to revenge his forced retreat from Camp V, was the obvious man to lead the forlorn hope. It was decided that Mallory should take full command of the final attack, choosing his companion, his route, and his method. With Norton's report to guide him, he concluded that the crest of the ridge offered more chance of success than the traverse across the face. And he would use oxygen. This last decision also, in effect, decided his choice of companion, for Odell had no faith in oxygen. Young Andrew Irvine was ready to believe in oxygen if Mallory believed in it. So on June 6th Mallory and Irvine shook hands with the now sightless Norton and set off for the highest camp. Odell moved up to Camp V in support; he was now the only climber fit to do so.

The weather on the day of the last bid for the summit was less clear. Mist hung about the upper part of the great ridge where the Charterhouse schoolmaster and the young Oxford man were grappling with the unknown. Odell, a fanatically keen geologist, clambered upward from Camp V that morning to examine the rocks at a height far above any that had been reached by a geologist before. Every now and then he looked up at the great ridge above him, especially at the two rock "steps" in it where Mallory had thought there might be difficulty. The cloud hung low across the crest, masking the black rock and dazzling snow. But suddenly it opened, revealing the whole summit-ridge and the final pyramid. Far away on a snowslope below the second rock step Odell saw a tiny object move, a second black pinpoint follow. Then the mist swept across like a curtain falling on the last scene of a drama. Odell looked at his watch. It was 12.50 p.m.

This was the last that was ever seen of Mallory and Irvine.

In the years that intervened between the Third Everest Expedition and the beginning of the Second World War there were three more British attempts to climb Mount Everest. On the first of these Frank Smythe, alone, reached approximately the same point as Colonel Norton's farthest. The other two attempts were defeated early in the campaign by the terrible and unpredictable weather that seems to lie in wait for all who approach Everest on its north and east flanks. All three expeditions followed the North Col route discovered by Mallory; and on the 1933 Expedition Wyn Harris and L. R. Wager, attempting the crest route on the ridge, found an ice-axe on a rock ledge sixty feet below the crest. It could have been either Mallory's or Irvine's, but in all probability it marked the place where a fatal slip had taken place nine years before.

Meanwhile, mountaineering in Europe had been steadily growing in popularity. In Britain as well as on the Continent new climbing techniques and improved equipment were being developed; these were to play their part, years later, in the final conquest of Mount Everest. And in America, eleven years before the first Everest Expedition, a curious and astonishing feat of mountain-climbing—now almost forgotten by British mountaineers—had been performed.

67 Mount McKinley 20,300 feet

5 The Conquest of Mt. McKinley

"M'KINLEY IS CONQUERED!" screamed the banner headline on the front page of the *Fairbanks Daily Times* of 12th April 1910, and added a dramatic subhead: "Stars and Stripes Placed on Top of Continent and the Hitherto Unscaled Heights of America's Highest Peak Mastered." Two months later the London *Daily Telegraph* devoted a whole inner page to the story, under the caption "ON THE 'ROOF' OF THE AMERICAN CONTINENT". The report from Fairbanks had been confirmed and there seemed no doubt that the summit of the great Alaskan peak, 20,300 feet above the sea, had indeed been gained.

The story of North America's highest mountain begins no earlier than 1897, when a party of explorers penetrated into the unknown territory north of Cook's Inlet and saw far off a huge peak, draped in ice and snow, rising from a maze of glaciers and dwarfing all the neighbouring peaks of the Alaskan Range. Following a deplorable custom of explorers, they named it after a politician of the period, in this case William McKinley of Ohio, who had just been nominated for the Presidency of the United States; McKinley's undistinguished career ended four years later when he was shot dead by an anarchist, so it would have been better, on the whole, to have left the mountain to its old Indian name of Denali, the Great One. The peak stands 100 miles inland from the inhospitable shores of the North Pacific, in the same latitude as South Greenland. All around it is a wild country of mountains, canyons, forests, and great rivers. In 1910 this country was inhabited only by a few small tribes of Indians, and there were huge timber-wolves and brown bears as fierce as grizzlies to add to the hazards of travel. On the credit side for the traveller, herds of caribou roamed the rocky slopes and the rivers were brimful of candlefish, a kind of smelt so fat that when dried they would burn like a candle. The fringe of this vast territory had been penetrated by Man when the second wave of the Yukon Gold Rush lapped over into Alaska and left a few tough prospectors "washing" or working placer-mines on the banks of the Sushitna River, but the interior was still unexplored country.

The news of the discovery of Mount McKinley in 1897 brought an exploring and surveying expedition near it five years later to establish its height as 20,300 feet. And in 1903 Dr Frederick A. Cook carried out a remarkable journey right round the mountain—a journey which has never been repeated—and made an unsuccessful attempt to climb it from the north. Frederick Albert Cook deserves some notice, for until his dying day he maintained that he had been the first man up McKinley. He was a resolute explorer, a great traveller, a fine writer and lecturer. Yet his claim to have reached the North Pole a year before Peary got there was proved completely false, and he is known to history as "the most impudent faker in the world's record of exploration". In 1906 Dr Cook and three companions made an attempt to climb McKinley and Cook claimed to have reached the top with one of them named Barrill. He produced in evidence a photograph said to have been taken from the summit. Later, Barrill deposed on oath that 'at no time did Dr Cook and he get nearer than a point fourteen miles in an air line from the top of Mount McKinley", and the supposed summit photograph was proved to have been taken from an insignificant foot-hill peak. From the first Cook's claim had aroused suspicion, for it was already known that the Alaskan giant would demand mountaineering of a very high order if its mighty glaciers and ice-draped ridges were to be climbed.

So McKinley in 1910 was a virgin, awaiting the great mountaineer with enough expert skill and experience to lead his party to the top.

The idea was born in Billy McPhee's saloon in Fairbanks. It was the middle of Alaska's ten-month-long winter, and the shacks and log huts of the little settlement were buried in deep snow. Outside the temperature was twenty below—so cold that when a man spat the saliva crackled in mid-air; inside, in the smoky light of the big hanging oil-lamp, McPhee's saloon was packed with bearded men in fur caps and clothes made of animal skins. Most of them were miners and prospectors for gold, and in Alaska that meant that they were also hunters and trappers; pioneers who had learned how to survive where the majority of men would die of starvation and exposure—"sourdoughs". Up at the bar, where the clamour of rough voices was loudest and Billy McPhee presided, they were arguing about the possibility of getting up Mount McKinley, not long ago revealed as the highest peak in North America.

The facts about the inception of the "Sourdough Expedition" are not easy to get at, but there are enough to build upon. It is clear that the plan arose from a challenge and a bet, and it seems not improbable that the challenge originated in whisky. At any rate, here was Tom Lloyd, sourdough and miner, proclaiming that he reckoned *he* could make McKinley summit, given time and the right pardners; one can imagine the uproar of jeers, oaths, and acclamation. Lloyd stuck to it, and his

14. The Teton Range, Wyoming   *U.S.T.O.*

mining partner, William Taylor, backed him up. The saloon-keeper came in on their side. The opposition challenged him to back his opinion with hard cash. And in the upshot Billy McPhee and his friend Dave Petree, having ascertained that Tom Lloyd meant what he had said, put up a forfeit of $5,000 that Lloyd or one of his party would reach the top of Mount McKinley before the 4th of July 1910.

It was December, the whole of Alaska would be covered in snow for many months, and the summit of McKinley is more than 150 miles as the crow flies—many more for men on foot—from Fairbanks. But Tom Lloyd set about making his preparations. Taylor would go with him, and two men who had worked with them for years—Charlie McGonagall and the Swede Pete Anderson. None of the four had been on a mountain or knew anything at all about mountain-climbing, but as Alaskans they had travelled more miles on snow than on dry ground and—since the snow was very often as hard as Alpine ice—knew a little of what they might expect when they reached the great glacier which was said to lead to the base of McKinley's final peak. Lloyd proposed to attack the peak by sourdough methods: snowshoes, dog-team and sledge, "staking" the snow-trail to the summit. His sole concession to the problem of climbing steep ice was to have four stout poles shod with steel points at one end and double-pronged steel hooks at the other, and these were made by Jim Johnson, the Fairbanks smith. The public-spirited McPhee grub-staked the party to the extent of $500. And on 20th December 1909 the oddest climbing-party that ever set forth to conquer a great peak departed, amid cheers and jests, from in front of the wooden Pioneer Hotel, Fairbanks. It consisted of six men with no mountaineering experience, two dog-teams, two horses, and a mule.

The two additional members of the party were Robert Horn and Charles Davidson. These two either quarrelled with the others or had no real intention of joining in the adventure, for they left the four sour-doughs before they got anywhere near the mountain; one account says there was a fight, after which Davidson and Horn "cleared out". Lloyd and his three companions travelled slowly on across the white wastes of Alaska, breaking their trail between the two forks of the great McKinley River, shooting for the pot, camping in the snow-laden cottonwood thickets. They possessed a large sheet of balloon silk which, slung between two saplings, made a tent eight feet by ten. There was no hurry, for the snow would last far beyond April; and the snow—so long as it was hard-frozen—was the highway for the expedition's transport. Not for the sourdoughs the army of laden porters and the expense of paying and feeding them. All the way from Fairbanks the teams of huskies pulled the sledges loaded with equipment and the flour, lard, and coffee which were all that was needed to supplement the meat won by their rifles; the dogs were fed on the meat of the caribou their masters hunted. It was February 14th before they were in sight of the big glacier. They made a camp—Willow Camp—by the last timber and for the next fortnight reconnoitred, hunted, and prepared for the advance up the glacier.

All books of mountaineering adventure mentioning the Sourdough Expedition state that the four frontiersmen left no written record of their climb. This is not so. Thomas Lloyd kept a diary, which he later made available to the *Fairbanks Daily Times*; and though there is good reason to believe that parts of the diary were "edited" before it was printed it remains the only authentic document, revealing on the one hand the climbers' ignorance of the mountaineering problems they were to meet with and on the other the unique and resolute way in which they tackled them. Whether by good luck or by the instinct of lifelong pathfinders—probably a combination of both—they had chosen the most practicable route to the base of the main peak. The glacier, now called the Muldrow Glacier, curved up for a dozen miles between the flanking ridges of McKinley until it steepened in an ice-slope leading to the final ridge. It was covered deep in snow, and snow fell recurrently throughout the long and patient assault. Tom Lloyd's first move was to establish a camp on the glacier, and this was done in mid-March after several journeys of reconnaissance.

> March 13.—Took stove, tent, and bedding up Wall Street Glacier. We called it that because you look straight up as at a wall. I would not like to estimate the height of the wall, but in places it honestly looked to me to reach 10,000 feet straight up. Of course, it cannot be anything like that distance or height, but it looked to be—stretching straight up in the air. It is the grandest thing I ever saw in my life, that long stretch of glacier. . . . The next eight miles are terrible for crevasses. You can look down in them for a distance stretching from 100 ft. to hades or China.
>
> London *Daily Telegraph*, June 1910.

The crevasses were anything up to fifty feet wide, but usually there was a snow-bridge strong enough to take them across. When there wasn't, Lloyd bridged them himself by bringing up trimmed tree-trunks from Willow Camp; the poles were laid across the blue-green chasms and snow thrown on them and left to harden. The dog-teams hauled these logs, and were able to pull sledges across the bridges, though sometimes a husky would slip off the edge and dangle in his harness until the rest of the team pulled him out. So long as the cold weather held—often it was 26 degrees below zero and more—the work of making the route could go on. Their chief fear was of a warm spell that would soften the snow. They had spent much of their time at Willow Camp in cutting and trimming stakes until they had 750 of them, and with these the whole route was marked out little by little so that they could go up and down their "Wall Street" with the dog-

S. Snow Saddle
M. Summit of Mount McKinley
N. North Summit.
W. "Wall Street" Glacier
H. Pothole Camp

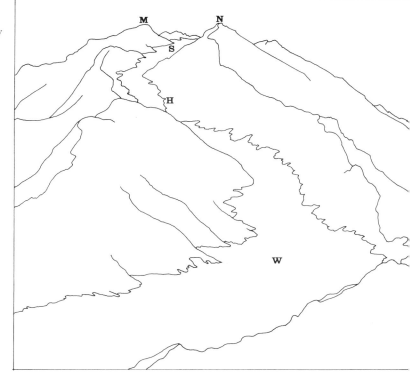

Diagram 5
Mount McKinley

teams even in thick fog. Fog delayed them for some time at the glacier camp. This was established in a snow-filled crevasse and called Pothole Camp. The balloon-fabric tent was sunk five feet deep in this snowy pit and snow piled round it to protect it against the storms which further delayed them with blinding snowfalls. The oil-burning stove was used only once; the heat it generated caused it to melt the snow beneath and subside below the level of the two caribou hides and three sheepskin robes they used for bedding. At Pothole Camp they weathered snow-storms that lasted for days on end. During the "warm spell" that threatened the success of their enterprise (the temperature rose to zero!) great ice-avalanches thundered down from the enormous mountain-walls that flanked the glacier.

> A slide seemed to be taking the glacier under the tent away, and startled by the sound like the report of a great gun (I had never heard anything like it before) I jumped up. It didn't seem to affect the other boys, and the Swede, who had crossed many glaciers, paid no attention at all. He simply looked at me and smiled, and said "It's just ripping a little below; it is safe here." . . . The ice comes tearing down the sides of the perpendicular walls with a most awful noise, tearing and grinding its way.
>
> London *Daily Telegraph*, June 1910.

Pete Anderson seems to have been one of those iron men common in fiction but rare enough in real life. He had a frostbitten toe before the party set foot on the glacier and this got steadily worse, but according to Lloyd he would admit only that it was "a little bit sore, as a fellow would say". All four of them, indeed, had to guard constantly against frostbite and snowblindness. The howling blizzards that swept down upon them, burying the tent in its "pothole" again and again, would certainly have defeated a party of Alpine climbers; but the frontiersmen merely "stormed-up", as they called it, and waited patiently for the next clearance and the subsequent hardening of the new snow. In snow, on snow, they were perfectly at home—and so were the huskies who lay buried in the drifts until they were required for the next haul.

Patiently, seizing their opportunities between snowstorms, they snowshoed farther and farther up the glacier with their sledge-loads of stakes. The ice-slope higher up was badly crevassed and covered with soft snow, but they trod out a way up that and took the dogs as high as 15,000 feet. When the snow hardened on the steep places they fitted roughlocks to the snowshoes, a harrow-like frame of points that gave them surer footing. Lloyd reckoned there were eight miles of trail to within striking distance of the summit, and they staked all of it. Much more recently, many thousands of feet of fixed ropes have been used to make safe the way up a great mountain; but never before or since has such a remarkable thoroughfare been established in order to reach a summit.

On March 17th they reached a narrow snow-saddle, and saw that "Mac" (as they called the mountain) had two summits, both about 5,000 feet above them and apparently of equal height. The crest of the saddle was a razor-edge of hard snow and there was no place for a tent, but where there was snow these men could always contrive a shelter. They drove a tunnel into the side of the col, about fifty feet below the crest, and that was their final camp for the assault.

> After we had driven that tunnel we climbed on to the roof of the ridge, and looked over the other side. If we had driven the tunnel a little further in, so as to have a back door to our home, and had we opened that back door, we would have found ourselves looking down a precipice which stood at about 80 deg. to perpendicular [*to the horizontal, Lloyd means*]. If our foot had slipped at such a back door there wouldn't have been a grease-spot left of one of us by the time we reached the bottom of that precipice.
>
> London *Daily Telegraph*, June 1910.

From now onwards the dogs could not be used. Taylor remained below to ferry meat up from Willow Camp with the aid of the sledge while the others began staking a trail, and cutting steps, up the last ice-ridge towards the summit. Nothing is said in Lloyd's diary about their

15. Unclimbed peak in the Logan Range, Canada   *M. Banks*

decision to climb the north summit instead of the south, a decision that must have been made when they reached the upper ice-basin, now known as Harper's Glacier, at 19,000 feet. But that decision came very near to ending their claim to have climbed McKinley, as we shall see.

At the Tunnel Camp the weather turned against them again. There were prolonged snowstorms, and Taylor was held at Willow Camp for four days with the vital food supplies; the others, fearing the worst, went back down to Pothole Camp, searching for him on the way, and met him "mushing" up the glacier through the last of the blizzard. By April 1st they had got everything they wanted up to the Tunnel Camp, including a fourteen-foot pole and the American flag. On the 2nd the four men started out at daybreak for the summit.

At this point the veracity of Tom Lloyd's diary begins to be doubtful by reasons of later discoveries. No details are given of the difficulties encountered on the summit climb, and (except for the statement that they used no ropes but "took their chances individually") nothing is said about the method of ascent. This is perhaps natural enough in a man to whom the technique of mountaineering art meant little or nothing. But his other assertions did not all stand the test of proof.

The entry for April 2nd says that they made the high ridge towards the coast summit (which is the south peak and the higher of the two) intending to follow that ridge to the summit. There is an addendum to this entry, probably inserted at a later date: "Note: there are two summits to Mount McKinley, apparently of equal height and connected by a saddle. We climbed them both." The diary adds that when they gained the coast summit Lloyd could find no rocks in which the flagpole which they had brought with them could be placed firmly. They thereupon resolved to return to the Tunnel Camp, climb the other—north—summit next day, and plant the flagpole there. The entry on April 3rd records this second climb and the planting of the flagpole; and this, at least, is known to be the truth.

We had little difficulty in reaching the saddle, as the boys had been there previously and had cut steps, which made the ascent easier. Once there we proceeded to cross the glacier between the two summits, to the north summit, where the rocks were. The distance from the left, or coast, summit to the right, or northern, summit (zigzagging as we had to go) must be about three miles, but it is a hard matter to estimate distance up in that air . . . We dug down 15 in. into the rocks until we had found a solid spot, where there will be no question but that the flagpole will stand, and into it we stuck that flagpole . . . a straight, seasoned spruce sapling full 4 in. at the butt, and tapering to full 2½ in. at the top, and is full 14 ft. long. The flag attached to it is 6 ft. by 12 ft. in size, is an American flag erected by four Americans of Welsh, Scotch, Canadian and

Swedish descent, and on the flag, written thereon in ink, is the name "M. W. Griffin". . . The flag was raised at 3.25 p.m. on April 3, 1910.

That is the story of the climb.

London *Daily Telegraph*, June 1910.

They got back to the Tunnel Camp at ten o'clock that night, and next day followed the staked trail all the way down to Willow Camp. "We travelled some," Lloyd wrote afterwards. Eight days later Thomas Lloyd, alone, arrived back in Fairbanks with his dog-team and told the story of the successful ascent, repeating his statement that both summits of Mount McKinley had been climbed. Fairbanks accepted the story as wholly true and Tom Lloyd as a national hero; but it was so fantastic a tale that when it reached a wider public many people, including some American mountaineers, doubted it altogether. When the doubters were able to interview Taylor, McGonagall, and Anderson, who had stayed behind to work at Lloyd's mining camp, they found that the stories of the other sourdoughs differed considerably from Lloyd's. In particular, it was quite evident from the accounts given by these three men that only one summit had in fact been climbed—the north summit.

Lloyd's claim was now widely disbelieved. Then, three years later, a climbing-party succeeded in reaching the south or higher peak of McKinley. Hudson Stuck, Archdeacon of the Yukon, made with Harry P. Karstens an ascent which confronted the *Fairbanks Daily Times* with a grave problem. For had not the paper already headlined the conquest of Mount McKinley in 1910? The editor compromised with a slightly ambiguous headline: STUCK CLIMBERS REACH SUMMIT OF SOUTH PEAK. And when the full report was received one part at least of Tom Lloyd's story was confirmed. From the summit of the south peak, 20,300 feet high, the north peak—less than 300 feet lower—had been clearly seen, and on it stood the flagpole placed there by the sourdoughs, denuded now of the Stars and Stripes but vindicating the courage and resolution of four genuine heroes.

What made Tom Lloyd falsify his account? Why did he claim to have climbed both summits when to have reached one of them was a sufficiently great achievement? Most probably, I think, he would be unable to estimate the relative height of a second summit so far away from him, when the difference was less than 300 feet. He would not *know* that the south summit was the higher. But doubt, perhaps, assailed him later on—for the story of making the second ascent in order to plant the flagpole more firmly reads like a later fabrication— and he had more to influence his lying than his own fame. There was that $5,000 dollar forfeit to be paid out by Billy McPhee and Dave Petree, his friends and backers, if some busybody pointed out that the

16. Mount Hunter, Alaska, seen from Mount McKinley   *M. Banks*

unclimbed summit could have been the highest point. It is more than likely that such a man as Lloyd would attach greater importance to being loyal to his friends than to telling a safeguarding lie.

Whatever the reason, the ascent of Mount McKinley's 20,000-foot north peak by the four sourdoughs of Fairbanks remains one of the great achievements in the history of mountaineering, a feat without parallel in the record of daring and resolute adventure.

6 New Routes and North Faces

Up to the beginning of the First World War rock-climbing was not accepted as a legitimate sport by the majority of mountain-climbers. Mountaineering was freed from the necessity of using scientific experiment as an excuse; the attempt to gain the summit of an unclimbed peak was applauded as a sporting effort. But to most Alpinists mountaineering meant climbing a mountain by a snow-and-ice route, and a climber without an ice-axe was not a mountaineer. Rock ridges, their sides too steep to hold snow, offered practicable routes to many an Alpine summit, and of course on some first ascents there were short passages of difficult rock; but the climber's choice was always for the snow wherever he could keep on it, for the technique of ascent on snow had been developed from the beginning of mountain-climbing and was highly efficient. Clambering up rocks was thought of as an undignified and dangerous form of gymnastics to be avoided as far as possible. One of the reasons why the Matterhorn remained unclimbed for so long was because it is a rock peak.

The hierarchy of older mountaineers represented in Britain by the Alpine Club were lagging behind the times, however. In widely separated corners of Europe young men were already developing a form of mountain-climbing that owed nothing (except perhaps the technique of safeguarding with the rope) to snowslopes and ice-axes. Deprived by circumstances of the chance of ascending greater mountains, they climbed the lower peaks that were more accessible to them. The limestone ranges of the Eastern Alps attracted Germans like Josef Enzensperger to climb their rock ridges and faces long before 1914. The great rock spires of the Dolomites challenged others; in this same period the 700-metre north wall of the Laliderwand, in the Karwendel mountains, was climbed by Angelo Dibona. As early as 1906 the northeast face of the Finsteraarhorn, a vast rock-wall, was the scene of a first guideless ascent by the American V. A. Fynn. In Britain the sport began earlier but took longer to establish itself.

In 1869 an Alpine Club member, J. Stogdon, reported finding "quite Alpine conditions" in the Great Gully on Bowfell, above Langdale. Thereafter a small but growing number of Alpine climbers visited the Lake District and North Wales in winter to get in some practice for

69 A Ben Nevis gully at Easter (Scotland)

the summer campaign in the Alps, and it was not long before some enthusiasts, discovering that the homeland mountains had a beauty and grandeur of their own, came at other seasons and were tempted to tackle the gullies and rock buttresses. The year 1886 is a landmark in British rock-climbing history—the year when W. P. Haskett-Smith, scrambling round the crags of Great Gable, came upon the now famous Napes Needle and made the first ascent solo. Haskett-Smith did not regard British crags as stepping-stones to Alpine climbing and found full satisfaction in going on climbing them, though he was regarded by more senior mountaineers as a mildly dangerous eccentric. His book

70 Napes Needle, English Lake District

Climbing in the British Isles opened the eyes of many a youngster to the possibilities of mountain adventure in his own country. And when, in the last decade of the nineteenth century, Owen Glynne Jones and the brothers Abraham began their association in rock-climbing and book-producing, the growth of the sport in Britain was assured. The photographs taken by George and Ashley Abraham (some of them are reproduced in this book) are still among the finest pictures of British crags, and had a decided influence in attracting men to the new sport.

The exploration of British mountains in a search for new rock-faces and first ascents now became the hobby of a small band of pioneers.

119

72 The "crux" on Eagle's Nest Ridge

73 New West Climb, Pillar Rock,
English Lake District

1 Eagle's Nest Ridge, English Lake District
Left

74 Central Buttress, Scafell, English Lake District

75 Scafell Pinnacle

By Alpine standards the mountains are far from high; but the rock-climbing on their crags can exact as high a technical standard as any to be found on greater mountains. North Wales and the Lakes, Ben Nevis and the far Coolin of Skye, yielded in turn their climbable precipices, and soon each precipice was a vertical maze of "routes" made by climbers seeking the mountaineer's paradise—a way no one had trodden before. Lliwedd, a neighbour of Snowdon with a rock-face more than 800 feet high, was the scene of a prolonged siege by J. M. Archer Thomson, a Llandudno schoolmaster. In 1909 a guide to the climbs on Lliwedd was published listing no less than thirty-six routes.

76 Innominate Crack on Great Gable, English Lake District

78 On Milestone Buttress, North Wales

79 Red Wall on Lliwedd, North Wales

Sunset from A' Cioch, Skye, Scotland
Left

80 The Chamonix Aiguilles

Whereas the first climbers had followed Alpine precedent and sought out the "lines of weakness"—the gullies and clefts—the new school looked for airy ridges and clean buttresses where balance and neatness were of more importance than physical strength, thus introducing a new technique of balance-climbing to replace the old clutch-and-struggle method. Some of those who took part in the pioneering of British rock-climbs still regarded it as training for the Alps, and were pleasantly surprised to find that on Alpine rock they were now as competent as their guides—and sometimes more competent. A. F. Mummery had already proved this on the steep granite of the Chamonix Aiguilles.

Rock-climbing as a part of mountain craft had come to stay. But in Britain the non-climbing public, ready enough to accept the first ascent of some distant snow-peak as legitimate and praiseworthy, still

81 Valkyrie route on the Staffordshire Roches (English gritston

regarded it as a foolhardy sport pursued by people who were not quite right in the head. The rare fatal accident on a mountain was the signal for the coroner, and after him the newspapers, to denounce and condemn the utter folly of rock-climbers. When the Great War of 1914–1918 arrested the progress of British climbing there was still a quarter of a century to pass before rock-climbing would be generally accepted as a sport for sane men and women.

The two decades between the world wars saw a vast increase in the number of active mountaineers, and also an overall improvement in technical standard. An almost feverish search for new routes on rock-face and mountain began. In Britain, at first, this took a characteristically light-hearted course; as when climbers from Oxford and Cambridge pioneered hair-raising new routes in rubber plimsolls and "oxford bags," to the music of a gramophone at the foot of the crag. Later, with the growth of Youth Hostels and increased leisure for workers, young people from the industrial North and Midlands swelled the ranks of the rock-climbers, many of them having learned the rudiments—and more—of balance-climbing on the steep and very difficult gritstone "edges" of Derbyshire and Yorkshire. The two men who are outstanding for their advancement of British climbing standards in this period, Menlove Edwards and Colin Kirkus, both came from Liverpool. Many of these youngsters added snow and ice craft to their skill on rock and went on to climb in the Alps and mountains even farther afield. The label of Privilege was gone at last from mountaineering.

On the Continent the progress of rock-climbing had taken a grimmer course. The resurgence of Germany after defeat, under Hitler and his National Socialists, relied largely on race-worship and the cult of physical courage. Young Germans were encouraged to attempt the apparently impossible in a do-or-die spirit that held prudence in contempt and extolled carelessness of death as a virtue. This attitude was transferred to mountaineering. It resulted in many fatalities and bred a cut-throat competition between the young climbers of the countries near the Alpine frontiers. Foremost among the groups of dedicated would-be heroes was the Munich "school" of climbers, who brought into use *pitons* and *karabiners*—steel pegs that could be driven into cracks in vertical rock and steel snaplinks for securing the climber to the pegs—by means of which they could ascend rock-faces so steep that they were unclimbable by ordinary methods. Thirty years later these aids were to be accepted almost universally as an extension of mountain craft; but at the time their connection with the perversion of a peaceful mountain sport caused them to be condemned by mountaineers in general.

The new trend—the Nazi intrusion, as it might be called—led inevitably to attempts on mountain-faces which had been left unclimbed

17. Loch Lomond, Scotland, early morning   *Frank Martin*

because they were dangerous. No true mountaineer ever courted danger for its own sake. The whole point of any sport is that it demands the acquisition of a special skill which cancels out the danger. It was the mountaineer's justification that he climbed by routes where his skill in mountain craft, supported by courage and resolution of no mean order, made him competent to ascend and descend *safely*. Edward Whymper (not the most prudent of climbers) had put this unwritten law of the sport into words long before.

> The line which separates the difficult from the dangerous is sometimes very shadowy, but it is not an imaginary line. It is a true line, without breadth. It is often easy to pass, and very hard to see. It is sometimes passed unconsciously, and the consciousness that it has been passed is felt too late. If the doubtful line is crossed consciously, deliberately, one passes from doing that which is justifiable to doing that which is unjustifiable.
>
> Whymper's *Scrambles Amongst the Alps*, 1900.

The great unclimbed faces were dangerous, and therefore unjustifiable, because they were known to be the flanks down which the mountains discharged rock-falls and avalanches. Skill and courage were essential, but even more essential was an inordinate share of Luck. The penalty for being unlucky was certain death.

By 1931 the greater Alpine ridges, and their "justifiable" faces, had been climbed by mountaineers during the Silver Age of new routes. The Matterhorn had been climbed up all its four formidable ridges. Among the mountain-faces that remained unclimbed, three gigantic walls challenged the new Supermen: the North Face of the Matterhorn, the North Face of the Grandes Jorasses in the Mont Blanc range,

82 Tools for "direct aid" climbing

and the North Wall of the Eiger in the Bernese Oberland. The first of these falls in one sheer, ledgeless, crumbling precipice from the summit of the Matterhorn to the glacier 4,000 feet below. Like all north faces, it is continually plastered with snow by the sudden storms which even in summer sweep across the great obelisk of rock. The snow melts, freezes, loosens the precariously poised rock of which the precipice is built. Only at night—and not always then—is the cannonade of falling debris arrested by the hand of frost. Yet a first-rate mountaineer willing to take a hundred-to-one chance of death might plan a route, in good weather and at the proper times of day, that offers hope of escaping the worst rock-falls. One of the gravest dangers would be from rocks dislodged by climbing-parties on the Hörnli Ridge of ordinary ascent, which rims the Face on its left side.

As things stood in the 1930's it was certain that the Matterhorn North Face would be attempted; and almost—but not quite—certain that the attempt would end in tragedy.

At two o'clock in the morning of 31st July 1931, the caretaker of the Swiss Alpine Club hut at the foot of the Hörnli Ridge was up and lighting his stove. As usual at that time of year, there were several climbing-parties in the hut and they would be starting early for the ascent of the Matterhorn by the easiest route. The caretaker was surprised by the entrance of two young men burdened with heavy rucksacks, and incredulous when they informed him that they were about to try the ascent of the North Face. At last he was persuaded that they were serious, and agreed to warn the climbers on the Hörnli route to be careful not to dislodge stones. The two then climbed rapidly down to the lower plateau of the Matterhorn Glacier and prepared for their desperate venture.

Franz and Toni Schmid, two brothers in their early twenties, had arrived from Munich on bicycles a few days earlier. They were engineering students who had made difficult climbing their hobby, and together they had accomplished many hard ascents on rock and ice. According to an Alpine Club member who met and talked with them, the Schmids were "not of the 'record-breaking' type" but were confident in their skill and fully cognisant, from careful study, of the risks they were taking. They camped in a small tent below the Matterhorn Glacier and spent the next day finding the way through the *séracs* of the glacier to the foot of the vast ice-slope which sweeps up to the base of the northern precipice. The following day was one of rest and preparation, but at 11.30 p.m. they crawled out of the tent into bright moonlight. Below them the huge black shadow of the Matterhorn stretched across the sleeping valleys and gorges; above them the dark shaft of the mountain reared itself sheer and forbidding against the night sky.

Laden with the gear for their attempt—two 40-metre ropes, steel pitons for hammering into rock and ice, a thin rubber tent-sack for the expected bivouac, and food—they made their way to the hut on the Hörnli and gave their warning; in the freezing darkness of early morning they gained the upper plateau of the Matterhorn Glacier and stood at the foot of the North Face.

Straight above them the ice-slope rose for 1,000 feet, a glimmering wall like white glass, to end beneath an enormous black wall that soared up, and up, in a near-perpendicularity that was no illusion of the night. Below the ice-slope was a lesser mountain of avalanche debris, separated from the ice by the deep cleft of the *bergschrund*. Already fragments of ice were whizzing down the polished snow-trough that made the easiest way up the mound, reminding them that they would have to climb at top speed up this lower section if they were to escape the heavier bombardment when daylight came; but it was still too dark to see their way. At last they were able to start. Up the avalanche-chute they went, unroped but wearing their steel-spiked crampons, with ice-fragments constantly bounding over the upper lip of the *bergschrund* above and bruising heads and arms. They reached the base of the ice-slope, found a practicable place for crossing the *bergschrund*, and tied on the ropes—two lengths of 130 feet linking them together. At 4 a.m. the sky began to pale and they started up the ice, Toni leading. To save time, no steps were cut. They relied on their crampons and the small security of a piton driven into the ice by the leader at the end of each rope-length. They were making for the rock-wall below the end of a long thin cleft or gully seaming the vertical wall for more than a thousand feet, which offered the only hope—a slim one— of getting up the first half of the Face. The ice was deeply grooved by the stones that had fallen from thousands of feet overhead and occasionally a piece of rock came shrieking through the air to strike the slope and go whirring down into the big crevasse far below them. There was no shelter whatever from these; but they were not hit, and after climbing without a pause for two hours reached the first ribs of rock protruding through the ice. It was sunrise, and the slanting rays were touching the vertical wilderness of rock and ice that hung above their heads. From near and far sounded the explosions and whistles of falling rock as the Matterhorn began its daily bombardment.

The base of the gully was still 200 feet above them, petering out on steep smooth slabs that overhung the upper ice-slope. These slabs were encased in *verglas*—frozen melt-water—and offered no hold or ledge for safeguarding, but they had to be climbed if the gully was to be reached. Toni Schmid led across that formidable and exposed traverse, cutting tiny nicks in the thin skin of ice to take the points of their crampons; it had to be done with the utmost delicacy, because a hard blow could have split away the whole frail shell and left the rock holdless. A rib of cleaner rock, reached at last, allowed them to move more directly upward and enter the mouth of the gully. Seventy feet farther, and they came upon a small knob of projecting rock, where they halted and ate some chocolate. That knob of rock was the only place, on the entire climb, where they were able to sit and rest.

The gully was like a constricted, twisting lift-shaft and its walls were of rotten rock, but down its bottom (or, more accurately, the cleft in its inner wall) there ran a ribbon of ice. Sometimes progressing by tiny holds nicked in the ice, sometimes using the rocks of the right wall, which seemed slightly less fragile than those on the other side, they very slowly gained height. There was never anywhere to loop the rope in a securing belay. One missed foothold, one rock handhold badly judged, and nothing could save them from hurtling down to destruction on the glacier that gleamed farther and farther below them as they looked down between their poised feet. And stonefalls thundered down incessantly from the great face far above, tearing past close to them but luckily never hitting them. Franz, who had been leading up the gully since noon, was tiring when he reached the upper exit of the shaft, but somehow he overcame a stiff vertical chimney and an equally steep wall of ice above it and emerged, with fingers bleeding and frozen, on the open precipice. Toni followed and joined him.

The sun was just setting. Overhead the snow in the shallow grooves between the topless ribs of rock was dyed blood-red. They had climbed more than half of the North Face, but 1,750 feet remained to be climbed, many hours of ceaseless and continuously dangerous work as hard as any they had yet encountered. Somewhere they would have to halt for the night—but where? They were standing on the smallest of footholds with no belay for the rope, and whichever way they looked there was only smooth verticality. Life depended on finding a niche into which they could jam their weary bodies, or a ledge for a standing-place, before darkness made it impossible to climb any more.

Toni took over the lead and they went on climbing. Night came welling up from the far-sunken valleys and the great Face grew shadowed and chill. Wreaths of mist began to form across the precipice, bringing a new fear for the future: if the weather broke while they were still on the Face their hopes of survival would vanish. A thin rib of shaky rock; then a runnel of black ice; another rib, another runnel. Up and up they crawled, with strength fast ebbing, with the rope frozen as stiff as a wire hawser and almost impossible to manipulate. Still there was no halting-place—not even a tiny projecting rock, or an inches-wide ledge. Nothing.

Very slowly, very painfully, they wormed their way upward through the gathering darkness, the down-drag of the abyss beneath them taking stronger hold on their stiffening limbs with each long minute. And then, suddenly, Toni gave a hoarse cry. Through the gloom on their

18. Buachaille Etive Mor, Scotland   *Frank Martin*

left hand he had seen, ten feet away, a break in the sheer fall of the crags. It was a low-relief boss of rock, whose outward-sloping top, no more than three feet square, made the only haven they were likely to find.

Close though it was, the few steps needed to reach it had to be made on a vertical wall of loose rock. Franz, who was precariously placed, called to his brother to hold the rope while he moved up to a safer stance whence he could safeguard Toni on that short crossing. It was just as well that he did so. Toni had scarcely started the crossing when his foothold, a rock that had seemed to be part of the solid mountain, broke clean away and went flying down the precipice. If he had fallen with it the rope would probably have dragged Franz after him. But with a desperate effort he got his hands clamped on a bulging slab and supported himself there until Franz was able to pull him up, inch by inch, to a better foothold.

Toni finished the traverse and pulled himself gasping on to the boss of rock. It was veneered with ice and slanted too steeply to stand on, but he managed to bang in two pitons and secure himself to them before taking in the rope—now stiff as an iron bar—as Franz moved across with infinite caution to join him. When Franz was tied on and more securing pitons driven into the very dubious rock above the boss, their first task was to chip away the ice from their tiny platform. Axes and crampons were hung on another iron peg, and carefully fastened there; if those came loose and fell, it meant death for the climbers as certainly as if they had fallen themselves. Then they got out the thin envelope of rubber which was to be their protection against the icy cold of 13,000 feet and spread it over them, and extracted their food— bread, bacon, cheese, and dried fruits. All these operations took a long time, for every movement had to be made slowly and with extreme caution. Their sloping boss was neither large enough nor level enough to allow any relaxation. They huddled together in a cramped, half-balanced position which they dared not change for fear of throwing too much weight on the shaky pegs from which they were partly suspended. All night they crouched there, cramped and frozen, and for both of them it was the longest night they had ever known. The writhing mists cleared, ending for a time the threat of storm, and brilliant green stars pricked the blackness of the void in front. Far, far below a few pinpoints of yellow light marked where the chalets and hotels of Zermatt lay. If some passing *djinn* had offered to waft them down to a warm and comfortable bed, one wonders, would they have accepted?

There was no rest, no relaxation even, for the brothers clinging to their lofty projection on the inhospitable wall. The cold that gripped them was like the cold of outer space. The first hint of dawn, bringing hope and the certainty of light, was greeted with croaking shouts of joy, but they found they were unable to move. They were literally frozen stiff, and the complicated movements required to get them into position for resuming the climb were impossible until the sun had brought a little warmth to thaw them out. And that morning the sun was long in rising. It came at last, out of a belt of cloud that had gathered ominously on the eastern horizon. By 7 a.m. they had managed to stand, to pack up their gear, to strap on crampons and begin the second half of the ascent.

The crampons were needed because although their way lay up steep rock the rock was cased in thin ice. The angle steepened slowly as Franz inched his way upward on tiny nicks in the ice, and at last it was too steep even for men who had climbed for twenty-seven hours on one of the steepest precipices in the Alps. The slabs above were vertical, and revealed not the tiniest crack where a piton could be inserted. There was no apparent way round. After only forty-five minutes' climbing on this second day they had reached an impasse.

It was 7.45 a.m. and the Shoulder on the Hörnli Ridge was about 1,600 feet away on their left, just possibly accessible by a very tricky traverse. But Franz made one attempt to get up that impossible wall of slabs. He gained three feet on it; and the inevitable retreat to his old precarious footing was the greatest effort of climbing he made on the whole ascent. His despairing glance towards the Shoulder brought a quick protest from Toni: "No! We *must* finish the North Face!"

All very well, thought Franz; but where is there a way? Pressed close against the ice-draped wall, tiny figures lost among its huge vertical wrinkles, they had no chance to look for alternative routes. And then, unexpectedly, came help. A party of climbers led by the guide Alois Pollinger had appeared on the Shoulder. (One of them took the photograph reproduced as *Plate 83*.) An exchange of shouts across four hundred yards of precipice followed, and Pollinger managed to convey to them his opinion that their only chance was to traverse— somehow—to the right and gain slabs which were at an easier angle there. Franz tried it. The first part led along a narrow moulding of snow frozen to the rock, so fragile that the wind that had risen flicked pieces of it away, and then across great reddish-yellow slabs coated with ice just thick enough to support their crampons. Beyond this were more slabs and more ice, but they could continue to creep slowly upward towards the summit-ridge which was now less than a thousand feet overhead. And they were climbing into cloud.

Cloud, the seething grey cloud of a Matterhorn storm, wrapped itself round the narrow head of the great mountain. Hail, snow, thunder, must follow very soon. If they came before the climbers had finished the ascent there would be an end of Franz and Toni Schmid. Franz began to climb as fast as he could, racing against the coming storm; and for the first time it seemed that the Matterhorn was disposed to help him. He reached the bottom of a deep cleft packed with snow and

83 Franz and Toni Schmidt on the Matterhorn North Face

cut and kicked his way up it with Toni close behind him. Another snow-filled crevice—a rock groove—a short, difficult wall. Then more grooves, the snow in them hard and safe. Now the angle was definitely easing—they could actually stand comfortably in snow-steps. Here came the first hailstorm, flailing down into their faces, but nothing could stop them now. Up the last steep snow-grooves they toiled to the snow-corniced crest, and hauled themselves, at 2 p.m., on to the narrow comb a few feet from the cross on the Italian summit of the Matterhorn. They had been on the North Face for thirty-four hours.

The Matterhorn had not finished with them yet. Thunder crashed as they reached the top, lightning played round them and forced them to place axes and crampons in a safe spot and huddle as far away from them as they could get. When the first fury passed they started the descent of the Hörnli Ridge, but again the storm struck at them. Snow and hail poured down the frozen crags like waterfalls and the rope became completely useless, a thick white bar of ice. Groping their way down (for they had never been on this ridge before) they came at last to the little Solvay Refuge perched in a nook of the ridge, and there found the shelter that saved their lives. They took off their frozen clothes and stood them up in a corner like suits of armour, wrapped themselves in the hut blankets, and slept until noon of next day.

There was a celebration banquet for them in Zermatt, and speeches, and adulation. If heroes are only very brave men, then Franz and Toni Schmid were heroes; but the comment of a great mountaineer on a similar ascent gives a sane and caustic judgement. "Let us be grateful to the men who did it," wrote R. L. G. Irving, "for they have removed any excuse or inclination for others to choose their way."

A few days after their ascent of the Matterhorn North Face the Schmid brothers set forth to attempt the second of the "Big Three", the North Face of the Grandes Jorasses. They were prevented by bad weather. The following year Toni Schmid fell to his death on the Gröss Wiesbachhorn, and it was another team of young men from Munich, Martin Meier and Rudolf Peters, who in 1935 made the first ascent of the 4,000-foot rock face which had been the ambition of the few top experts since 1920. Two days after their climb the ascent was repeated by two Swiss climbers, a man and a woman, who were unaware that the Germans had been there before them; they were Raymond Lambert and Loulou Boulaz, the latter an exceptionally brilliant woman skier and mountaineer. Lambert was later to play a leading part in the Swiss attempt on Everest.

The North Face of the Grandes Jorasses is a harder climb than the Matterhorn North Face, demanding an extremely high standard of rock-climbing technique, but there is less danger from falling stones and avalanches—it is more "justifiable" from the standpoint of traditional climbing. It must be emphasised that none of these formidable precipices could be attempted by any but the very best of climbers, and these had also to be men of the highest moral and physical courage. For one of the thousands of ordinary Alpine mountaineers to try the climbs could hardly be called suicidal, because it would be literally impossible for him to overcome the first real difficulty. In short, every climber who got any considerable distance up one of the Big Three faces proved himself to be a first-rate mountaineer by so doing, whether he succeeded or failed. He had to be thoroughly expert on snow, ice, and rock and also to be a master of the use of rope and pitons in "direct aid" climbing. Nowhere was this more essential than on the North Face of the Eiger; here, on the first ascent at least, it was equally essential that the climbing party should have Luck on their side.

The three great peaks of the Eiger, the Mönch, and the Jungfrau stand on the northern edge of the Bernese Oberland above Grindelwald, fronting the storms that gather high over the lower foothills. On the summit of the Eiger, 13,042 feet above sea-level, a furious snowstorm may be raging while people in Grindelwald are sunbathing on the balconies of their hotels. From this summit a very steep ice-slope falls to the rim of the most formidable precipice in the Alps—the Eigerwand, a 6,000-foot wall of rock plastered with snow and ice and swept continually down its whole height by falling stones and avalanches. So frightfully steep is this wall that its many verticalities and overhangs give, in places, some protection from the bombardment. Often the thousand-foot perpendicular base of the wall, far too steep to hold snow, is clean and dry, no more difficult to climb than (say) the wall of the Empire State Building; but rain or melt-water after a warm day can freeze on the rock during the night, coating it with *verglas* and making retreat impossible for men who have climbed beyond it. Above this first obstacle another thousand feet of fly-on-a-wall climbing up mixed rock and ice leads to the middle third of the Eigerwand, three ice-fields one above the other separated by over-

84 Grandes Jorasses (left): North Face in shadow

hanging cliffs. "Ice-field" is here a misleading term; these are huge sheets of ice clamped to the precipice. To gain a footing on the lowest of the three it is necessary to traverse leftward across a vertical wall, swinging sideways on a rope attached to a piton hammered in above. A slanting groove called the Ramp runs up to the left above the third ice-field. It ends in impossible overhangs, but a long traverse back to the right on an exposed snow ledge brings the climber to the centre of the cliff—and the most dangerous obstacle of all. This is the White Spider.

The Spider is an ice-filled scoop three-quarters of the way up the Eigerwand. Its name, given by the first climbers, comes from the long narrow troughs which stretch out like legs from the central mass. These are the channels by which the ice and snow loosened from the summit ice-field plunge down the upper part of the face, so that the White Spider is a kind of main spout collecting avalanches and discharging them again down the 4,500-foot wall below its steeply tilted white plaque. And there is no way of avoiding it. Like hypnotised flies, the climbers must creep across to it and up its glassy face, hoping to escape a fatal avalanche, until they can gain the ice-draped cliffs above. A long series of vertical grooves, the Exit Cracks, lead to the base of the summit ice-field—800 feet of difficult and dangerous climbing by ordinary Alpine standards but to the few men who emerge safely from the Exit Cracks a very heaven of relief. (*Plate 85* and *Diagram 6* show these features.)

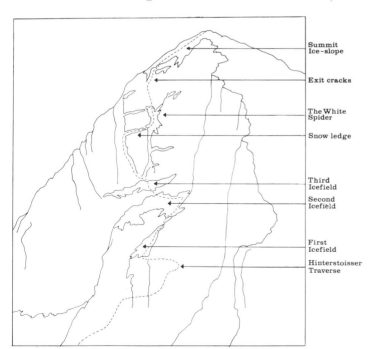

Summit Ice-slope

Exit cracks

The White Spider

Snow ledge

Third Icefield

Second Icefield

First Icefield

Hinterstoisser Traverse

Diagram 6 (corresponding to plate opposite)

The Eigerwand, showing route by which the first complete ascent was made.

138

85 The Eigerwand

The sport of climbing is very different from that of motor-racing. But the climber who attempts the Eigerwand is not unlike a racing-motorist who—to test his skill and luck—drives at top speed round the track in the opposite direction to the rest of the speeding cars. "Luck is the output of one's last reserves," a great German climber once said. Out of all Earth's millions, only a dozen or so men at any given time possess the skill and strength, *and* the phenomenal reserves, to climb the North Wall of the Eiger.

The first attempt came in 1935. Again two young climbers, experienced and expert, came from Munich. The unknown difficulties they had to face proved even worse than they had anticipated, and when they had spent two days and nights clinging to the Wall the weather broke. In their third bivouac at 10,800 feet they were frozen to death.

Sedlmayer and Mehringer were the Eigerwand's first victims, but their fate did not deter others. Next year there were two teams of candidates on the huge wall at the same time—two Austrians and two Germans. Andreas Hinterstoisser, the German leader, achieved the perilous passage that now bears his name, the Hinterstoisser Traverse, and they gained the First Ice-field. Above it one of the Austrians, Angerer, was injured by a falling stone and the two parties joined up. Together they made a first bivouac below the Second Ice-field and the next day climbed that and the Third Ice-field, making their second bivouac just below the place where the first pair had died the previous year—the "Death Bivouac". Down in Grindelwald telescopes and binoculars watched their every move. On the third day they were seen to be beginning the descent; evidently the injured man was unfit to climb any more. The weather was worsening now. Hail, rain, melting snow poured down the lower half of the face, to freeze in a skin of ice on the Hinterstoisser Traverse. The four men were cut off, for they had left no fixed rope on the Traverse. Their only hope—a chance in a thousand—was to lower themselves straight down 700 feet of ice-glazed overhangs and vertical walls. Avalanches and falling stones bombarded them as, frozen and exhausted, they set about that impossible task; and the thick cloud that now drifted across the terrible Wall veiled them as with a winding-sheet.

To the anxious watchers in the valley it had long been obvious that a tragedy was inevitable. A rescue-party of guides started from Grindelwald and a special train was run for them up the Jungfrau Railway, which tunnels up inside the mountain and connects with the outer face by an opening at the Eigerwand Station. Out into the freezing mist these gallant men traversed, across the vertical Tom-Tiddler's-Ground of stonefall and avalanche. From the invisibility 300 feet above their heads came a faint cry and then a shout: "Help! The others are all dead—I'm the only one left. Help!"

19. Loch Coruisk and the Coolin, Skye, Scotland   *T. Hough*

The survivor was twenty-three-year-old Toni Kurz. Hinterstoisser had fallen to death. Angerer, pulled off by the rope, had been strangled by it. The other Austrian, Rainer, had frozen to death. Kurz was hanging in a rope-sling against a wall of ice with one arm frozen into a shapeless, lifeless lump. Already it was growing dark and there was no hope of reaching him that day—the guides had only time to call up that they would try to reach him next morning before night forced them to retreat, back across the vertiginous ice-glazed rock, back to the safety of the tunnel.

At the first glimmer of daylight the rescuers started again to climb across the wall. They hardly expected to find Toni Kurz still alive, for he had been four nights on the Eigerwand; but alive he was, and calling down urgently that the only way to reach him was from above. The guides did their best, but when they had reached a point about 130 feet below Kurz they could climb no higher. An icy overhang blocked the way and hid the half-frozen man overhead from sight. If Kurz had another rope he might be able to lower himself on it; there was no other chance of life for him. The rescuers called up to him, directing him to climb to Angerer's body—if he could—cut the body loose, un-twist the rope so obtained, and from the strands make a line long enough to lower to them. Then they could send up a spare rope and pitons and a hammer. Incredibly, Toni Kurz managed to do all this, one-armed as he was. It took him five hours of agonising effort, and during that time there were snow-avalanches and rock-falls that narrowly missed him and his rescuers. Then Angerer's body came hurtling past through empty air. At long last the thin twisted line came snaking down to the guides. They fastened pitons and a hammer to it, and attached a strong rope; the first rope proved to be too short, so they knotted another to it. An hour passed before Kurz, having hauled up this lifeline with evident difficulty, called down that he was about to lower himself.

Perched on their insecure footholds below the overhang, the guides could hear the slow scraping of his movements as he descended. As they made their preparations for receiving him they knew that he must be at the very end of his strength—that by normal human standards the limit of endurance had been passed long ago. But Kurz continued to descend, on a rope-sling hitched to a snap link on the dangling rope. Now his boots, cased in blocks of ice, appeared on the edge of the over-hang. And there he stuck. The knot joining the two ropes had jammed in the snap-link.

The rescuers could almost touch those frozen boots with their ice-axes. They could hear the young man groaning as he attempted to free the knot, and urged him to try—to go on trying. One of them, leaning desperately outwards, could just see him endeavouring to free the jammed knot with his teeth. But the last reserves had been called out and used, the will to live stretched to breaking-point. Toni Kurz spoke only once more: "I'm finished." His body sagged forward and the rope-sling slid a little way to dangle below the overhang. The man in the sling was dead.

After the four-fold tragedy of 1936 the authorities in Berne issued a ban on all climbing on the Eigerwand. It was withdrawn as being obviously impossible to enforce, and in 1937 several intending assault parties were encamped on the flower-strewn pastures below the mighty Wall. Bad weather frustrated all but two of them: Ludwig Vörg and Hias Rebitsch, who had just previously taken part in a gruelling search for two Italian climbers missing on the Eiger, climbed to 11,000 feet—the highest yet reached—before a storm forced them to retreat from their second bivouac. They came down safely, the first men to escape alive from the death-trap. Perhaps encouraged by this, two young Italian climbers started up the Face in the early summer of 1938. Sandri and Menti were expert rock-climbers but had insufficient knowledge of the Eigerwand, which was in bad condition. They fell to their deaths from the "Difficult Crack" below the Hinterstoisser Traverse. A month later four men who had studied the problem of the Wall until they knew the utmost that was to be known about it decided that prolonged fine weather had put it into climbable condition. On July 20th the two Austrians, Kasparek and Harrer, started up; next day they were joined by two Germans who had profited by their steps in the ice to mount quickly. These were Vörg (who had retreated from the Wall the year before) and Heckmair. Later on the two "ropes" united as a single party.

Individually and as a team, these four men were superior to any that hitherto attacked the Eigerwand. They were all expert on rock and ice, they had perfected themselves as far as possible in knowledge of the climb; they had nerves of finest steel, iron wills, and that intense fire of the spirit that can all but conquer death itself. On the third day of their climb they were caught by a tremendous avalanche on the lower rim of the White Spider, but superhuman skill and tenacity saved them from being swept down. Their third bivouac was above the Spider— above the most dangerous part of the ascent—but the fine weather broke in storm, and torrents of hail, snow, and water poured down from the summit ice-field. They climbed on through the mist and driving snow. Kasparek had fallen sixty feet and been held by the rope; both Vörg and Kasparek had the skin ripped off their hands by falling rocks; the Exit Cracks were masked with ice, small avalanches rushed down the rock grooves every minute or so to pile their suffocating snows on the climbers' heads and shoulders. But they climbed on—out on to the great ice-slope under the summit. "If we hadn't just come off the Eiger's face we would have said it was steep," wrote Heinrich Harrer afterwards. "Now it seemed flat."

So the Eigerwand was behind them, vanquished. But the Eiger very nearly took its revenge. They hewed their way up the ice-slope through a blinding snowstorm, came to softer snow—and leaped back in the nick of time. The soft snow was the cornice overhanging the other side of the summit-ridge, and they had nearly fallen down the *South* Face of the Eiger!

The men who made the first ascent of the Eigerwand knew the risks they were taking and were confident that they possessed the means of overcoming them; but their venture was as much an escape as an achievement. One of them sums up his feelings after the climb thus: "We had made an excursion into another world and we had come back." Others were not so proficient in pushing mind and body to the utmost limit—or just not so lucky. When, after the Second World War, the Eigerwand again became the target for ambitious experts, nine more men died on the Face between 1946 and 1958. But twelve of the twenty attempts were successful. Improved technique and equipment, increased knowledge of the vagaries of the mountain and the weather, were lessening the chances against the climber.

The first British pair, Chris Bonington and Ian Clough, ascended the Eigerwand in 1962, having first brought off the rescue of another British aspirant whose partner had been killed. I have heard Bonington, one of our finest all-round mountaineers, give it as his opinion that the great Wall is now a justifiable mountaineering exploit; but only, he added, if the climber has previously made such ascents as the Matterhorn North Face and the North Face of the Grandes Jorasses, and made them with a wide margin of strength and endurance in hand. The events of recent years seem to bear out his contention. The Eigerwand has been climbed solo, by the Swiss, Darbellay. And in September 1964 a twenty-six-year-old German girl, Daisy Voog, became the first woman to climb it, with her companion Werner Bittner.

It is not the Eigerwand that has changed, but the standards of mountaineering prowess. The great North Wall remains one of the most perilous climbs in the Alps. Its challenge is only for the expert of experts, the man or woman who have so perfected themselves that they can face with confidence every hazard that Fate and the Eigerwand can provide.

20. On Crib y Ddisgl, Snowdon   *Showell Styles*

87 On the ridge of the Moine, above Chamonix

88 Rock face on the Meije, Dauphiné

86 Roping down
Left

89 "Artificial": North Face of Cima Grande, Dolomites

90 Bivouac on the East Face of the Grand Capucin

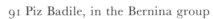

91 Piz Badile, in the Bernina group

92 The Salbitschijen, near Andermatt   93 The Second Tower on the
Salbitschijen

94 The "crux pitch", Salbitschijen South Ridge

21. Napes Needle, Lake District, England   *Showell Styles*

96 On the face of the First Sella Tower,
Dolomites

97 *Facing page*
   ''Free abseil'' from the
   Petit Charmoz, Chamonix

98 Nanda Devi

7 The Secret Goddess

In July 1936, while four young mountaineers were dying on the Eigerwand, eight other mountaineers were travelling through the Himalayan foothills towards Nanda Devi, an unclimbed giant 25,645 feet high.

The love of mountains, like all human passions, has many facets. It may bring one man to the great hills merely to look at them, to be near them; another finds he is drawn to reach their summits, no matter by what route. As the great lovers of history seem always to have chosen a mistress difficult of attainment, so the great mountaineers have put apparent inaccessibility high on the list of the charms that make their inamoratas desirable. Tastes in mistresses differ widely. And there is a marked contrast between the savage cliff perched just above a popular Swiss resort—the hardest way up a mountain which has several easier routes to its summit—and the beautiful peak whose easiest route of ascent must inevitably demand the utmost in human skill and courage.

"Romance" is hardly a term that can be used in connection with the grim saga of the Eigerwand; but the story of Nanda Devi is surely the most romantic of all recorded mountaineering adventures.

Hidden in the icy mazes of the Kumaon Himalaya stands an inaccessible peak—inaccessible both by reason of its towering height and steep sides and because it is defended by a ring of impassable ridges. Hither, in the far-off days when the gods lived on earth, fled the Princess Nanda, pursued by a prince of the Rohillas who had slain her father. Nanda took refuge on the summit of the peak, thus preserving her virginity; and from that day she became one with the mountain, which received her name—Nanda Devi, the Goddess Nanda. No man can ever reach the virgin goddess, for the great mountain-wall that surrounds her is built of sheer rock and ice. Nowhere in its circumference of full seventy miles is the wall lower than 18,000 feet. True, it is cleft at one place by the tremendous gorge whereby the waters from the Inner Sanctuary escape in fury to the lower lands, but this gorge too is impenetrable, which is why the Seven Rishis—the wisest men in the world—dwelt there during their residence on earth. Afterwards they departed to the heavens and became the seven stars known elsewhere as the Great Bear. From them the torrent in the gorge takes its name, the Rishi Ganga.

This is the legend current in Garhwal, the birthplace of the Hindu religion, and when the first European explorers and surveyors entered Garhwal to unravel the mysteries of the Kumaon Himalaya they found that the facts fitted the legend with uncomfortable closeness. In 1883 the mountaineering explorer W. W. Graham determined to try and reach the secret Goddess in her Sanctuary and probed at the ring-wall of mountains. Finding it impassable, he tried to get through the only possible breach—the gorge of the Rishi Ganga—and found it too steep and perilous even for a skilled climber. Dr Longstaff gained a col on the ring-wall twenty-two years later and was the first man to look down into the Inner Sanctuary; but he could not descend and explore that 250 square miles of untrodden territory because of the great steepness of the ice-slope on the inner side of the col. A second try by the Rishi gorge in 1907 failed. Other climbers, in later years, attempted to get up the Rishi Ganga but without success. Hugh Ruttledge, later to lead two Everest Expeditions, tried more than once to penetrate what he described as "one of the most terrific gorges in the world", and could make no headway along the sheer cliffs that stand high above the torrent. Since Garhwal was then part of British India, Nanda Devi was the highest peak in the British Empire, and if climbed would be the highest summit yet gained, so it had for mountaineers two attractions besides its beauty and romantic isolation. But not until 1934 did two men, building on the experience of the first explorers, succeed at last in climbing through the gorge of the Rishi Ganga and viewing the great south face of Nanda Devi.

Eric Shipton was at this time twenty-six years old. Tall and of fine physique, he had climbed in the Alps before a brief period as a coffee-planter in Kenya gave him the chance of first ascents on 17,000-foot Mount Kenya and a subsequent invitation to join Ruttledge's Everest Expedition of 1933. After his adventures on Everest he had resolved "to spend the rest of my life doing this sort of thing". Like Longstaff, Shipton was a born traveller and adventurer; and when Bill (H. W.) Tilman came out to try his hand at prospecting and coffee-planting in Kenya, Shipton found in him a like-minded companion. Tilman had gone through the 1914–1918 war with distinction as a Regular Army officer. Stocky, wiry, with the alert look of a Cairn terrier, there is something indestructible about him—as indeed he has proved throughout a lifetime of hazardous ventures. (In 1964, at the age of sixty-six, he set sail in a small cutter for East Greenland, there to ascend unclimbed peaks.) To Tilman mountain-climbing has always been a means to an end, the choicest means in modern times of achieving the adventure of travel and discovery. He and Shipton, alone, found a way up the unclimbed lower peak of Mount Kenya and made new climbs on Kilimanjaro and Ruwenzori; and when Shipton, on fire with enthusiasm for the Himalaya after his Everest experiences, determined to

99 Nanda Devi beyond its sanctuary wall

100 The gorge of the Rishi river

try and solve the problem of Nanda Devi, he chose Tilman for his only European companion. Neither of them was the type of climber who would have felt any desire whatever to attempt the Eigerwand, and competitive mountaineering was utterly abhorrent to both of them. But if the only way to Nanda Devi had been barred by an Eigerwand they would have tried to find a way up it.

With three Sherpas selected by Shipton from the tried and tested Everest porters, the two made the ten-day march through the exquisitely beautiful wonderland of the Himalayan valleys and reached a place on the northern rim of the Rishi gorge whence there was no onward way except along the wall of the gorge itself. This wall, of crumbling rock to which cling flowers and tufts of vegetation, drops sheer to the foaming river in its canyon far below—a depth of from 5,000 to 8,000 feet along the two-mile length of the gigantic cleft. It took them eight days of probing and retreating, crawling along the rickety face carrying their tents and supplies, rounding sheer corners with a vertical drop of thousands of feet beneath them, sleeping in chance-found caves on the precipice, before they emerged above the gorge at a height of about 15,000 feet above sea-level and found themselves in the untrodden Inner Sanctuary.

22. The Matterhorn   *Hester Norris*

101 Load-hauling on the wall of the Rishi gorge

102 The route up the Rishi Ganga

Nanda Devi, the secret goddess, was unveiled at last. The enormous south face of the mountain towered above, 10,000 feet of snow and ice and rock with a very long and steep ridge rising diagonally up it to abut against the even steeper precipice below the summit. Great glaciers spread out from the foot of the face and from the other 20,000-foot peaks that rimmed the Sanctuary, but between them lay a wide undulating tableland of soft, springy turf where herds of bharal—wild mountain sheep—roamed, and Himalayan flowers bloomed. Even at this great height there were many birds. In a lost Eden as romantic as Conan Doyle's "lost world" the explorers camped and surveyed for three weeks, and when the breaking of the monsoon drove them back down the hazards of the Rishi gorge they withdrew only to return. In September, when the snowstorms of the monsoons were past, they made a second ascent of the Rishi and spent another three weeks completing the map of the southern Nanda Devi basin.

The ground-plan of this basin or Sanctuary, larger than the county of Rutland, can best be grasped by visualising a circle representing the enclosing mountain-wall. From the right-hand side of the circle a short line drawn towards the centre is the great ridge linking Nanda Devi to a peak on the circumference called East Nanda Devi; a dot at the inner end of the line is Nanda Devi itself. Opposite this line, on the left-hand side of the circle, a mark on the circumference would represent the

103 Peaks above the Rishi: Changabang (22,520 feet) in centre

gorge of the Rishi, by which the rivers flowing from the glaciers of the Sanctuary rush out and down to join, after a hundred turbulent miles, the waters of the Ganges. (See *Diagram 7*).

Tilman and Shipton had known from the outset that their five months' work could not possibly end in an ascent of Nanda Devi; their party was far too small. Five men were quite insufficient to carry the high-altitude tents and equipment necessary for an assault up the gorge to the base of the mountain. But this small compact party, in which Sahibs and Sherpas worked together and shared the load-carrying, had set a new high standard in Himalayan exploration and mountaineering. They had not only made a detailed survey, but also, in the course of it, had climbed Maiktoli (22,320 feet) and reached a height of 20,500 feet on the south ridge of Nanda Devi. The latter climb was made to satisfy themselves that this ridge, the only practicable route they had seen after viewing the mountain from all sides, could at least be started. The complete ascent—or an attempt at it— would have to wait for another year and a larger party of first-rate mountaineers.

It was from the United States that the impulse came that was to end the frozen isolation of the Secret Goddess; but it came obliquely. A

Diagram 7
The Nanda Devi Sanctuary

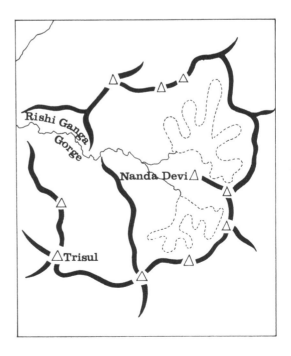

British-American expedition to attempt Kangchenjunga was proposed
by the Americans, to start for the mountain in July 1936. Four mountaineers from each nation were to form the team, which would be led
jointly by T. Graham Brown, Professor of Physiology in the University
of Wales, and Charles Houston, a young American physician who had
climbed with Graham Brown on the first ascent of Mount Foraker
(17,000 feet), the second highest mountain in Alaska. Three experienced climbers—W. F. Loomis, Adams Carter, and Arthur Emmons—
completed the American half of the team; the other three Britishers
were H. W. Tilman, Peter Lloyd, and N. E. Odell, the last-named having been on Everest in 1924. Odell took the place of Eric Shipton, who
in 1936 was with Ruttledge's Everest team. Application to go to
Kangchenjunga had to be made to the Indian Government, and it was
made too late. Permission was refused, and the party turned its
ambitions to another objective: the ascent of Nanda Devi. Tilman and
Loomis went out before the monsoon to prepare the way and to engage
the best half-dozen Sherpas they could get.

By this time parties of Himalayan climbers had come to place great
reliance on Sherpas, without whose help in carrying loads on dangerous
ground at great heights their plans were almost certain to be abortive.
This small tribe or race (they are said to number less than 4,000) had
originally crossed the frontier from Tibet and settled in the mountains
near Sola Khumbu in Eastern Nepal. From their earliest youth
Sherpas are accustomed to cross passes of 19,000 feet and more,
carrying loads of trade goods; and when the demand for expedition
porters arose in the 'twenties they found a profession for which they
were better suited than any men in the world. On the Everest Expedition of 1924 the few porters who carried to 27,000 feet were all of the
Sherpa race, and were dubbed "Tigers" by the sahibs. Short of
stature but amazingly strong, loyal, unselfish, capable of the highest
courage, these men have a strange affinity with the British. The idea of
facing the unknown hazards of a high mountain in order to climb it to
the top was perfectly comprehensible to them, and the best of them
not only acquired the technique of rope and ice-axe with surprising
rapidity but also became climbing-partners as cheerful and reliable
as any British mountaineer.

Tilman, of course, hoped to get six Tigers for the Nanda Devi assault;
but he was unlucky. The big German Expedition to Nanga Parbat in
1934 had chosen the best Sherpas available, and in the terrible disaster
that overtook the party eight of them had been killed. Ruttledge and
his 1936 Everesters had taken the pick of the few who remained.
Tilman managed to get only one genuine Tiger and five other Sherpas
who were either elderly or completely inexperienced. The Tiger was
Pasang Kikuli, whose name deserves (perhaps more than any other) to
be written in letters of gold on the scroll of Himalayan heroes. Pasang

Kikuli had already carried loads to 25,700 feet on Everest in 1933, had been on two Kangchenjunga Expeditions, and was one of the five porters who came safely down from the Nanga Parbat disaster. As it turned out, he was not to perform any great feats on Nanda Devi. The final test was to come on K2 in 1939.

With two Sherpas and some Dhotial porters from the remote village of Mana, Tilman and Loomis forced their way along the precipices of the Rishi gorge with preliminary loads of food and equipment. Rock-falls had altered the crumbling sides of the cleft, but they contrived to link up the precarious ledges by which Tilman and Shipton had come in 1934, at one place hauling the loads by rope up a wall of sheer rock. Here Tilman, superintending the hauling operations, was knocked off his ledge by a big flake of rock dislodged from above and fell down the precipice, luckily coming to rest on a narrow shelf 1,400 feet above the vertical drop to the river with no worse injuries than a cracked rib and the loss of a lot of skin. "It was necessary to get moving before stiffness made this impossible," is his comment on an accident that would have made a stretcher necessary for most of us. They went on up the gorge, dumped the loads (which included 900 lb. of food) two days' march— or climb—from the Sanctuary, and returned all the way to Ranikhet to wait for the passing of the monsoon and the arrival of the rest of the party. This preliminary journey, which occupied twenty-eight days, turned out to be vital to the success of the Expedition.

When the complete Anglo-American team reached the lower end of the Rishi gorge in late July the snowy fury of the monsoon was over. But the huge snow-deposits on the mountains of the Sanctuary far above were still melting, and the immense volume of water rushing down the gorge, its sole exit, rendered the route very nearly impassable. At the first difficult crossing of the river thirty-seven of the forty-seven porters who were carrying the main supplies of food and equipment refused to go any farther. Left with only ten Mana men and six Sherpas, the climbers might well have decided to abandon the journey; they had already cut down their supplies to the absolute minimum to ease the very hazardous climb up the Rishi, and every load was now essential. Luckily, however, the advance party had carried some loads up already, and they revised their plans. Every sahib would now carry the same load as a porter, and double or treble journeys would be made back and forth between each bivouac-spot to relay the loads. This gruelling labour had to be done on the two-mile-long face of a precipice where small grass-tufts clinging to the sheer rock were often the only footholds; where, through many hours of each day, the heavily laden men clung and crept along 2,000 feet above the shrunken white thread of the river far below their boot-soles; where protection with the rope was generally useless. It took them five days. By August 1st the climbers and all their supplies were in the Sanctuary, with the variegated rocks of Nanda Devi's pedestal—rust-red, yellow, and black—merging into the higher slopes of snow and ice that soared to the summit more than 10,000 feet overhead. Next day a Base Camp was established at 15,500 feet, a mile above the snout of the south-eastern Nanda Devi glacier. The ten Mana porters were paid off and sent back down the Rishi to the lower lands, taking with them one of the older Sherpas who was unfit to do any more climbing. The American Emmons, who had been badly frostbitten on the Chinese peak Minya Gongkar in 1932, was left in charge of Base Camp and the further survey of the Sanctuary. The men who were to attack the ultimate shrine of the Goddess Nanda now numbered five Sherpas and seven sahibs.

In *Plate* 104 Nanda Devi is the farther of the two peaks, to the left of Nanda Devi East. Its left-hand skyline is the great south-east ridge. This ridge, on which the climbing-party was to live for the next three weeks, was called by them the Coxcomb Ridge because of the serrated ridge of crumbling yellow rock that protruded from the snow of its lower reaches. The reconnaissance made two years earlier by Tilman and Shipton had established the fact that there were no great difficulties below 19,000 feet, and the first need was to place Camp I at the top of this easier section and stock it with food for twenty-five days. Beyond

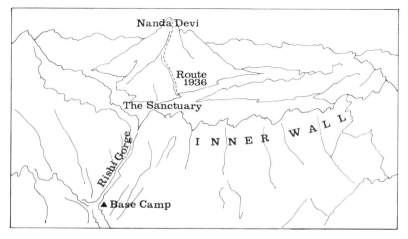

Diagram 8 Nanda Devi

104 Nanda Devi and East Nanda Devi

that it was impossible to plan times and distances. The ridge was something like three miles long, all of it tilted at a very high angle and the last section, at least, formidably steep. There was no knowing what obstacles awaited them higher up or whether some quite impassable pitch would defeat them utterly. Moreover, there were plenty of other unknown quantities: the weather, the state of the snow, the rate of climbing, the ability of the Sherpa porters, and—especially—the powers of acclimatisation of men only two of whom had been higher than 17,500 feet before.

Acclimatisation, the gradual accustoming of the human body to living and functioning at high altitudes, was essential to the success of the Nanda Devi party. The heavy and cumbrous oxygen apparatus of the 'thirties was no use to them; one oxygen cylinder had been brought out from England, but it had last been seen spinning down towards the Rishi torrent, nearly taking a porter with it. It had been intended only for use in the treatment of frostbite. Some men acclimatise slowly, others quickly, and for many people the "mountain sickness" which is the effect of oxygen-lack is felt as low as 10,000 feet. The twelve climbers had been living above 12,000 feet for a week or more and were well acclimatised to this height, but it remained to be seen how each man would adapt himself to greater heights as they rose up the ridge. On this factor depended the human possibility of the ascent, as well as the choice of the two men who would make the bid for the summit from the final camp—if they got that far.

A day's hard climbing with heavy loads brought them to the ridge above the yellow Coxcomb, and at once they met difficulty. The ridge was very narrow, a precipice on one hand and an ice-slope on the other, and nowhere was it broad enough to site the camp. After vain prospecting higher up the rib of snow and loose rock, they fell to work digging and building and at last had three small platforms with a tent pitched on each. Then they retreated to Base Camp, where the tail-end of the monsoon caught them with a blizzard that left four inches of snow and prevented any climbing for two days. On the third day, though the snow was still falling, Camp I (19,200 feet) was occupied, three Englishmen and two Americans remaining there while the Sherpas descended to Base Camp to bring up more supplies next day.

And now began the slow, toilsome, and always perilous task of fighting a way foot by foot up the great ridge. The lingering monsoon had by no means finished with them. Rain, turning to snow, belaboured Camp I and again kept the party in their sleeping-bags for a day: a nuisance which was to recur throughout the ascent. At such close quarters in tiny tents the best of comrades become acutely conscious of the personal deficiencies of their tent-fellows. "Some of us" (to quote Tilman) "talked too much or too loudly, some did not talk enough, some smoked foul pipes, some ate raw onions, some *never* washed. . . ."

23. Roping-down on the Rötihorn *H. N. Collinson*

105 Camp I

106 Camp II

They kept intolerance at bay by a system of "musical chairs", by which tent partners were changed at intervals. They lived chiefly on porridge, dried milk, and pemmican, all of which require hot water to make them palatable. The water had to be obtained by melting snow on a Primus stove; a very slow and arduous business, for a packed saucepan of snow yielded only a teacupful of water and the hapless cook had then to go out into the blizzard and collect more—not only in the saucepan but also down his neck and on his clothes. The interior of a small tent on a Himalayan peak—sopping wet from melted snow, foul with the soot from a flaring stove, thick with the mingled odours of paraffin, stale food, and long-unwashed clothes and bodies—is not the snug and romantic place one might imagine. It is a vast relief (and I speak from experience) to get out of it even into bad and dangerous conditions.

So it was with the Nanda Devi men. In spite of the soft new snow, Tilman and Odell climbed up to find a site for Camp II next day. The ridge was now much steeper. Fearfully loose rock on the crest, followed by great overhanging cornices, forced them to traverse on the steep slopes falling to the glacier, flogging away the soft snow to cut steps in the harder snow or ice beneath. One of the two (the record does not say which) slipped and fell; the other saved him with the rope hitched round a swiftly driven axe. A species of trapdoor had to be hewn through a snow overhang. And they found the only possible site for Camp II—a sloping ledge six feet wide beneath a rock overhang, with a 2,000-foot drop to the glacier beneath its edge. Next day, in a snowstorm, two tents were carried up and placed here and from these

Graham Brown and Charles Houston made the next advance. First occupying the new camp, they worked their way up the increasingly difficult ridge for a further 800 feet. "We descried what looked like two flies crawling up the steep snow arête," says Tilman, "and we watched them anxiously, making ribald remarks about their rate of progress and frequent halts." Everyone was feeling the effect of altitude now, and after half a dozen upward steps it was necessary to halt while gasping lungs struggled to take in oxygen from the thin and freezing air.

Camp III was placed snugly under a sheltering snow-hump at 21,000 feet. It was August 18th; in eight days the climbers had gained little more than 5,500 feet, and the worst part of the ascent rose above them. At this point Fate—or perhaps the Goddess Nanda—delivered two cruel blows in succession at the attackers. Only two Sherpas—Nima and Pasang Kikuli—had been fit enough to help with the carry to Camp III. It had scarcely been decided to send the two ailing men down to stay at Base Camp when it was discovered that both the others were out of the fight. Nima was sick, and Pasang Kikuli—who had unwisely removed his snow-glasses while clearing a platform for the tents—was completely snowblind. They, too, were sent down to Base Camp. All the carrying, as well as the climbing, would henceforth have to be done by the seven sahibs.

This tremendous handicap only spurred the determination of the British-American team to press on with the assault. Lloyd and Loomis were coming up from the lower camps, Adams Carter—who was suffering from slight frostbite—escorted the disabled Sherpas down the

167

hazardous ridge, Tilman and Odell climbed with heavy loads to Camp III and occupied it. That evening there was an ominous halo round the sun, and two 'mock suns', even more ominous, hung on either side of it. Next day it was snowing. They got down again to Camp II for more loads while the others carried the equipment for Camp IV to a snow saddle at 21,800 feet, and that night all seven climbers were in the tents at Camp III when the storm broke.

Out of the south-east came the icy, snow-filled gale, smiting the three little tents high on their narrow ridge, tearing at the thin fabric until it seemed certain that all would be whirled away into the void. For forty-eight hours, without cessation or lull, the blizzard drove like the wrath of the Himalayan gods. Outside the tents movement was suicidal and even breathing was impossible. Inside, huddled in their sleeping-bags with an eye—and sometimes a steadying hand—on the rocking tent-poles, the seven men who had dared the vengeance of the Secret Goddess lay and waited. Their one consolation was that the tremendous wind would not allow the snow to settle for any great depth on the mountain; if it had done so, not only would the rest of the climb have been physically impossible but also their retreat down the ridge would have been cut off. The snow drifted and packed on the sagging tents, reducing the space inside by one-half. There was little rest for anyone; and when, on the morning of August 24th, the weather cleared and a move could be made they felt (according to Tilman) "complete physical and moral wrecks".

But the day was calm and sunny. From the dazzling snowslope falling away at their feet they looked across a great purple void to the ivory wall of the Sanctuary, with the black notch of the Rishi gorge its only gap. To the east, wave on wave of snow-peaks rolled to the far horizon. And above them their narrow ladder, powdered with new snow, soared for more than 4,000 feet to the longed-for summit. That very day they carried up the three tents for Camp IV, and five climbers occupied them: Lloyd, Loomis, Odell, Houston, and Tilman.

They had been more than a fortnight on the mountain and further delay might easily end their chance of climbing it. Speed, continuous action, was now essential. The plan agreed upon was that all five men should carry food and the tiny bivouac tent as high as possible from Camp IV; the two fittest men would remain in the bivouac and try next day to reach the summit. Houston and Odell were at this time going extremely well and they were chosen as the summit pair. The plan was a great deal more difficult to execute than to devise. The beginning of the route beyond Camp IV lay across an exceedingly steep snowslope where steps had to be cut and the greatest care exercised. This led to a slabby gully whose smooth rocks were only thinly covered with snow. At the foot of this they rested, but—"it was no place for a long sojourn without prehensile trousers . . . boots, hands, and ice-axe

108 Houston and Lloyd at Camp IV, 21,800 feet.

were all needed to prevent the beginning of a long slither which would only end on the glacier 6,000 feet below". The gully was climbed without mishap, and above it there was safer but harder going, kicking and cutting their way up very steep snow. It was a beautiful day, and the sun, even at more than 22,000 feet above the sea, was too hot for comfort. Away to the right the 22,500-foot peak of Nanda Kot sank lower until at last they were looking above it. Ahead of them the final broad face of Nanda Devi rose in a precipice of snow with a central rock-ridge protruding from it like a Roman nose, and they climbed towards the ridge, making for a tower of rock that seemed as if it might have a flat summit on which the bivouac tent could be placed. For on all that day's ascent they had found no level spot big enough for a tent. The only way on to the tower was by a difficult rock chimney, up which Lloyd—a brilliant rock-climber—led in grand style. There was no site for a tent on top. It was four o'clock; if the three descending climbers were not to be overtaken by darkness on the perilous slopes they must turn back at once. Leaving Odell and Houston to find a site—if they could—before nightfall, Tilman, Lloyd, and Loomis went down to Camp IV.

109 In the "shallow gully," at 23,000 feet.

It was fairly certain that the summit pair would have to spend another day moving their bivouac higher up before they were in position to make a dash for the top, so the others expected to have a two-day wait at Camp IV. They spent the first day helping Graham Brown and Carter, who were coming up to join them, to carry loads from Camp III. Mist shrouded the upper mountain and nothing was to be seen of the two above, who (as they later reported) climbed to 24,000 feet and then returned to move the bivouac higher, having found the distance to the summit too great. On the next day, August 27th, mist still hid the great final precipice. In the tents at Camp IV the five men were eating porridge and discussing a fresh blow of Circumstance—both Loomis's feet were frostbitten and he could climb no farther. Suddenly, unexpectedly, there came to their ears a high, faint call. It was Odell's familiar yodel, and it sounded urgent.

Outside the tents there was nothing to see. But from the mists above that shrill cry came again. The bivouac was at least 1,800 feet above them—Odell must have climbed some distance down to make them hear him. Carter, who had the strongest lungs, shouted his loudest to ask what was wrong. The answer, barely audible, shocked them as nothing else could have done: *"Charlie—is—killed!"*

110 Traversing across the gully

It was a moment, a moment of paralysing consternation, before any of the five could move. There had been a fatal accident. Houston was dead. Odell had sounded sure of that, but he might be mistaken. It was imperative to get up to the bivouac at once.

Tilman and Lloyd were the first away, carrying bandages and spare clothing. Graham Brown and Carter followed with a hypodermic syringe and other medical supplies. The immediate need was to get to the scene of the accident; but in all their minds was a foreboding that nobody mentioned. Houston and Odell would have been climbing roped together. If Houston had fallen and Odell had not checked the fall with the rope, it meant that he also had been dragged down and badly hurt. They pictured him crawling down the ridge with the last of his strength to shout for help, and the picture grew more vivid when their own shouts, as they climbed higher, were not answered. With Loomis barely able to manage the descent himself, with the Sherpas out of action 6,000 feet below, the party was reduced to four climbers. The chances of getting a helpless man down the mountain were too remote to bear thinking about.

Of all their days of climbing on Nanda Devi that morning's climb from Camp III was one they would remember most clearly afterwards. Speed was vitally necessary—and speed was literally impossible. The slightest effort above that required for normal climbing rendered them instantly breathless and exhausted and required a halt for recovery. They could only mount as before, slowly and with continual care. The tricky snowslope was crossed, the edge of the gully gained. Remembering the difficulties here, and the hard chimney above (how could an injured man be got down that chimney?) they tried another route, and found it worse than the first. Hauling themselves panting on to the steep snow-ridge beyond, they toiled up the last stretch. There was the little tent not thirty paces above, and no one to be seen. Instinctively they tried to run to it, but could only advance slowly and step by step. What would they find in the tent, if anything?

They heard voices talking quietly in the tent. The curtain was pulled aside. "Hullo, you blokes," said Odell cheerfully. "Have some tea!"

Houston had been violently sick all night and was very weak. The message Odell had tried to convey was *"Charlie is ill!"* The reactions of the rescue-party may easily be imagined: first a profound relief; then a natural disgust at having been made to suffer so much mental torture; then, of course, deep concern for Houston. The symptoms suggested food-poisoning from some tinned beef Houston had eaten the day before, and the results had left him able to stand and walk but capable of little more. In spite of his illness, the young American took charge of the situation. He insisted that the assault should go on without a break; he could get down to Camp III, he declared, with one man leading and two behind to safeguard him. Thus Tilman would be

able to occupy the bivouac tent with Odell straight away, move it higher next day, and make the summit attempt on the following morning. After some demur this plan was adopted, with one modification: the whole party went down with Houston, who climbed steadily despite his helpless state of weakness, and then Tilman and Odell ascended again to the little tent in which Odell and Houston had passed two miserable nights.

"Site" was a somewhat misleading term for the position of this camp. A wall of snow swept up from the depths on the west side to a razor-edge with a vertical precipice falling from it. The platform that had been scraped out of the snow was so narrow that one side of the tent floor hung like a flap down the icy western steeps, much reducing the floor space and any sense of security the inhabitants could feel in such a place. "Odell, who was the oldest inhabitant and in the position of host, generously conceded to me the outer berth, overhanging space," comments Tilman. Next morning, the weather continuing to hold, they climbed 500 feet up the ridge to a more comfortable site on a snow-shelf discovered by Odell and Houston two days earlier, placed the bivouac tent there, and descended for the remaining loads of equipment and food. The height of this second bivouac was about 24,000 feet. Above it rose the final 1,600 feet of Nanda Devi—a saw-like ridge of rock steps and snow edges leading to a great snowslope under the last steep wall of snowy rock. The weather, the condition of the snow on that long snowslope, the unknown difficulties of the final wall, were factors any one of which could defeat them on the morrow. The two men turned in, resolved upon an early start.

The day of the assault dawned clear and bitterly cold. Tilman and Odell were away before sunrise, struggling with a rope that was frozen stiff. "What mugs we were to be fooling about on this infernal ridge at that hour of the morning!" This sentiment—perhaps to be applauded by most non-climbers—gave way before the enthusiasm of the mountaineer as they slowly gained height. Slowly indeed. Both men had acclimatised remarkably well, yet each delicate upward step demanded five or six gasping breaths. They climbed at the rate of 200 feet in an hour, and this was fast going at such an altitude. The last part of the great ridge was a tilted knife-edge of rock, bridging—like Mahomet's sword—the dizzy gap between earth and the throne of the Goddess. It was of sound rock, the first they had climbed on since leaving Base Camp. The sun rose as they stepped on to the great snowslope.

The snow was fearfully soft. At each step they went in more than kneedeep, and when the next step was made they merely sank in deeper, back to the previous level. Every movement of this kind cost them eight deep breaths. Their hopes of the summit began to fade, but they forced themselves to think of nothing but the lifting and plunging of their leaden feet and went on, literally inch by inch. Now the sun smote down from a glaring sky, sapping the energy from mind and body and scorching the few inches of skin left exposed by their masks and snow-glasses. But to the south-west Trisul was below them and they were level with the crest of East Nanda Devi on the Sanctuary rim. A little after one o'clock that execrable snowslope was below them and they were at the foot of the final wall, where they halted to try and force some chocolate down their parched throats by eating snow with it.

They had been heading towards the only place in the final wall that seemed to offer any hope of effecting a lodgement on it. There was first a difficult rock wall, then a very steep snow-gully, likely to prove unclimbable if the snow in it was soft, and lastly a snow ridge with an easy-looking corridor beside it just below the summit crest. Odell led up the rock wall. They were only 300 feet below the top and both men felt that nothing could stop them now. Tilman, taking the lead, climbed the snow-gully after a hard struggle; it was even steeper than it had looked but the snow was hard enough because of that steepness. He drove in his axe at the top, to safeguard Odell as he climbed up. The summit was almost within their grasp—they could choose between the steep snow ridge or the more gently sloping corridor. As Odell came gasping up to him, Tilman proposed that they should use the snow corridor.

Nanda Devi made one last effort to dislodge the violaters of her shrine. Scarcely had Tilman finished speaking when there was a sudden splitting sound and a hiss. The snow broke away to the depth of a foot all round the ice-axe to which he was holding, and forty yards of the corridor floor peeled off to go plunging down the terrific south face beneath in an avalanche. By a miracle the two climbers were not dragged down with it. But—"the corridor route had somehow lost its attractiveness", and they finished the climb by the snow ridge. At three o'clock on August 29th they stood at last on the summit of Nanda Devi.

Surprisingly, the summit was the most comfortable place on the whole mountain. It was a broad, almost flat tableland of snow twenty paces wide and 200 long, where it was perfectly safe to unrope and walk about. Cessation of effort brought comparative ease of breathing and with it the power to appreciate their position. They were on the highest summit yet reached; the nearest rival to their peak was Dhaulagiri, 200 miles away, and every icy peak in sight was below them. They and their companions had achieved a feat of mountaineering that would rank in history among the greatest. "I believe we so far forgot ourselves," says Tilman, "as to shake hands on it." But he spared a moment from the golden time of rest and triumph to be sorry for Charles Houston, who—but for the defective contents of a bully-beef tin—would have stood here in his place.

Forty-five minutes was all they dared spend on the hard-won summit of their mountain, for the long and dangerous descent had to be made before nightfall. The avalanche had swept the steep gully in the final wall, obliterating the steps they had laboriously cut, but they passed that and the narrow ridge safely and were snug in the little tent shortly after sunset, brewing and drinking mug after mug of weak, sweet tea. On September 1st all the climbers were back at Base Camp.

The Secret Goddess was conquered. But she had exacted her sacrifice. The veteran Sherpa Kitar Dorje, who had remained at Base Camp with stomach trouble, had died of dysentery on the day following the successful assault. His fellow Sherpas had erected a large cairn on his grave among the mountains to which he had given his life.

Dr Tom Longstaff, one of the earliest worshippers at the shrine of Nanda Devi, had written in the Lonsdale Library Volume on *Mountaineering* that the climbing of this beautiful and cloistered peak would be a sacrilege too horrible to contemplate. Tilman himself had felt, after the first joy of victory, a sadness that the proud head of the goddess was bowed; he likened his remorse to that of the hunter who, having shot his elephant, feels that all the skill and courage of the hunt and the rich gain of ivory cannot atone for the fall of a giant. The conquerors of the Eigerwand would not, I think, have understood this feeling. But there is no sacrilege when a virgin peak is climbed for the love of its beauty and majesty; and in the last words of his preface to Tilman's book about the climb Dr Longstaff admitted it: "A laconic telegram reached me in Shetland: 'two reached the top August 29.' No names; they had deserved the honour. Here was humility, not pride, and gratitude for a permitted experience."

111 Nanga Parbat (26,620 feet) from 120 miles away

8 The Siege of Nanga Parbat

THE greatest precipice on earth rises at the extreme north-western end of the Great Himalayan Range. Here the Indus river, after flowing north-west for 600 miles between the parallel crests of Karakoram and Himalaya, makes a sudden dramatic bend to run due south through the mountain barrier to the plains, carving a gigantic trench whose floor is only 3,000 feet above sea-level and forming a moat round the base of Nanga Parbat, one of the ten highest peaks in the world. Hardly twenty-five miles map distance separates the Indus trench from the 26,620-foot top of Nanga Parbat—a difference in relative height found nowhere else on the surface of the globe. In no other place can the traveller pass in so few miles from the blistering heat of rocky barrens where nothing will grow, through the zone of grass and trees and flowers, to polar conditions of eternal ice and snow. No mountaineer will ever gaze in awe at a greater precipice than the South Wall of Nanga Parbat, which drops in one terrific sweep of rock and ice to the glacier-blocked Rupal Valley 16,000 feet below. And no other mountain has defended itself more savagely against the assaults of besieging mountaineers than Nanga Parbat. Viewed from 120 miles away (*Plate 111*) it still stands supreme.

In 1895, when the great Alpine mountaineer A. F. Mummery journeyed out with his friends Collie and Hastings to make the first attempt on Nanga Parbat, very little was known about climbing at high altitudes. Mummery underestimated the size and strength of the fortress he was attacking. He treated it as an outsize Alpine peak, with its rock-faces and snowslopes and avalanches conforming to Alpine standards of behaviour though on a slightly increased scale. "I don't think there will be any serious mountaineering difficulties on Nanga," he wrote home to his wife. "I fancy the ascent will be mainly a question of endurance." It took five weeks of hazardous probings and retreats to disillusion him, and even then he was only partly aware of the dangers he was facing. He was quite unaware of the fact that on a 26,000-foot mountain the real climbing problems begin above 20,000 feet. That was the height he reached, with one Gurkha porter, on the Diamir or western face of Nanga Parbat; an almost incredible performance. It was while he was attempting to cross one of the flanking ridges to get a look at the north-west face of the mountain that Mummery and his two Gurkhas disappeared for ever. They were almost certainly over-whelmed by one of the unpredictable ice-avalanches which are Nanga Parbat's most terrible weapons.

Mummery had tackled the mountain from the south and west only because the northern approaches were barred to him. In 1895 the warring Hunza tribes prevented access to the upper Indus gorge, and the British Raj had not yet succeeded in bringing law and order to this debatable land between the Himalaya and the Hindu Kush. Thirty-seven years later all this was changed. An expedition led by Willy Merkl of Germany and including seven other first-class climbers—one of them a young American, Rand Herron—set out in 1932 for the 200-mile journey from Srinagar to the mountain. They had better maps, fuller knowledge of Himalayan conditions, and far more efficient equipment than Mummery's party. Much of the dark mystery sur-rounding life at high altitudes had vanished, for on Everest men had climbed to 28,000 feet without oxygen and had even slept comfortably at 26,800 feet. In place of Mummery's tiny carrying-party of two Gurkhas the German-American Expedition had an army of 150 load-carriers and a dozen Hunza porters for the higher camps. Improved knowledge of Nanga Parbat's topography brought them to the attack from the north, where the long Rakhiot Glacier pushes far in between flanking ridges to the North Face of the mountain—a face to all appearances much less difficult than the south and west faces.

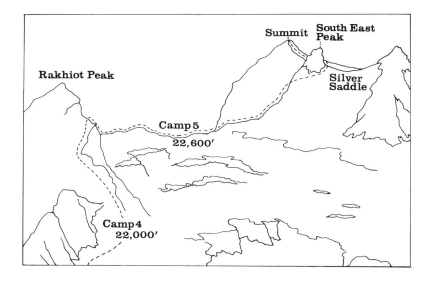

Diagram 9. The upper camps and route on Nanga Parbat

Superficially, the conformation of the great slopes and the route up them were not unlike those of Everest on the North Col route: a climb from the glacier to a snow-ridge, the crossing or by-passing of a subsidiary peak (the Rakhiot Peak), and a long final ridge to the summit. But whereas the East Rongbuk Glacier provides an easy way throughout its rise of 4,600 feet, the Rakhiot Glacier begins lower, rises higher, and is a difficult climb up icefalls. The climb to the ridge is twice as high as the North Col climb, three times as dangerous, and four times as long in point of time. Like Everest's north face, the north face of Nanga Parbat is swept by tremendous storms; but instead of a bare precipice there is here a mighty wall hung with ice—hanging glaciers that may discharge thousands of tons of ice down the face at any moment of the day in summer. And summer, between the heavy snowfalls of late spring and the coming of the monsoon in July or August, was the only time for an attack.

Merkl's party, with Rand Herron playing a leading part, encountered a long spell of fine weather which enabled them to push their attack as far as a camp on the ridge west of the Rakhiot Peak, at 22,800 feet. This was Camp VII. It had taken them thirty days and seven camps on the mountain to get this far, and they were still a long way from the top. Then a fearful snowstorm that lasted for eight days drove down on them and they had to retreat from the chain of tiny tents almost isolated by the deepening snow. One climber had acute appendicitis, two had strained hearts. Only superb mountaincraft and Merkl's wise leadership brought them off the mountain safely. This time, it seemed, Nanga Parbat had exacted no toll. But on the way home young Rand Herron, sight-seeing in Egypt, fell in descending the Pyramid of Gizeh and was killed.

Merkl had learned a great deal from this expedition. He had found a practicable route and knew its enormous length and difficulty. He knew that on Nanga Parbat the weather in one camp could be fine and calm while in the camp above it might be so bad that movement outside the tents was physically impossible. But he did not realise that the long spell of fine weather, not the eight-day snowstorm, was the exception to the rule on this terrible mountain. In another year, he told himself, no such unlucky chance would rob him of the coveted prize— a prize needed, among other things, to restore lost prestige to a resurgent Germany. In 1934 he led an all-German expedition to Nanga Parbat.

No more competent climbing expedition ever set forth than the party that reached Base Camp below the Rakhiot Glacier in May 1934. The twelve Germans included eight of the finest mountaineers in the world; they had thirty-five picked Sherpas, more than 200 porters, and the full co-operation of the Indian Government and the Himalayan Club. By June 6th their third camp had been established on the side of the ridge below the Rakhiot Peak, in spite of poor weather with frequent snow-falls. They planned to cross a high shoulder of the Rakhiot Peak to avoid the avalanche-threatened steeps below it, and thence to move along the very narrow snow-crest towards a great black pillar of rock known as the South-East Peak. This pillar was far too steep to climb over, but by traversing across the icy wall below it on the north they might gain a beautiful snowcrest called the Silver Saddle, slung between the pillar and another gigantic rock tower dubbed the North-East Peak or (by later expeditions) the Silver Crag. Once on this saddle, the way to the summit—still nearly two miles distant along a difficult ridge of rock and ice—lay open.

Nanga Parbat got in the first blow. Alfred Drexel, one of the best climbers, went down with pneumonia and died at Camp II. A sort of funeral oration, made by one of the party beside Drexel's grave near Base Camp, spoke of "an epic of battle and heroism and national self-sacrifice". The spirit here was very different from that of Mummery and his fellow-venturers, or of Tilman and Odell on Nanda Devi.

The assault went on. Nanga Parbat sent down warnings in the shape of vast ice-avalanches which narrowly missed the clustered tents in their snowy hollows below the Rakhiot Peak. Fritz Bechtold, a member of the party, describes one:

> High overhead, 11,000 feet above us, the first rays of sunshine struck the immense ice-cliff at the edge of the summit plateau. Then came the first salvo. The blue glittering mass of ice spread itself out slowly across the wall, as the glacier gave birth to the avalanche. A wave 700 feet high rolled over the fearful north face of Nanga Parbat. Cataracts of ice beyond the powers of imagination roared down, striking against the mountainside, bursting over the citadels of granite, and finally hissed their way as fine ice-dust on to the level glacier below. After a breathless silence the cloud of dust grew up in white bubbles, climbing higher and higher and covering us with its icy breath.
>
> *Nanga Parbat Adventure*, by F. Bechtold, 1935.

The mere blast of air from such an avalanche, several miles distant, could have blown tents and men from their precarious perches. But they continued to fight their slow way upward, establishing a route through the maze of giant crevasses and ice-pinnacles to the ice-wall on the flank of the Rakhiot Peak. The weather on the whole was favourable now; but men descending from one camp where clear sunshine had reigned were surprised to find the lower camp digging itself out from the aftermath of a blizzard. It was another of Nanga Parbat's grim warnings.

Twenty-six days after Drexel's death the ice-wall on the flank of the Rakhiot Peak had been crossed with the aid of fixed ropes and the first camp placed on the snow-ridge—Camp VI. The meticulously planned

25. The Summit-ridge of the Eiger   *Picture-point*

advance continued; a climbing-party would go forward as far as possible and set up the tents, a supply party come up to stock them, the camp would be occupied for a further push upwards, and so forth. Nanga Parbat gave a final warning. One of the upper camps could not be stocked according to plan because of a snowstorm which half-buried the camp below, though on the ridge the weather was clear and a climbing-party had reached the Silver Saddle. It was July 6th, and Camp VIII had been pitched at 24,560 feet. Two climbers, breaking the track from this camp, had got as high as 25,280 feet and considered the summit only four or five hours beyond. The mountain struck its second blow.

During the afternoon of the 6th the wind rose. By nightfall it was a hurricane blowing dense clouds of snow across the mountain. Tents were damaged, movement was totally impossible. Imprisoned at nearly 25,000 feet were five German climbers and eleven Sherpa porters.

At that time little was known about the effect on the human mind and body of bad conditions at high altitudes. Today we know that survival in such conditions is not just a matter of endurance and moral courage. The combination of exhaustion, great height, and intense cold produces, at a certain point, an exceedingly rapid decay of the actual tissues of brain and muscle leading to physical and mental collapse and death. Even in good conditions, altitude can so affect mentality that the strongest-minded may have his judgement warped and experience vivid hallucinations. It could be assumed that something of this evil effect had already overtaken the climbers; for when the storm hit the high camp there was no support party nearer than Camp IV. Below them was 4,000 feet of difficult climbing, a linear distance of more than three miles where every foot of descent demanded the utmost care, and nowhere on this terrible journey was there any help. All next day the storm raged, piling the insides of the tents with fine snow, preventing the stoves from being lit, bringing the limit of bodily endurance nearer with every freezing hour. On the morning of the 8th, though the blizzard was as fierce as ever, Merkl—who was with this advance party—gave the word to retreat.

Down below at Camp IV the weather was fairly good and the climbers there had no suspicion of the tragedy that was being enacted 4,000 feet above them. There had been some snowfall between Camps IV and V, and on July 7th they decided it would be a good thing to remake the route. They found the snow so soft and deep that it was impossible to force a way up to Camp V. Even then the frightful possibilities were not apparent to them. On the morning of July 8th, when they saw through a gap in the clouds a string of tiny specks descending from the Silver Saddle, they thought it likely that the advance party were coming down in triumph from a successful assault. Then, at seven that evening, two reeling, exhausted figures floundered down through the waist-high snow to Camp IV. Peter Aschenbrenner and Erwin Schneider, cased in ice from head to foot, were able to tell of the storm and the retreat. Merkl had sent them ahead to break the trail while he and the other two Germans followed with the eleven porters; in the blinding snowstorms they had lost touch with the others, but the main party could be expected (they added) before long.

But no one came. The morning broke after a night of heavy snow, and the watchers at Camp IV scanned the vast slopes anxiously through clearer weather. Grey-white cloud still surged below the Silver Saddle, but through a momentary break they glimpsed—far, far overhead—a party descending the slopes beneath the Saddle. Two days ago they had been seen only a little higher up. It seemed incredible that they had gained such a small distance towards safety.

It was now certain that the men on the ridge were engaged in a desperate struggle for life. There was no possibility of helping them. Repeated attempts to climb upward through the deep soft snow failed completely. And that night more snow fell, removing all hope of ascent on those great white walls but leaving open the faint chance of descent. Next morning, July 10th, seven men were seen coming down from the Rakhiot shoulder, and hours later four of them—Sherpa porters, terribly frostbitten—crawled into Camp IV with the first news of tragedy: their three Sherpa comrades had died of cold and exhaustion on the way down, and a Sahib, Uli Wieland, had on the previous day lain down in the snow below the Silver Saddle and had died instantly.

As if to quell any desperate hope of rescuing those who might still be alive on the ridge, a blizzard now swept over Camp IV and continued for thirty-six hours. As soon as it ceased, three Germans and three Sherpas left the tents determined to break a way through to Camp V at all costs. The difference in height between the two camps was 1,600 feet, a distance which might occupy between one and three hours on a British or Alpine mountain. It took the six men all day to accomplish their task, and the effort required was enormous, but they reached Camp V. There was no one there, and another fierce snowstorm broke and continued all that night. The morning was July 13th; for five days the storm had been blowing across the ridge, and the ridge was 23,000 feet above the sea. No human being could still be alive up there after such an ordeal, the Germans told each other. If they themselves were not to die in the snow-avalanches that must result from the vast new snow deposits, the high camps would have to be evacuated, and quickly.

As though Nanga Parbat read their minds, they were given another unexpected glimpse of hope. The curtain of snow-cloud was swept aside again and they saw three men moving down the ridge. The three tiny figures halted, and one of them moved forward. Down some freak current of the storm-wind floated an agonised cry for help. Then the cloud drew across once more and all was blotted out.

To be within sight and sound of their dying friends, yet to be power-less to help them—this must have been the very refinement of torture to the men in the lower camps. It did little to ease their mental agony when, after yet another night of storm had passed, one more man succeeded in struggling down to Camp IV and brought the terrible story of what was happening on the ridge. The man was Ang Tsering, a young Sherpa who had been Willy Merkl's servant. He was in the last stages of exhaustion and his hands and feet were badly frostbitten, but he managed to gasp out his news: Welzenbach was dead, two of the remaining three Sherpas were dead. The only men left alive on the snow-ridge were Merkl and a Sherpa named Gay-Lay. Ang Tsering told how the little party of two Sherpas and the expedition leader had started down from Camp VII to try and reach Camp VI, leaving the body of Welzenbach in the frozen, snow-filled tent. Merkl, in whom the spark of life was nearly extinct, had been unable to crawl up a slight rise in the ridge and had collapsed. The two Sherpas had managed to scrape out a hollow in the snow, and then Gay-Lay, who was the senior of the two, ordered Ang Tsering to try and reach Camp IV; Gay-Lay would stay with the Sahib.

Frantic with anxiety, Aschenbrenner and Schneider made desperate attempts, on the two succeeding days, to climb up through the con-tinuing blizzard and the impassable drifts. Once or twice the wind brought to their ears the sound of human voices crying for aid. On July 17th, while the injured and feeble Sherpas were escorted down to safety, a last attempt was made. It failed, as they had known it must fail. But there had been no cries from above for two days then.

Four German climbers, six Sherpa porters, died on Nanga Parbat in 1934. The death-toll of the mountain was now thirteen human lives.

The *Sportsführer* of the German Reich ruled German mountaineering in 1937. Under a dictatorship the officials—indeed, the dictator him-self—must produce victories if they are to survive; but the cruel triumph of Nanga Parbat in 1934 had drastically reduced not only the funds available but also the number of German climbers capable of taking effective part in such expeditions. However, German prestige was (according to the Germans) heavily involved, and it was con-sidered essential that another attempt to climb Nanga Parbat should be made as soon as possible. Nanga Parbat was *Unser Berg*—"our mountain". When it became known that Eric Shipton and another great British mountaineer, Frank Smythe, were contemplating a small expedition to Nanga Parbat, they received many letters of protest from German mountaineers. There was no British expedition, and the preparations for a German expedition in 1937 went ahead, actuated in part by a motive new to mountaineering: the motive of vengeance.

Paul Bauer, who had led two daring but unsuccessful assaults on Kangchenjunga, did much of the organisation but took no part in the third Nanga Parbat attack, which was led by Karl Wien and included seven other young German climbers of the first rank. Once again the long march to the mountain was made, and the slow establishing of camps up the Rakhiot Glacier began. Twelve experienced Sherpa porters had been enlisted for the high carrying. Nanga Parbat might be called a cruel mountain, but never a treacherous one; it gave, as before, fair warning of its power. A huge ice-avalanche fell from above Camp II on the glacier, some distance from the camp but smashing tents and knocking men flat with its blast of air. No one was hurt seriously and the climbing went on. By June 14th Camp IV was completely established, in nearly the same place as the 1934 Camp IV to which the few survivors of the tragedy had staggered down. Overhead was the Rakhiot Peak with its perilous traverse to the snow-ridge; and on the lip of the snow-ridge close to the peak was a thin blue line, looking insignificant from 4,000 feet below, indicating a slightly overhanging cornice. All the climbers, experts in such matters, agreed that even if the cornice broke away and fell it could not reach the camp. Preparatory to pushing up Camp V, seven Germans and nine Sherpas were at Camp IV. The remaining climber, Ulrich Luft, was given the task of bringing up more stores with five porters. It was afterwards thought very strange that all but one of the climbing-party should have congregated in Camp IV at this early stage of the build-up, and it seems not unlikely that over-eagerness to press the attack was responsible. Wien was a young leader with a young team; and all of them were eager to show that danger meant nothing to them beside the glory of Hitler's Germany.

On June 18th Luft led his carrying-party up the route to Camp IV, threading a difficult way by ice-slope and crevasse to the snow-plateau where the four tents were. Ahead of the Sherpas, he topped the last snowy rise and saw the white level before him. It was empty. The tents had gone. Luft rubbed his eyes and peered incredulously about him, looking for some sign or message to tell him why and whither Camp IV had been moved. And then he saw that where there had been a broad depression in the plateau, giving some slight shelter from wind for the tents, there was now a broken sea of solid ice. An avalanche had buried tents and occupants many yards deep.

Frantically Luft called up the porters and they all began hacking at the avalanche debris with their ice-axes. It was quite hopeless. The mass of ice-blocks, 1,300 feet long by 500 feet wide, was already frozen solid, for the fall had occurred two days before. Luft raced down to Base Camp, runners were dispatched to the nearest inhabited places, telegrams eventually reached Germany with news of the disaster. Bauer and two others flew out to India at once and a plane placed at their disposal by the R.A.F. took them to Gilgit in the Indus Valley. Bad weather and changes in the ice-route up the Rakhiot Glacier delayed their search-party and it was not until July 15th that they reached the plateau at 20,300 feet where Camp IV had stood. Six days of hard work were needed before three tents were discovered, and the bodies of nine Sherpas and five German climbers extracted. The climbers' diaries had been written-up to the evening of June 14th and their watches had all stopped at a little after midnight; and it was evident that they had been overwhelmed by the avalanche as they slept. The fourth tent and the bodies of the other two Germans were not found, though the searchers trenched the ice ten feet deep in every direction. Sixteen men perished in this catastrophe. The death-toll of the mountain was now twenty-nine.

Paul Bauer, no longer young but the most experienced German mountaineer at this time, resolved to avenge the deaths of his friends. In the next year, 1938, he led a strong expedition to complete the conquest of the terrible mountain. It was a grim and ghastly progress towards the Silver Saddle; first the body of a Sherpa was found hanging on an ice-wall—it had been there for four years—and then the bodies of Willy Merkl and the faithful Gay-Lay were discovered on the snow-ridge above. And the Silver Saddle was never reached. The weather broke, and Bauer, a fine mountaineer and no death-or-glory climber, wisely gave the order to retire. In 1939 Nanga Parbat was again attempted by Germans. This time the party was a small one of four expert mountaineers including Heinrich Harrer, who had been on the first ascent of the Eigerwand in the previous year. Their plan was to try the Diamir face, the route attempted by Mummery forty-four years earlier, thus exchanging the incalculable dangers of the Rakhiot ice-avalanches for the severe difficulties of very steep ice and rock. The difficulties proved too great for porters carrying tents and stores and the weather again put an end to their somewhat desperate venture. For the four Germans that was the end of all mountaineering for six years, for the outbreak of the Second World War found them still in India and they were all interned; though Harrer escaped to Tibet and later became tutor to the young Dalai Lama.

Nanga Parbat had spared these last two assault-parties. But when, after the war, mountaineering in the Himalaya began again the mountain snatched two more human lives. Three young Englishmen—Crace, Thornley, and Marsh—went to "take a look at" Nanga Parbat in winter conditions. Their official purpose was to examine winter temperatures and snow and avalanche conditions, and it seems fairly certain that they had no intention of going high on the mountain. They approached by the Rakhiot Glacier, and here their Sherpas (among whom was the now famous Tenzing) refused to carry higher. Thornley and Crace went on alone and pitched a tent at about 18,000 feet. Cloud blotted out the upper slopes of the glacier and snowstorms blew over. When Marsh, who had stayed behind with frostbitten feet, went up to look for his friends a few days later they and their tent had disappeared. They were never seen again.

Thirty-one lives had been sacrificed on Nanga Parbat, and eleven of them were German lives. To the Germans of 1953 the mountain was more than ever *Unser Berg*, the triumphant ascent of it a German prerogative. A younger step-brother of Willy Merkl, Dr Karl Herrligkoffer, resolved to promote another expedition, the eighth to attempt the mountain. "I determined," he wrote, "that I would myself organise a new German Himalayan expedition, whose task it would be to set the seal of victory upon the heroic efforts of our dead comrades, to fulfil, in fact, a sacred trust." The Rakhiot Glacier route was to be taken, every modern device used; the finest climbers of a new age composed the strongest party ever to go to the mountain.

Remembering the splendid mountaineers who had succumbed in the past half-century to Nanga Parbat's fury, most onlookers felt a grim foreboding of disaster when the 1953 Expedition set forth. It seemed as though no ordinary man, however skilled as a mountaineer, could ever attain that summit. The man who would tread the final snows of Nanga Parbat would have to be a superman, a being beyond

112 The south face of Nanga Parbat

the normal weaknesses of flesh and spirit. There was such a man with Karl Herrligkoffer's team. His name was Hermann Buhl.

Hermann Buhl was an Austrian, the son of a poverty-stricken family living in the back streets of Innsbruck. As a boy he disdained the companionship of other boys and went off by himself into the mountains that surround Innsbruck, invariably returning with his stockings torn to shreds; a circumstance that always led to shrill scoldings from his mother. Young Hermann took his scoldings in sullen silence, not deigning to disclose that—unable to afford *kletterschuhe*—he had been climbing in stockinged feet, and alone, on the dizzy and difficult cliffs frequented by the crack Innsbruck rock-climbers. Alone. That word is the key to the superhumanity (or, perhaps, abnormality) of this remarkable man. For him mountain-climbing was less a sport than a duel. Throughout the record of his phenomenal climbing career one feels that the presence of even a single companion, though sometimes necessary to ensure success, deprived him of full satisfaction on a great ascent. The single-handed triumph, the vindication of personal skill and courage, were what he chiefly sought in the mountains.

Lightly built, beak-nosed, dedicated from early youth to the great crags, Hermann Buhl quickly perfected his rock-climbing technique. A great vertical precipice in summer no longer gave him the narrow

113 Hermann Buhl

margin between life and death that he craved; he began to make "first winter ascents". The terrible south face of the Marmolata in the Dolomites was climbed by Buhl in winter, a feat that disregarded all sane mountaineering traditions. The Salzburg Route up the 6,000-foot precipice of the Watzmann, the most severe climb on a face which none but the expert of experts could ascend, was not challenge enough for him; he climbed it in winter, alone—and *at night*. The north face of Piz Badile, one of the sheerest rock-faces in the Alps, had been climbed for the first time by a party who spent two nights clinging to the precipice; two men of that party had died of cold and exhaustion on the mountain. Buhl cycled 100 miles to the base of Piz Badile and repeated the climb, solo, in four and a half hours. Cycling back the next day, he fell asleep from sheer weariness and pitched over his handlebars into the Inn river, narrowly escaping drowning; he carried his damaged bicycle to the nearest house and hitch-hiked back to Innsbruck. Inevitably the great North Walls attracted him. Gaston Rébuffat has given us a picture of him on the Eigerwand, leading the final ice-bound precipice in a terrible storm with a mixed party of French and German climbers behind him. The men had joined forces to battle their way out of the death-trap contrived by repeated snow-storms and avalanches and had spent three agonising days and two nights together on the great wall. All this time Buhl hardly spoke at all. When he and his Austrian companion reached the safety of the Eiger summit-ridge they began the descent at once, without a look or a word for their late companions who were toiling up the final ice-wall a few metres below them. "That was the last I was to see of them," writes Rébuffat, obviously unable to comprehend this attitude. To Hermann Buhl it was a perfectly natural attitude. His own duel with the Eiger-wand was fought and won; how other human beings climbed, felt, or lived was of no interest to him. This was the man—in some ways a near approach to the Overman of Nietzsche's prose-poem—who in 1953 fixed his ambitions on Nanga Parbat.

Buhl was included in Dr Herrligkoffer's team at the request of the Austrian Alpine Club, which was helping to finance the Willy Merkl Memorial Expedition, as it was called. The climbing party now included six Germans and four Austrians, though its leader seems to have persisted in regarding it as an all-German expedition. Perhaps this was one cause of the dissension and ill feeling which from the beginning upset the unity of the party. Another cause was Buhl. "His inclusion in the team", Herrligkoffer says, "was objected to by some of his Tyrolese colleagues, but his unquestionably unique position among all German and Austrian climbers fully justified the decision to retain him." This objection raised by Buhl's own countrymen may well have been rooted in the fact that he seemed to have no human weaknesses. A man of iron can have no sympathy for the failings of other men.

Dr Herrligkoffer, regarding himself as ordained "to fulfil a sacred trust", used the best equipment and modern means of transport. The climbers were flown from Rawalpindi to Gilgit in two planes; a fleet of jeeps took the equipment as far as possible, 300 Hunza porters carried it to Base Camp. Radio sets enabled communication to be maintained between the leader and the assault parties. With a picked team of Hunzas doing the carrying up the Rakhiot Glacier and the slopes above, the attack proceeded methodically, following the general pattern of the earlier ones. Herrligkoffer had been severely criticised in the German papers for deciding to try the dangerous Rakhiot route yet again, but he had stuck doggedly to his decision, maintaining that the incurring of known dangers was justifiable in the fulfilment of a sacred trust and the raising of German world-prestige. Nanga Parbat appeared to sympathise with his view. During the eight weeks of hard climbing before a camp—Camp V—was established on the snow-ridge below the Silver Saddle the party experienced delays, minor ailments, and a four-day snowstorm, but there were no casualties and no near-escapes from avalanches. Yet the party was far from happy. For one thing they were dogged by memories of the past disasters; there was Drexel's grave to be ceremonially visited, a memorial tablet to Merkl and his comrades to be erected, a camp to be placed on the very ice-plateau where sixteen men had been crushed to death while they slept. For another thing, the system of controlling the assault was irksome to some of the climbers. Dr Herrligkoffer proposed to make the decisions for advance or retreat, basing his orders (which he would transmit by radio from a lower camp) on reports radioed to him by the assault parties. Hermann Buhl in particular was impatient of this tight rein. There were angry words, defiances, ultimatums. It was a disunited team that prepared, on July 2nd, for a determined attack on the summit.

Meanwhile, news had been received by radio of the British success on Everest. Another powerful motive was thus added to those of the "sacred trust" and the glorification of Germany: the Nanga Parbat party must at all costs triumph on their lesser peak now that the British had triumphed on the highest mountain in the world. So tension increased, and with it a grim and humourless resolve to conquer or die. This war to the death had no link at all with sport. Very far away, now, was the spirit of Mummery.

On July 2nd Hermann Buhl and Otto Kempter, the pair chosen for the assault, spent the night in their small tent on the snow-ridge at a height of 22,640 feet. The Silver Saddle was still above them, and the summit was far beyond that and 4,000 feet above the tent. They had no idea what might await them on the unknown last section of the climb. "The assault plan," says Herrligkoffer, "was therefore regarded from the outset as being one which carried exceptional hazards." The weather, however, was unprecedentedly fine and the two men, both top-flight mountaineers, in excellent condition. It was admittedly a desperate scheme to attempt the final 4,000 feet of a great Himalayan peak without placing an intermediate camp, but this would take extra days and the fine weather might break. Besides, the assault pair had both been provided with lightweight Perlon tent-sacks for protection in case they were forced to bivouac.

There was high wind at Camp V that day, but it died away about midnight. Buhl and Kempter had agreed to start out at 3 a.m. Shortly after midnight Buhl roused his companion and announced that he proposed to start at once for the summit. Kempter reminded him of their agreement and declined to start so long before dawn, whereupon Buhl packed some food in his rucksack and set off alone towards the Silver Saddle. An old and wise law of mountaineers lays it down that a climbing companion must never be left alone on a mountain; but Hermann Buhl accepted no law but his own. There is sound basis for the suggestion that he did not want Kempter to go with him—that he was determined to make this a duel between himself alone and the most dangerous opponent of his career. The accounts given by the two men of what took place in the tent that night differ considerably and one can only guess at what passed between them.

The night was starlit, calm and bitterly cold. A crescent moon set the narrow ridge gleaming silvery-white as Buhl began his solitary climb. The steel spikes of his crampons bit into good hard snow and he moved exceedingly fast for a climber at 23,000 feet, rising steadily up the icy undulations of the long arête. At 5 a.m. the sun rose in golden splendour from behind the vast shapes of the Karakoram peaks—Masherbrum, Rakaposhi, K2, the Mustagh Tower—and he halted below the Silver Saddle for his first rest. Beyond this point, on the traverse to the Saddle and across the tilted snow plateau that rose behind it, breathing became difficult and rests more and more frequent. Every step forward demanded a concentrated effort and two or more gasping breaths. He kept on, hour by hour, and through the utterly still air the noonday sun smote down on the blinding field of white. Once, looking back, he saw a tiny figure moving slowly on the skyline of the Silver Saddle. It was Otto Kempter, doggedly trying to catch him up.

> I saw him stop and sink down. Otto had given up. This in itself was more or less immaterial to me but with my tongue parched and my stomach rumbling I could not but think of the bacon in Otto's rucksack which was now lost to me.
>
> *Nanga Parbat*, by Dr Herrligkoter, 1954.

Ahead of him rose the snow-flecked rocks of a minor height on the ridge known as the Fore-Summit. Beyond it the ridge dipped again and then ascended to the white shoulder that supported the distant

114 Route to the Silver Saddle

summit. Buhl, unwilling to climb the extra 300 feet to this intervening top, decided to traverse round it.

It was now long after noon, the hour by which he had hoped to gain the summit of Nanga Parbat. The timetable that would ensure sufficient daylight for the descent to Camp V had proved hopelessly inadequate, but nothing mattered now except to keep on. Finding the weight of his rucksack intolerable, he left it at the foot of the rise to the Fore-Summit; in it were food, spare clothing, and the lightweight tent-sack. His anorak he tied round his waist by the sleeves. In its pockets were a camera, spare gloves, drinking-flask, a Tyrolese pennant and a small Pakistan flag; he had also some Padutin tablets for delaying frostbite and some capsules of Pervitin, the booster drug used by German airmen during the Second World War. Thus equipped, he went on.

The traverse brought him directly above the terrific east face and confronted him with steep snow and ice. He passed it safely and was on the main ridge again at 2 p.m. Still the ascent rose in front, and more formidably—" a steep rocky ridge crowded with snow-towers, vertical pitches of sharp-edged granite, badly exposed cornices and steep flanks of compressed snow". Buhl, doubting his flagging powers, remembered the Pervitin capsules and took two of them. Gasping for breath, forcing himself to treat each obstacle in turn as the goal of all his remaining energy, he climbed slowly towards the snow shoulder that hid the final peak. It was 6 p.m. when, after very hard climbing, he stood on the shoulder at an altitude of 26,000 feet and saw the last broken declivity of rocks rising in front. And suddenly he knew that the end of endurance had come. He was physically incapable of getting up that final slope.

But somehow, unaccountably, he was going on. Crawling on hands and knees, he dragged himself up the rocks and found himself standing upright on hard snow. There was nothing higher to climb. He was on the summit of Nanga Parbat. It was seven o'clock in the evening.

All round him was the vast sea of snow-peaks, Himalaya and Karakoram, Pamirs and Hindu Kush, but the lone victor of Nanga Parbat could not afford the time for more than a glance at them. The ice-axe, with the pennant of Tyrol attached, was planted in the snow and photographed. Then it was photographed with the Pakistan flag tied to it. More photographs of the distant views, to prove beyond doubt that the summit had been reached, and then immediate descent. At ten minutes past seven the sun went down and at once it was bitterly cold. Buhl knew he could not reach the tent; he had been climbing for more than sixteen hours and was literally at the end of his strength. He managed to climb some 450 feet down from the summit, a task that took him two hours, and as darkness flooded across the mountain he groped his way to a large rock that projected from the 50-degree slant of frozen snow, the only flat standing-place within reach.

His precarious perch would be in shadow when the moon came up and he would have to remain there until dawn. The rucksack containing his spare clothing and tent-sack was on the other side of the Fore-Summit, many hours of climbing away. Beneath his anorak he had only a thin pullover—and he knew the night temperature at that height would fall far below zero even if the windless calm continued. Ill-equipped, alone, and shelterless at nearly 26,000 feet, his chances of survival were a hundred-to-one against; if the wind rose, death was certain.

Hermann Buhl swallowed several of the anti-frostbite tablets and prepared to spend seven hours on the borderline between life and death.

From Camp IV two members of the climbing-party had seen Buhl, followed at a distance by Kempter, reach the Silver Saddle and disappear. All that day, July 3rd, they kept watch on the route, and at five o'clock saw a single figure on the Saddle, descending very slowly. Two hours later Kempter staggered into Camp IV in a state of collapse, and later reported that Buhl had gone on alone. The men at Camp IV had oxygen with them, but—incredibly—they made no attempt to go up and look for Buhl next morning, though the weather was as clear and calm as ever. Not until late afternoon did they make any move, and then it was only to start fixing a memorial tablet to Willy Merkl on a rock pinnacle called the Moor's Head, a ceremony which had been arranged beforehand. The party began to go back to camp. Two men, one of them the photographer Hans Ertl, lingered a moment. And they saw, high above them on the traverse from the Silver Saddle, a tiny black speck that moved, and stopped, and moved downwards again.

A little later Hermann Buhl staggered and swayed down the last few yards of the ridge to fall into Ertl's arms. His face, deeply lined and skeletal as a mummy's, bore the imprint of suffering, and blood-stained saliva trickled from his mouth. His feet were severely frostbitten. But he had won his duel with Nanga Parbat, and—as we shall see—lived to climb again in the Himalaya.

Dr Karl Herrligkoffer's description of Buhl's arrival ends with this passage:

> He looked aged by twenty years . . . From his lips fell the words: "Yesterday was the finest day of my life." Although torn with grief at the sight of his friend's agony, Ertl filmed Buhl's last steps to the tent and so put on permanent record the final moments of this unique adventure.

115 Entrance to the Western Cwm; Lhotse behind, centre

9 Everest

Achttausender became the magic word in top-flight mountaineering during the years between the two World Wars. The German word indicates a mountain whose height is 8,000 metres (about 26,250 feet) or more, and there are fourteen such mountains in the world, all of them in the Himalaya. (Professor Kenneth Mason, historian of the Himalaya, lists fifteen, but includes the second peak of Kangchenjunga; fourteen is the number generally accepted.) To climb an *Achttausender* became the ambition of the foremost mountaineers of several nations —notably Germany and France, with Italy and America and Japan entering the competition later. For with such a limited number of giant virgins to be deflowered, international competition inevitably and deplorably entered into the spirit of Himalayan mountain-climbing. It was suddenly of the first importance to plant a national flag on the newly climbed summit, to photograph it (preferably in colour) as proof of the national triumph, to publish a long account of the ascent emphasising the feats and heroism of the climbers.

Annapurna, the tenth highest mountain in the world, was the first *Achttausender* to be climbed, and that was not until 1950. A party of nine French experts set out on the do-or-die venture which was to be "for the honour of France" By a mingling of fine climbing with dare-devil recklessness the Tricolour was duly planted on the summit; and though members of the party were carried down in avalanches, nearly killed by a blizzard while they were snowblind, and terribly frost-bitten, they escaped with no worse consequences than the loss of a total of ten fingers and fifteen toes. Before this, however, small parties were having more sport and less agony on Himalayan peaks that did not come within the German-established list of the Big Fourteen. Frank Smythe and his party climbed Kamet (25,443 feet), C. R. Cooke and G. Schoberth climbed Kabru (24,002 feet) and F. Spencer Chapman with one Sherpa, Pasang Dawa Lama, climbed Chomolhari (23,997 feet). Nanda Devi, climbed in 1936 by Tilman's party, remained for fourteen years the highest summit reached. These men, and the mountaineers who were devoting their holidays to new sporting ascents in the Alps like Graham Brown's "triptych" on the Brenva Face of Mont Blanc, had a different concept of mountaineering from that of the big international teams. To them there was something ridiculous, even disgusting, in the idea of planting a national flag on a summit; it was as though a visiting Mahommedan should carve his initials on the door of Westminster Abbey. Many mountaineers had a similar feeling about Everest, but no one contended that the highest peak on earth ought to be left unclimbed.

There had been seven expeditions to Mount Everest between 1919 and 1939, all of them British and all of them unsuccessful. There had also been the tragic attempt of Maurice Wilson, an English eccentric who had never been on a mountain before and seems to have thought that spiritual power could compensate for lack of skill; he reached the foot of the North Col alone and died there. It is unjust to say, as climbers of other nationalities did say, that the British were keeping Everest to themselves. The mountain was then accessible only through Tibet, a country that believed (not unwisely, as the sad events of 1950 were to show) that foreigners should be kept out, and permission for entry was rarely granted. The British applications were favoured because the Dalai Lama, ruler of Tibet, came to consider that the British could be trusted to do nothing beyond what they proposed, which was to attempt the ascent of Everest. In fact, the real opening of the way to the top of Everest only came when the conquest of Tibet by the Chinese Communists closed the Tibetan frontiers completely. At about the same time the Nepal Government, loosening its traditional bonds of isolation, began grudgingly to open its frontier for the passage of selected expeditions from the Western nations. The southern approach to Everest was available for the first time.

The first expedition to take advantage of this was a small American reconnaissance party including Dr Charles Houston, later joined by H. W. Tilman. Houston and Tilman examined the approaches to the "Western Cwm" (into which Mallory had looked in 1921) and saw part of the Cwm itself. They considered the route possible, but very hazardous. The next year, 1951, Eric Shipton led a British reconnaissance party which included a New Zealander named Edmund Hillary to examine the Western Cwm more closely. This, which was to prove the key route to final triumph, needs a little description.

Travelling northward up the deep valley of the Imja Khola beneath the superb peak of Ama Dablam, 22,700 feet, the climbers reached the snout of the long Khumbu Glacier which runs like a moat along the western ridges of Mount Everest. Six miles up the great ice-stream they came suddenly to a mighty opening in the mountain-walls on the right or eastern hand. Down through this narrow gateway the glacier came tumbling in a giant cascade of broken ice 2,000 feet high, from a high inner basin of snow and ice slopes extending three miles beyond it (*Plate 115*). Looking up into the Cwm, they saw at its head a long containing-wall 26,000 feet high running for two miles between

26. Mount Everest (*left*) and Lhotse   *Tom Weir*

Everest on the left and the subsidiary peak of Lhotse on the right. The lowest point of the ridge they named the South Col, and it seemed possible to climb the ridge leftward from the South Col—the south-east ridge of Everest—to the summit. Shipton's party had four problems to solve:

Could the great Icefall be climbed at all, and if so would the route be safe for an army of porters?

Were those vast slopes leading to the South Col climbable?

Was the south-east ridge from the Col as technically simple as it looked?

Was it better, from the point of view of weather, to make an attempt in spring or in autumn?

Shipton and his men solved the first problem at least. Toppling ice-pinnacles and avalanches of snow repulsed their first determined attempts to climb the Icefall, but at last they found a very difficult but reasonably safe route up the south side and gained its top—only to find their way into the upper basin completely blocked by an enormous crevasse stretching right across the Cwm. They could see nothing of the south-east ridge, but it looked as if a steep and very hard route could be made up to the South Col. As for the weather, their reconnaissance was made in September and October, after the monsoon, and there seemed little to choose between that time of year and late spring.

The first part of the trail had been blazed, but all the upper part remained doubtful. One thing only remained as certain as it had been

W.　West Ridge
S.　　South Col
E.　　Eperon des Génévois
L.　　Lhotse
L.F.　Lhotse Face

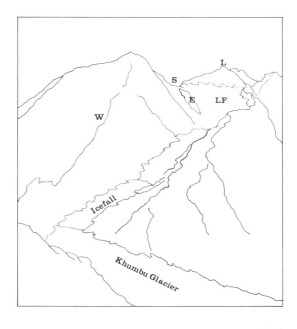

Diagram 10
K 2

from the first: to climb the highest mountain in the world would require perfection in organisation, lavish and efficient equipment, the best mountaineers that could be got together—and luck with the weather. Organisation of a British expedition began in 1952. But it was a Swiss expedition that made the first attempt and proved that the route was feasible.

Switzerland had obtained permission from the Nepalese Government to make two assaults on Everest in 1952, one before the monsoon and one after. Thus they had hope of a successful counter-attack if the notorious Everest weather repulsed them in the spring. The party of twelve who went out for the first attempt included eight top-flight climbers, among them Raymond Lambert and Gabriel Chevalley; and the Sherpas were led by a certain Tenzing Norgay. Base Camp was established on the lower Khumbu Glacier on April 20th, Camp I at the foot of the Icefall five days later; and from Camp II halfway up the Icefall a third camp was carried to its top and placed in the Western Cwm itself. In fourteen days they had done the first quarter of the ascent. The three parts remaining were the advance up the Western Cwm to the foot of the fearfully steep Lhotse Face at its end; the ascent of the Lhotse Face to the South Col; and the final mile of ridge to the summit 2,000 feet above the Col. All this was unknown ground. And the monsoon, with its winds and snowstorms impossible for human beings to face, could be expected at the end of May.

The Western Cwm was no mere three-mile walk up a snow-valley. It was filled with a steep snow-covered glacier whose treacherous surface was split by enormous crevasses, a maze of dangers where hours might be taken over an advance of a few yards. One crevasse, sixteen feet wide, proved impassable until Jean-Jaques Asper, the youngest of the Swiss climbers, had himself lowered sixty feet into the chasm to a point where the walls were only six or seven feet apart and thence managed to hack and claw his way up the vertical ice to the other side. With ropes stretched across and anchored, the rest were able to pull themselves over. Swiss and Sherpas worked like demons at the relaying of loads and tents farther and farther into this white Valley of Silence, as they called it, and by May 9th had placed Camp V at the foot of the Lhotse Wall, a little more than 3,000 feet below the South Col. For the first time they had a close view of that mighty barrier—and saw, to their joy, that a practicable though hazardous route could be made up the sweeping ice and snow of a wide couloir beside an upper spur of rock.

Now began the real high-altitude work, for loads for the stocking of the higher camps had to be carried from 22,000 to 25,000 feet. There was no place for a camp on the bare wall of the Lhotse Face, so the

first step was to dump loads at the foot of the rock spur, which they named the Eperon des Génévois or Geneva Spur, preparatory to the last carry up to the South Col. And now, too, Everest showed its teeth. Hitherto the weather had been favourable, but when the long job of stockpiling below the Spur was finished it broke in fierce snowstorms. The party starting up for the Col was beaten back and for three days no climbing was possible. Then, on May 25th, Lambert with two Swiss climbers and Tenzing with six Sherpas set out in better weather to try and gain the Col. Their plan was to place Camp VI on the South Col, move up a seventh camp on the ridge at 27,500 feet or higher if possible, and then make the final dash for the summit—a "dash" that would be an agonisingly slow crawl under conditions in which none but one or two men out of all Earth's millions could remain alive.

The climb to the South Col proved to be steep but not technically difficult; that is, though for the whole distance there was no place where a slip by an unroped man would not have meant death, skilled climbers were able to overcome the recurrent mountaineering problems with confidence. But the dreaded effects of altitude were making themselves felt. Climbers and Sherpas moved at snail's pace up the vast sheet of white. Every step was a supreme effort of unresponsive muscle and gasping lungs. At the steeper places handrails of rope and steel spikes were fixed, and each of these safeguarding measures took ten times the effort and time it would have taken at sea-level. They had started as early as possible, but darkness began to fall when they were still far below the Col. Two porters had already turned back exhausted. The others hewed a tent platform out of the freezing slope and bivouacked there on the Lhotse Face. In the morning, after a sleepless night, the rest of the porters—with one exception—refused to go higher. The exception was Tenzing; he and the three Swiss, all carrying maximum loads, went on and reached the South Col, where they set up Camp VI in a fierce wind.

The South Col, the goal of so much planning, is perhaps the most terribly desolate place on earth. Here is no narrow snow-crest wrought into beauty by wind and sun but a grim, bare plateau of grey ice streaked and dotted with rock, across which the wind tears with unceasing fury. Above it on the north rises a ridge of shattered rock draped with ice, leading to the sharp summit called the South Peak which hides the final rise to the top of Everest. Only 3,500 feet—about the height of Snowdon above sea-level—has to be climbed from the Col to the top. But if that 3,500 feet was as technically easy as the ascent of Snowdon, it would still require the utmost in human endurance to climb it at this altitude; and it is far from easy, as later climbers were to discover.

The four men who had reached the Col knew little of those unclimbed difficulties except what they could see from their flapping, snow-plastered tent. But they did know that their effort was wasted unless more food and equipment could be got up to the Col. Thanks to that miserable night on the Lhotse Face they had reached the Col early in the day. Tenzing volunteered to go down again and bring up porters and stores. Somehow he managed to persuade three Sherpas to climb with him to the South Col carrying loads—the bare minimum for an assault. That night the terrible wind gave them no rest, but in the morning the weather was at least clear. The three Sherpas, however, were too weak and demoralised to go in any direction except down, and down they went, leaving Tenzing and the three Swiss—Aubert, Flory, and Lambert—once more alone. By a great effort these four succeeded in carrying a small tent and some supplies up the snow and rock of the south-east ridge to a height of 27,560 feet; and at this point it was proposed that two men should camp and next day try for the summit, while the other two returned to the Col. This proposal came from Tenzing.

To realise the boldness of the suggestion one must consider that this would be their third night at over 25,000 feet. Every hour, almost every minute, their physical and mental deterioration from the effects of altitude was increasing. The Sherpas had failed to bring up sleeping-bags or stove and there was very little food. The only thing in their favour was the weather, and that could not be expected to hold much longer. It was perhaps this that led Lambert to agree to Tenzing's proposal. The little tent was pitched, Aubert and Flory (both suffering severely from exhaustion and cold) went down; and the Sherpa and the Swiss climber prepared for the night and the assault that would follow it.

Again there was no rest for them. Instead, they spent most of the night thumping and rubbing their limbs to keep frostbite at bay, for their tent was higher than the highest summit yet reached and the temperature was far below zero. A little snow melted over a candle-flame was their only drink. When at last the long hours of darkness ended and there was light enough to see, they were almost exhausted by the violent movements that had been necessary to retain circulation of the blood. Yet from somewhere they found the courage and will to go on. They began to climb at 6 a.m. It took them five and a half hours to gain 650 feet of height on the ridge, though the climbing was no-where difficult. They had three cylinders of oxygen with them, but the manipulation of the supply required so tremendous an effort that they could only use it while standing still. The wind rose, cloud swept across, the temperature dropped still lower—and still they fought their infinitely slow way upward. At about 28,200 feet they stopped. The will to go on was still fiercely alive, but all else in them seemed to be dead. "We had reached," says Lambert, "some sort of physiological limit." With the utmost difficulty they made their way down again, to reach the tents on the South Col at nightfall literally more dead than alive. The spring assault had failed, but failed in an almost incredible display of human courage and resolution.

In September of the same year the second Swiss attack was mounted. Lambert and Chevalley of the first team joined it, and Tenzing again led the Sherpas. There was an accident on the last day of October, when a mass of ice broke away above and came down on three roped parties who were climbing the Lhotse Face. One Sherpa was killed and another suffered a broken collar-bone. After this a new route up the Lhotse Face was found, longer but safer; and it was not until November 19th that a camp was once more established on the South Col. It was now even colder than it had been in the spring, and it was almost impossible to face the wind that shrieked at gale force across the Col. The thermometer stood at −30° Centigrade. Again Lambert and Tenzing set off, with seven Sherpas, to carry the final camp up the south-east ridge. They turned back before they had reached the highest point of the spring attempt—it was *not possible*, Lambert said, to live in such wind and cold. From a man like Lambert the words were absolutely final. There was no chance of wind or cold abating and every chance of their getting worse, for the Himalayan winter had arrived. Saddened by the loss of the Sherpa Mingma Dorje, the Swiss retreated from the mountain in the knowledge that they were lucky to have escaped so lightly.

Most people are unaware (for it was not publicised) that at this time Raymond Lambert had to wear very short boots specially designed for his toe-less feet, which had been crippled by previous severe frostbite. Yet, with Tenzing, he had been higher on Everest than any man before them. Great as was his personal achievement, however, the real achievement of the two Swiss attempts was that they had opened the way to the South Col and shown that laden porters could get there. It was the knowledge that this had been done that made possible the detailed planning by which the final triumph was won.

Dr Tom Longstaff's message to one of the British Everest party implored him to climb the thing, for heaven's sake, so that mountaineers could get back to the real enjoyment of their sport. Many British climbers shared this sentiment; but all were agreed that Everest must be climbed and that it would be fitting, after so many British attempts, if the party that climbed it was a British one. The selection of Colonel John Hunt, a forty-two-year-old Regular Army officer who had taken part in three tough Himalayan Expeditions, as leader of the 1953 Expedition was greeted with approval. Mallory's comment that climbing Everest was "more like war than sport" had been proved over and over again. Even those mountaineers who disapproved of words like "attack" and "conquest" being applied to mountain-climbing were convinced that the only sure way of getting to the top of Everest was by planning the campaign by military methods and on a military scale. This, in effect, was what John Hunt did.

In addition to Hunt, there were nine first-rate climbers and an Expedition doctor. Unlike the French, Swiss, and German teams the British party did not—could not, in fact—include professional mountaineering guides. Charles Evans was a surgeon, Alfred Gregory a travel agent, Tom Bourdillon a physicist; Michael Westmacott worked as a statistical investigator at a research station, and Wilfred Noyce was a schoolmaster. Charles Wylie got leave from the War Office, and George Band—at twenty-three the youngest of the party—had just taken his degree at Cambridge University. The doctor, twenty-seven-year-old Michael Ward, was also a very fine Alpine climber. The re-remaining two climbers came from New Zealand, where lanky Edmund Hillary made his living by bee-keeping and George Lowe taught in a primary school. It was thus a Commonwealth expedition. The reason for this narrow choice was not national pride but psychological necessity. One of the greatest of Himalayan climbers has said that the most essential quality in a mountaineer on a big Himalayan expedition is

117 Sir John Hunt

the quality of selflessness. Give-and-take between members of a team is always an essential of success; but on Everest a man must be ready to take one and give ninety-nine. This exceptionally close bond is almost impossible between men of different nationalities and different languages. Hunt, determined to ensure that every detail of his planning conduced to success, resolved that all his team must speak the same tongue and possess similar ideals and ways of thought.

The rest of his plan shows the same meticulous attention to detail. Obviously Everest would have some surprises in store and parts of the plan might have to be modified; but as far as was possible the campaign was mapped out in advance. New oxygen apparatus was designed and tested. A five-section ladder of light metal was made for crossing crevasses. (A giant elastic catapult for shooting grapnels across impassable gaps was also tried out, in the garden of the Royal Geographical Society, but was rejected after the grapnel had gone off course and lodged in a tree.) Other inventions suggested by helpful enthusiasts included a spring-loaded harpoon gun which could fire a grapnel with line attached from the South Col to the summit of Everest, thus providing a hand-line for the final climb; moreover, the line was to be coated with luminous paint so that the ascent could be made, if necessary, in the dark. The suggestion was rejected—"with some regret," says Hunt. He and his "staff" devoted themselves to selecting the very best in the way of high-altitude tents, boots, windproof clothing and down jackets, gloves, sleeping-bags, stoves, and—of course—food. March rations, Base Camp rations, Assault rations, all carefully devised for their special purpose, were packed in hundreds of numbered boxes. Ten different kinds of vitamin capsules, in bulk supply, were taken to supplement the diet and combat the effects of altitude deterioration. A hundred-and-sixty oxygen cylinders, thousands of feet of climbing-rope, hundreds of steel pegs and pitons—these and much more beside had to be taken something like 8,000 miles to the foot of Everest. Colonel Hunt issued *Memorandum Everest* to all his men; it laid down, as a complete though provisional plan, the programme and timetable of the grand assault that was to require this mass of equipment. The basic points of the plan were that it aimed at making three successive summit-assaults possible during the short spring climbing season; that the period before May 15th should be devoted to establishing all camps up to the South Col and "stockpiling" supplies; and that in order to ensure the best possible acclimatisation of the party a break should be made halfway through the stockpiling operation so that the climbers could rest at an Advanced Base Camp on the Khumbu Glacier.

In March a huge army of porters left Katmandu with the loads of expedition stores. By the end of the month the climbing party was at a temporary base camp whence climbers and Sherpas made practice

118 The first Base Camp, at Thyangboche

119 "Mike's Horror"

ascents and accustomed themselves to the use of oxygen apparatus. Not until April 13th did the expedition begin to prepare a route up the Khumbu Icefall; and here, at the outset, Everest had a surprise for them.

A steep icefall is the fastest-moving part of a glacier, and this 2,000-foot-high cascade of giant ice-blocks is continually in motion. Since the Swiss ascent of it six months earlier the Khumbu Icefall had completely altered. A new route had to be found, marked, and fitted with fixed ropes where it was difficult or dangerous for porters carrying loads. There were some fearsome obstacles to be passed, inevitably nicknamed—Mike's Horror, Hillary's Horror, Hunt's Gully—and passages where toppling ice threatened the ant-like procession of porters with bombardment, such as Hell-fire Alley and the Atom Bomb Area. Ice-cliffs forty feet high and chasms "measureless to man" interrupted the route, and it took them nine days of bridging and marking and hard climbing before the Western Cwm was gained and Camp III established there. Now began the great build-up of material in camps placed at higher levels in the vast white trough of the Cwm. Another ten days, and Camp IV had been placed near the foot of the

Lhotse Face with fifty loads dumped beside it. The ferrying-party, which had worked like clockwork, was now retired to a lower camp for a well-earned rest.

So far the weather had not interfered with the plan, but when the attack on the Lhotse Face was launched high winds and snowstorms threatened to set back the timetable. Hunt, distrusting the first Swiss route up by the Geneva Spur, had decided to make a long detour across the Face by way of the ice-ledges of the Lhotse Glacier, which offered sites for small camps, and in spite of the weather this route was pioneered and rendered safe for porters. Wilfred Noyce and the Sherpa Annullu, by a superb effort, completed the route to the South Col on May 21st, in clearing weather, and the stocking of Camp VIII on the Col began.

All this time the Sherpas had been carrying out their difficult and often dangerous tasks under their Sirdar, Tenzing Norgay. For Tenzing, who had already been twice to the South Col, was back again—not only as leader of the Sherpas but also as a fully fledged mountaineer. His experience and skill, his cheerfulness and resolution— never more apparent than when he was tackling difficulty or danger— and of course the fact that of all the party he was the only one who had been above the Icefall before, quickly made him one of the outstanding *climbers* of the expedition. The small, smiling man had been asked to join the climbing-party by Hunt in Katmandu two months earlier; but this promotion from hired porter to "sahib" had not turned Tenzing's head, nor had it detracted from his energy as Sherpa leader. Hunt, watching carefully for signs of fitness for the summit assault teams, had his eye on Tenzing already. It was not the least remarkable thing about this remarkable Sherpa that he "got on" excellently with Englishmen and New Zealanders, men of different race, colour, and creed. When, immediately after the achievement of Noyce and Annullu, Hillary and Tenzing led seventeen Sherpas from Camp IV to Camp VII in one day, to the South Col next morning, and down to Camp IV again the same day, it was plain that here were two exceptionally fit men who worked well together. Evans, Bourdillon, Gregory, and Lowe were equally fit candidates, with Noyce in reserve. Hunt, who at forty-two had considered himself too old for the climbing-party, resolved to go to the South Col to support and assist his men. On May 24th he reached Camp VIII on the Col with Bourdillon and Evans and two Sherpas; the following day the second assault party, consisting of Hillary and Tenzing with Gregory, Lowe, and three Sherpas in support, was ready at Camp VII below the Col.

This was the culminating moment, the apex of a pyramid of human endeavour whose base spread across thirty-two years. Eight major expeditions had failed in the all-out attempt to get to the top of Everest. Hunt and his companions were determined that this one, building on their experience and better-equipped than any of them, was going to succeed.

The South Col was no less inhospitable than it had been to the Swiss party. The terrible wind blew constantly across it, no invigorating gale but a freezing stream that sapped vitality and breathed slow death into unprotected lungs. The plentiful supply of oxygen enabled the men at Camp VIII to rest and sleep, in spite of their awareness that any further strengthening of the gale might well tear their tents from the Col and hurl them into the Western Cwm 4,000 feet below. Bourdillon and Evans were to make the first attempt, but on the morning of May 26th Evans's oxygen apparatus developed a defect that delayed the start, and one of the two Sherpas was ill. Hunt started out with the remaining Sherpa, carrying the tent and stores for the final bivouac on the south-east ridge which the summit pair would occupy on their descent, and was overtaken by the other two fairly soon. A couloir of bare ice and brick-hard snow needed slow and laborious step-cutting. Evans and Bourdillon gradually drew ahead and vanished among the snowy rocks of the South Peak, while the expedition leader and the Sherpa Da Namgyal, gasping and tottering under their heavy loads, toiled on. At 27,500 feet Da Namgyal—perhaps the toughest of the Sherpas next to Tenzing—could do no more, so they dumped the tent and stores on a ledge just big enough for a camp site and returned to Camp VIII, utterly exhausted.

Meanwhile, Evans and Bourdillon had climbed on and reached the top of the South Peak at one o'clock. For the first time the final stretch to the summit was revealed. There was first a very steep descent on snow to a narrow col, and then the ultimate ridge to the top—a narrow crest capped with bulging snow-cornices and set at a very high angle. The two men had a difficult decision to make. Some very hard climbing lay before them, perhaps three hours of it, but they had little doubt that they could reach the summit in spite of the defective apparatus that was depriving Evans of his full oxygen supply. But it was more than doubtful whether they would be able to return and get down to the bivouac before night. The risk of a one-way journey to a glorious death was not one a mountaineer would take. They made the only decision possible to sane men: to turn back.

The wisdom of that decision was shown on the descent. The terrific effort they had made had brought them very near the end of their strength. In the lower couloir Evans, who was descending last, slipped and fell, hurtling down towards Bourdillon "like a bullet", as the latter said. Bourdillon was dragged from his axe-belay, but as the two slid down the icy slope towards the fearful depths below he contrived to force the pick of his axe into the surface and gradually brought them both to a standstill. At half-past four they staggered down to the camp on the South Col, with faces covered with ice and limbs incapable of any further effort. They had climbed to more than 28,700 feet, hundreds of feet higher than any man had climbed before; and they had opened the way to the summit of Everest.

The night on the South Col was a test of fortitude. The second Assault Party had come up and with them Lowe and Gregory and seven Sherpas. Crowded in the tents, with the wind risen to gale force and sheets of frozen snow blowing across the Col, all of them passed a sleepless night, for the oxygen had to be reserved for the second attempt. In the morning, May 27th, the gale was hurling clouds of snow from the south-east ridge and climbing was out of the question. All day and the next night they stayed in the tents, and by the following morning only one Sherpa, Ang Nima, was fit enough to start with the climbers. But the weather was clear and fairly calm. Hillary and Tenzing prepared for the greatest climb of their lives.

By 9 a.m. the assault was under way. Gregory, Lowe, and Ang Nima started first, carrying the remainder of the stores for the bivouac on the south-east ridge. Hillary and Tenzing, wearing open-circuit oxygen apparatus, joined them at the point where the skeleton of the Swiss

120 Hillary and Tenzing nearing the top of the Lhotse glacier

tent, relic of Lambert and Tenzing's gallant attempt of the previous year, still stood on its lofty ledge. The immediate plan was to establish one tent high up the South Peak with plentiful supplies; this would allow extra time for the climbing of the final ridge if its still unknown difficulties proved hard to overcome. At 27,900 feet the tent was placed—the highest habitation ever built by man. Hillary and Tenzing watched their comrades descending again to the desolate Col and settled themselves in for the night. With the help of oxygen they were able to doze intermittently although the temperature fell to —27° Centigrade and the wind tore alarmingly at the tiny tent; and in the morning, having thawed out their frozen boots over the Primus stove, they crawled out and shouldered their 30-lb. oxygen sets.

The luck of the weather was with them. In almost windless air they moved off, Tenzing leading, up the last few hundred feet of the South Summit. The snow was unstable and treacherous and needed the most careful choice of footing, but they gained the South Peak at 9 a.m. Hillary now took over the lead and kept it right to the summit. Down the steep hard snow to the gap, up the narrow white crest above. The oxygen supply ceased, frozen up; Hillary managed to get it going

121 View from the South Peak
   Makalu on right, Kangchenjunga in distance, left

again for himself and Tenzing. Vast overhanging cornices drove them off the crest at intervals to traverse perilously across the frozen walls below. It was infinitely slow work, and Hillary began to doubt whether they would have enough oxygen for the climb and return. The "mental arithmetic" of calculating the amount of oxygen left to them was one of his main preoccupations all the way up to the top. And then—they topped a knife-edge of snow to see before them an obstacle that looked like cutting them off from all onward progress.

It was a step in the ridge, a face of bare rock forty feet high. A huge snow cornice overhung its right-hand side, on the left the rock fell sheer to the mighty ice-walls dropping to the Western Cwm a vertical mile below. One hazardous way alone appeared possible. Where the great cornice was plastered against the perpendicular rock there was a gap, a narrow crack between snow and rock running up the whole height of the obstacle. Hillary jammed himself into the base of this crack, praying that the cornice would not break away, and by kicking his crampon-spiked boots backwards against the snow and clutching at the rock with his hands climbed inch by inch to the top. Tenzing struggled up after him, on a tight rope, to collapse exhausted on the snow above.

The two men rested and checked their oxygen sets. Above them the ridge reared up as before, cornice upon cornice like a succession of snowy wave-crests. On they went again, now very slowly indeed—one foot of height gained in one minute was the best they could manage at this altitude of nearly 29,000 feet above the sea. It was nearly half past eleven when Hillary found suddenly that there were no more cornices in front of him; only a short and narrow apron of white, ending in a cone of hard snow. A few minutes later Edmund Hillary and Tenzing Norgay stood together on the top of Mount Everest.

What were their emotions at that tremendous moment? At great altitudes all feelings are dulled, but their first reaction was to thump each other on the back, grinning their delight through the icicles that encrusted their oxygen masks. They were on top of the world, and on this clear day the whole world seemed to lie at their feet; but Hillary's glance went down the gigantic spine of the North Ridge, down to the North Col whence the first climbers had made their valiant attempts thirty-three years ago. He took a photograph of that ridge and the winding glaciers that flanked it far below. He photographed Tenzing holding aloft the inevitable flags—a string of them this time, United Nations, British, Nepalese, and Indian. Hunt had given him a small crucifix to be left on the summit, so he dug a little hole in the snow and placed it there, beside the gift of chocolate and sweets Tenzing had brought as an offering to the Buddhist gods. Fifteen minutes after reaching the top the two were on their way down, forcing their fast-deteriorating minds and bodies to exercise the utmost care on every step of the dangerous way they had come.

122 Hillary and Tenzing after their successful ascent

Late that afternoon George Lowe, at the South Col camp, saw two weary figures coming down the last snowslope of the south-east ridge and went to meet them. The taller of the two moved cracked, ice-coated lips as Lowe came up to him.

"Well, we knocked the bastard off," croaked Edmund Hillary.

A section of the non-mountaineering public in 1953 held the belief that the ascent of Everest meant the end of all mountain-climbing. The climbing of earth's highest summit, they felt, had been the aim of all the otherwise incomprehensible fuss about mountains. This, of course, was very far from being the case.

Throughout the world the sport of mountaineering had attracted an increasing number of adherents ever since the end of the Second World War. In England, particularly, the use of mountains and steep rock-faces in the training of troops had set the seal of authority on climbing, so that the man-in-the-street no longer looked upon a rock-climber as a kind of suicidal lunatic. Climbing-clubs sprang up all over Britain, weekends and holidays found ever-growing swarms of people, young and not so young, flocking to the great rough crags that offered them the finest sport in the world. The standard of achievement was pushed higher and higher on rock-faces in Britain and America, and in Europe the overhanging Dolomite precipices that had been called impossible were climbed many times in a season by means of pitons and slings and the rope used pulley-wise through snap-links.

123 Members of the 1953 Expedition and Sherpas

Nor had the triumph of Sir John Hunt, Sir Edmund Hillary, Tenzing Norgay, G.M., and their team ended the epic of Mount Everest. In 1956 a Swiss expedition gained the South Col and got two assault parties to the summit on successive days; they also made the first ascent of Lhotse, then the highest peak still unscaled. Seven years later the first American expedition to Everest took the mountain by storm, not only climbing it twice by the South Col route but also sending a third party to the summit by the west ridge, thus opening a new route and making the first traverse—to the summit by one route, down by another—of the peak. This very large expedition included twenty climbers and thirty-two Sherpas, and employed 909 porters. Everest was no less formidable, nor had the effects of altitude altered. Dan Doody, one of the climbing party, was stricken by thrombo-phlebitis (as Gilkey had been on K2 ten years earlier) and only rapid evacuation from the high camps and expert medical attention saved his life. Another climber, Jake Breitenbach, lost his life when an ice-wall in the Khumbu Icefall collapsed.

By way of contrast, four young American climbers in that same year of 1963 reached the North Col of Everest without Sherpas or porters. Risking capture by Chinese Communist patrols, they had crossed the Tibetan frontier to make an attempt on the great mountain by the original route of the first British expeditions. The attempt failed. But the story of Woodrow Wilson Sayre and his three friends is the surest proof that a summit gained is not an end but a beginning.

124 K 2, the Second Highest

10 The Second Highest

WHAT happens when a climber is taken seriously ill high up on a great Himalayan peak? When a descent taking several days has to be made with a helpless man, down places which the fittest of expert mountaineers would find exceedingly difficult? When the terrible high-altitude weather turns against the party?

These are no idle questions. Deterioration of a man's physical state at great heights is a fact, and though the Himalayan climber is a chosen specimen of humanity he is subject, like all of us, to the unpredictable weaknesses of the flesh. It is likely enough that a hidden defect will suddenly show itself and strike disastrously when men are expending their utmost energies in conditions where human life could not normally exist at all. This risk is present on all high mountains, and it is the chief reason why every major Himalayan expedition includes a skilled doctor in the party. Fortunately for all concerned, such maladies have nearly always revealed themselves before the mountaineer reached the higher camps in that tenuous chain of little tents whose links could so easily be severed by storm or heavy snow; and though one man might die—of pneumonia like Drexel on Nanga Parbat or abdominal trouble like Kitar on Nanda Devi—his illness did not endanger the lives of his companions. The chance was always there, however. And in 1953, the year of the British success on Mount Everest, it turned up on another great mountain a thousand miles from Everest, in a tragedy that came within a hair's-breadth of being the most terrible disaster in mountaineering history.

K2 is the second highest mountain in the world. Its height of 28,250 feet, 752 feet lower than Everest, gives it pre-eminence among the giants of the Karakoram Range, which contains thirty-three peaks of more than 24,000 feet in height. The Survey of India numbered the Karakoram peaks for its own convenience during the opening years of the survey, with K as the prefix for the range, so that the name "K2" was purely a temporary one; but when it was found that four different native names for the mountain existed there was a long delay in deciding on the final name for the map, and by the time the mapmakers had resolved to name it Mount Godwin-Austen (after a famous English geographer) the designation "K2" had become widely known and used throughout the world. Somehow the simple letter and number seem entirely appropriate as a name for this shapely and formidable peak, less complicated in structure than other great ones yet appalling in its steepness and severity. Here are no convenient ridges or cols offering a way on to the upper structure of the mountain. It is in form a pyramid, and all the faces of the pyramid fall in sheer precipices of rock and ice for 12,000 feet to the glaciers of its plinth; the ridges between them appear to be totally unclimbable because of overhanging rock, and nowhere on the mountain is there any obvious ledge where a camp can be placed. For half a century K2 was considered to be the classic example of an inaccessible peak.

There was tragedy on K2 before 1953. The problem of the mountain had become well known to mountaineers through the extremely thorough reconnaissance made by the Duke of the Abruzzi in 1909, when every ridge and face of the huge pyramid was examined and an actual attempt made by the one way that offered any hope—a very

125 The K 2 Glacier and K 2

thin ridge of rock running up the south face. He reached a height of over 21,000 feet on this Abruzzi Ridge, as it was afterwards called, and then abandoned the apparently impossible route because it offered no halting-place anywhere. Sir Martin Conway's comment summed up the problem of K2: "Every foot of a route may be climbable, and yet if it cannot all be climbed in one day and there is nowhere to spend the night, what can you do?" Thirty years later improved mountain tents and equipment seemed to have answered his poser. Dr Charles Houston, who had been on the successful Nanda Devi ascent, brought out an American Karakoram Expedition in 1938 to attempt K2. Its preliminary reconnaissances proved beyond doubt that the only practicable way was by the formidable Abruzzi Ridge, and up this they climbed, hacking out or building platforms for six tents on the unyielding arête of rock. A vertical cliff of limestone that completely blocked the upper part of the ridge was climbed by William House up a difficult rock chimney and the party reached a height of 26,000 feet before being forced to retreat by lack of food. The following year saw a second American Expedition on K2, bent on making the complete ascent by the Abruzzi Ridge. There were new personnel, and a new leader, Fritz Wiessner.

As a German, Wiessner had been with Willy Merkl on the Nanga Parbat expedition of 1932. He was now a naturalised American. A man of great strength and indomitable will, he had in him something of the dogged independence and the lack of "selflessness" that characterised Hermann Buhl. In this lay the root of the imminent tragedy.

With Wiessner were five American climbers, none of them as experienced as the leader or such strong climbers. One of the youngest, Cranmer, fell ill at base camp and was left there in charge of the transport officer during the six weeks of the assault. Another, Durrance, sickened a week or two later and was brought down with difficulty. Soon only Wiessner and Dudley Wolfe, a forty-two-year-old climber, were left to push on up the ridge, with five Sherpas to help them carry and Pasang Kikuli in charge of the Sherpas. Already the party was far too weak for safety. All the reserves were unfit and down at Base Camp or Camp I; there was no responsible climber to occupy the camps in support of the advance party, and between each camp was a day's climbing on rock or ice of the greatest severity. To add to the danger, the weather was bad and several of the active men were slightly frost-bitten. Yet Wiessner climbed on. Camp VIII, at 25,234 feet, was placed on its tiny ledge on July 14th and occupied by Wiessner and Wolfe with one Sherpa, Pasang Dawa Lama; Pasang Kikuli had frost-bitten feet and had been sent down to Camp II. Then came the storm of wind and snow that held the three men helpless for three days in the highest camp. On July 17th, when the storm passed, Wolfe was ill and unable to move from the tent.

And now follow the incredible incidents which gave rise to this comment from the Himalayan historian Professor Mason: "It is difficult to record in temperate language the folly of this enterprise."

Leaving Wolfe ill and alone at 25,234 feet, Wiessner set off with Dawa Lama and a light bivouac tent to make a bid for the summit. He proposed at first to go on climbing all night, but Dawa Lama—a veteran Sherpa who wore the coveted Tiger Badge—anchored his ice-axe in the snow and refused to let him proceed with this suicidal plan. They bivouacked that night, sought a route next day and failed, bivouacked again; for five days this went on, with no successful issue, and then they descended to the lonely invalid in Camp VIII. Wolfe's food was nearly all gone and no one had come up to him from the lower camps. Wiessner, expecting to find supplies at Camp VII, descended with Wolfe and the Sherpa on the rope; the sick man slipped on the way and lost his load, which included his sleeping-bag.

There was no one at Camp VII—no reserves, no sleeping-bags. If the weather had not remained good the three might not have survived the night. Wolfe could not be moved, so Wiessner and the Sherpa went down next day to bring up supplies from Camp VI. There was nothing there either. Not unnaturally, the few Sherpas, leaderless and bewildered, had assumed that there had been a bad accident when nothing had been heard from the upper camps for over a week and had gone down to Base Camp. Wiessner and Dawa Lama went on down, camp by camp, after them. Dudley Wolfe was again left alone in Camp VII at 24,000 feet, sick and without adequate food.

It seems incredible that Fritz Wiessner should still have entertained hopes of climbing K2, almost single-handed as he was and with one of his party in a position of fearful danger. But he did. His plan required Durrance—who was far from well—to start up on July 25th with three Sherpas and bring Wolfe down from Camp VII; Wiessner himself, with two Sherpas, would start two days later for the high camps, to make another attempt to reach the top of K2. "It was inconceivable folly," is Professor Mason's comment on this. But it is fair to add that another account, put out later, states that Wiessner was so weak that he could hardly eat or speak, and this was why Durrance started out first.

And Durrance could not get higher than Camp IV. He and one Sherpa, both sick men, turned back here. Pasang Kita and Pintso Sherpa went on as far as Camp VI. They did not know it, but they were climbing to their deaths. Back at Base Camp, the exhausted Durrance reported their failure. It was the Sherpa Pasang Kikuli who volunteered to try and get help to the man who had now been up there for two weeks.

Pasang Kikuli's name deserves to head the list of heroes in the Himalayan record. At this time he had been on Nanda Devi with

Tilman; had escaped from the 1934 catastrophe on Nanga Parbat; had been on Kangchenjunga with Cooke and on Chomolhari with Spencer Chapman; and had been badly frostbitten on the North Col of Everest. Frostbitten again, able to climb only with pain, he nevertheless left Base Camp on K2, with one Sherpa named Tsering, and on July 28th accomplished the amazing feat of climbing that hazardous ridge right to Camp VI in a single day—a climb of more than 6,000 feet. Next day the Sherpas reached Wolfe in Camp VII. His tent was almost down and he was hardly able to stand. The Sherpas re-pitched the tent, brewed tea for Wolfe and fed him; but he refused to go down with them because he was as yet too weak to climb safely. They were to leave him to rest and eat, he told them, and come up for him next day. Since there was only one sleeping-bag among them this was good sense. Pasang Kikuli and his men descended again to Camp VI.

It was the night of July 30th. A storm of wind and snow swept across the Abruzzi Ridge and was still blowing next morning. Seizing the first lull, Pasang Kikuli, Pasang Kitar and Pintso Sherpa climbed up into the mists, leaving Tsering at Camp VI. Tsering waited for two days, increasingly cold and hungry. Then he climbed down, alone, to Base Camp to tell his story. Wolfe and the three gallant Sherpas were never seen again.

This was the first American tragedy on K2, the result of decisions as imprudent as Houston's on the 1938 attempt had been wise. Though an Italian had been the first to tackle the Second Highest, K2 now came to be regarded as "the American mountain," and the next attempt on the mountain, in 1953, was made by another American party.

When seven Americans and one Englishman occupied Camp VIII at 25,500 feet on K2 the hardest part of a very hard climb was below them. A month and a half had gone by since they first reached Base Camp on the Godwin-Austen Glacier; six weeks of toil and hardship and ver-tiginous clinging to rock or ice lay between the three little tents on their snow-ledge and the safe ground at the foot of the Abruzzi Ridge. Ten thousand feet of treacherous and sometimes vertical ridge had not been the only obstacle facing Charles Houston's American K2 Expedition.

Racial and religious enmity in the Himalaya had drawn a new frontier. K2 was now in Pakistan, and Sherpas—Indian nationals— were barred from entry. Deprived of the willing and heroic little men who had carried loads high on so many expeditions, Houston had to make use of Hunza men from the valleys of Baltit, good rock-climbers but inexpert on ice and snow. He could use them for carrying loads up to the lower camps only, which meant that above 20,000 feet all the carrying had to be done by the climbing-party itself, and also—a fate-ful circumstance—that there would be no reliable men in the camps between III and VIII when the final assault was launched. The weather, too, was unfavourable. When the route to the next camp-site had been opened by resolute climbing up crumbling knife-edges of rock and glassy walls of ice it had to be ascended and descended again and again with loads of food and camp equipment before the camp above could be occupied; and when the camp was ready a storm would swoop down on the ridge, obliterating the ice-steps and masking the rocks so that all the painful and dangerous work was to do again. One-day storm—three-day storm—two-day blizzard—two days' bad storm. K2 played cat-and-mouse with this fourth attempt on the Second Highest. But in spite of it they fought their slow way higher and higher on the inhospitable ridge that ran like a dark moulding up a white wall three miles high. The last weeks of June passed into July as they struggled and retreated and struggled upwards again. By mid-July House's Chimney—a narrow crack in a 150-foot precipice over-hanging space—had been overcome and loads hoisted up it by means of rope pulleys. So continuously steep was the whole gigantic ridge that loose rocks dislodged by climbers crashed down the whole route be-tween Camp VI and Camp II, often threatening to destroy the tents perched on their tiny ledges. There was no rock ledge for Camp VII. Forced by unclimbable black rock to take to a wall of ice on the right, the leaders discovered the one place where a platform six feet by four could be carved out of a pocket of hardened snow. Only one tent, accommodating two men, could be put here. From it they climbed on up the ice-wall and gained a narrow collar of snow beneath the final 3,000-foot slope of snow and ice—a much better camp-site where snow-ledges for three tents could be made. Since Camp VII on the ice-wall was almost useless as a support camp, the tiny bivouac tent was left there rolled up in case of emergency and all the climbers gathered at Camp VIII on August 2nd.

There were Charles Houston, the leader, and Robert Bates, who had both been on K2 before; George Bell, Robert Craig, Peter Schoening, and Dee Molenaar, all first-rate mountaineers; and young Arthur Gilkey, who had already shown himself to be one of the best and strongest ice-men in the party. The eighth man was Captain Tony Streather of the Gloucestershire Regiment, who had been to the 25,264-foot summit of Tirich Mir, highest of the Hindu Kush, in 1949. Streather was officially transport officer to the American expedition, but Houston had invited this tough and experienced Englishman to join the climbing-party.

It was a cheerful eightsome that occupied the four cramped tents at 25,500 feet. Every man was fit and eager for the final assault. Though the tents down the long ridge below them were unoccupied they were

27. Kangchenjunga   *Everest Fdn.*

all stocked with food. Their Pakistani liaison officer, Colonel Ata Ullah, was in charge of the six Hunza porters at Base Camp and in touch with the climbing party by radio. The weather was not altogether promising, but if it remained merely gloomy and exceedingly cold the bid for the summit could be made. Tomorrow the whole party would move two men to a point as high as possible on the summit-cone, leave them there in a two-man tent, and descend. Next day the chosen two would try for the summit while a second assault pair moved up to the tent. Houston intended to hold a ballot of the whole team to select the four most likely to reach the summit. But he did not hold it that night. The weather became bad and grew steadily worse. The wind screamed and blown snow hissed continuously on the tent fabric, penetrating through the ventilators to cover everything inside with fine white crystals, and in the morning there was no clearance. Men who tried to pass from one tent to another were almost choked by the flying stream of ice-particles. Death filled the air and there could be no hope of climbing that day. At six in the evening they heard on the radio Colonel Atta repeating the weather forecast he had picked up from Radio Pakistan: "Cloudy with heavy snowfall above 24,000 feet. Winds westerly, blowing 40 to 45 knots, occasionally gusting to hurricane velocity." That night and the next day the tents were shaken and flailed by the snow-gales, but the men in them remained cheerful. Food was in good supply and they could afford to wait. Houston, stumbling through the white fury between the tents, completed his ballot for the summit teams: Bell and Craig were to have first chance,

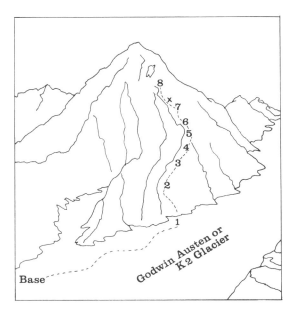

Diagram 11

K 2 from the south.
Figures indicate camps.
X indicates site of accident.

Gilkey and Schoening second. But the storm continued with unabated savagery. The third day was no better, and the fourth night worse—so bad that the fabric of the tent shared by Houston and Bell ripped and the poles snapped instantly before the onslaught of the snow-laden hurricane. The two men grabbed their sleeping-bags and half-stumbled, half-crawled into the shelter of other tents.

Still they remained cheerful. Such fury could not last much longer. No one spoke of the shocking conditions that must exist on the long, long ridge below them, cutting them off from the rest of mankind, but each must have followed in his mind's eye the successive drops of that descent which was for them the one link between life and death. First the short snowslope heeling over to the ice-wall with its empty bivouac ledge; loose rock and bad snow down to Camp VI; then the long, relentless steepness of the Black Pyramid—sheer slabs of granite—at the foot of which was Camp V; after that, the Chimney down the face of the vertical limestone precipice; and after that again, crumbling rock-edges, gullies filled with ice, dangerous snowslopes, for another 6,000

126 Camp V

feet of fearfully hazardous climbing. And every part of this route was now impassable, plastered with freezing snow and swept by terrific winds. But in the three days of better weather they needed for the final assault those bad conditions would clear away and the descent would again be possible.

The storm lasted, in its full fury, for six days; for the climbers, six days of lying crowded together in the tents while altitude slowly but surely lowered their physical condition. All of them were weaker than they had been and Bell had frostbite on two toes. Craig, too, had developed the first marks of frostbite on his feet and Molenaar was feeling ill. Houston wisely decided that their only hope of gaining the summit was to retreat to Camp VI as soon as the weather allowed it and there replenish their dwindling supplies and rest for a day or two before moving up again. *As soon as the weather allowed it.* Every man realised that on that vital phrase depended much more, now, than the climbing of a peak.

On the morning of August 7th there was a slight lull in the storm. For the first time in a week all the occupants of the tents crawled out among the wreaths of wind-blown snow. Arthur Gilkey, after emerging from his tent, suddenly collapsed unconscious. They took him back into shelter and Houston, the doctor, examined him. His left leg was swollen and discoloured—it had been like that, Gilkey explained, for a couple of days, but he'd been hoping it would clear up. Houston reassured him as he bandaged the leg; it would be a day or so before he could move, maybe. Then he went back to the tent he was sharing with Bates and Streather and broke the terrible news to them.

Gilkey had developed thrombo-phlebitis. In ideal conditions he might recover from it, but in conditions like those at Camp VIII he was absolutely certain to die. There was the slimmest of chances that he would survive if he could be got down to Base at once. And the route down to Base was closed.

> I knew, we all knew, that no one could be carried, lowered, or dragged down the Black Pyramid, over the dreadful loose rock to Camp V, down House's Chimney. My mind's eye flew over the whole route. There was no hope, absolutely none. Art was crippled. He would not recover enough to walk down. We could not carry him down. . . . But we could try, and we must.
>
> *K2, The Savage Mountain,* by C. Houston, 1955.

So Houston describes their plight and their decision. He told the others, but Gilkey was told only that he was seriously ill and that Houston had decided to retreat. Quickly they wrapped the helpless man in the wrecked tent, making a kind of stretcher-bundle of him. The lull was continuing and they could see their way to start the descent; it had to be started now if Gilkey was to have a chance of life.

The snowslope below the camp was a deep mass of powdery snow

223

bending over to the rim of the steeper ice-slope beneath it. They went some distance down it, lowering the bundled man in front of them. And stopped. All knew what would happen if they descended any farther on that loosely-poised layer. They had seen hundreds of powder-snow avalanches plunging down K2, and they were on the point of starting one that would carry them down with it.

The exertion of dragging Gilkey back up the slope was completely exhausting to his companions, but they regained the tents and got into them once more. By this time the wind was rising again and snow clouds were lowering across the grim faces of K2, but Schoening and Craig proposed a desperate plan. It would be days before that snow-slope would be safe, but beside it a ridge of rock and ice fell towards Camp VI. It was frightfully steep, but at least they would be safe from avalanches as they tried to lower Gilkey down it. Houston agreed and the two went out into the gathering storm to reconnoitre their route. Two hours later they staggered back up to camp through whirling mist and snow: the route was just possible. It could be tried tomorrow. But —if only Gilkey could recover sufficiently to help himself just a little!

They spent another night in the tents. Already they had been eight days above 25,000 feet, far longer than any other climbers had lived at such a height. And the next day, a day of thick cloud but a moderated wind, Gilkey declared that his leg was better; a little more rest, he said cheerfully, and he'd be able to climb down himself. Houston could not tell him that there was no hope of such a recovery, but he decided to allow one more day before starting down. So it was the morning of August 10th when the retreat, perhaps the most desperate mountaineering venture that ever was made, began in earnest—through a furious storm of wind and snow.

Houston had had to make a difficult decision. During the night he had discovered that Gilkey's phlebitis had spread to his lungs, and the blood clots were developing in his other leg as well. To order a descent in these conditions meant that they would probably all die. But to linger up there any longer meant certain death for Gilkey. Ought he to condemn a very sick man to death in order to make survival more probable for the rest of them? There was only one answer for men such as these.

Again they lashed the helpless man in the tent and attached four lowering ropes to him. Colonel Atta at Base Camp nearly 10,000 feet below was informed by radio of their intention, the smallest of the tents—all they could carry—was taken in case of emergency, and they began that terrible descent. A blizzard drove at them, rendering the work more difficult. It was several hours before they were descending the icy, snow-plastered rock-ridge. Steep though it was, projecting crags prevented the lowering of the inert 185-lb. bundle that was a just-living man. To one side of the ridge, between it and the wide face of the ice-slope, was a gully, a sheer chute walled with ice. Down this Gilkey could be lowered—but at terrible risk to his supporters. They started down it, Houston and Bates bracing back on the ropes above, Craig and Bell holding from the sides, and Schoening and Molenaar climbing down in front to find the route. Streather, between the carrying-party and the pioneers, acted as relay for the shouts of the men below, for the great gusts that shrieked across the mountain drowned their voices and they could scarcely see each other through the white turmoil of driven snow.

A step, two steps, in a minute. A halt, clinging to the ice, whenever a gust fiercer than the rest threatened to hurl them all into oblivion. The task of lowering was an agonisingly slow one, but the hours flew past almost unnoticed in the vital need for unceasing vigilance. At one time Craig had to unrope and go down in front of the bundle to direct operations. There came a sudden yell from Streather, a little to one side of the party: "*Hold tight!*" An avalanche, broken loose by the ropes, swept down over Gilkey and Craig, momentarily burying them. Houston and Bates strained back on the taut ropes with all their waning strength—and held. Streather's muffled shout came up to them: "They're still here!"

There were still eight men alive on the face of K2. The grim descent continued. But the strain was too great to be withstood much longer. Knowing that they could never get down to Camp VI on this day, they decided to try and reach the tiny ledge on the ice-wall, the ledge six feet by four that had been deemed hardly large enough for a two-man tent. It was their only chance to recover their fast-waning strength, the only possible resting-place.

Schoening and Molenaar shouted that they could belay Gilkey safely while the others climbed down to begin the crossing of the ice-wall. Bates and Houston descended, to find Schoening standing on the lip of a twenty-foot cliff with his axe planted behind a large boulder frozen into the snow. Gilkey was belayed to the axe. At the foot of the cliff an ice gully fell away into the white tumult of the storm towards the Godwin-Austen glacier two miles below. The tiny ledge which was now the goal for all of them was 500 feet away to their left on the face of the wall of ice and some distance below them. Eight of them, one unable to stand, had to get on that ledge, so Craig cut and clung his way to the haven first, to try and enlarge it. Meanwhile the others lowered Gilkey over the short cliff until he was resting against the ice-wall below. Schoening now held him there on a single rope while the rest climbed down to Gilkey's level. The plan was to pull him across the ice as on a pendulum, so Molenaar attached one rope to the strapped-up bundle and moved back across the slope. Bell and Streather on one rope, Bates and Houston on another, began to prepare rudimentary stances on the steep ice where they could anchor themselves while performing the hazardous operation of getting Gilkey across to the ledge. And through all this the thick, stinging snow lashed relentlessly at the eight tiny creatures—insignificant, invisible on the immense façade of K2—who struggled so doggedly for survival when, by all the rules of Man or Nature, they were doomed. One misjudged step of a frostbitten foot, one slip, and all would be over.

And Bell slipped. He flew down the ice-wall past Streather, dragged him instantly from his hold. Their falling bodies with the rope whipping between them fouled the rope between Bates and Houston and they too were flung headlong down. Both ropes pulled across Molenaar's rope, which linked him to the suspended Gilkey, and Molenaar went hurtling with the rest. Five men were falling to death. Barring a miracle, nothing could save them now.

But the miracle happened. The crossed ropes did not jerk free—and Molenaar's rope was tied to Gilkey. Far above on the tip of the twenty-foot cliff Pete Schoening stood, supporting Gilkey. The tremendous jerk of five falling bodies came on the helpless man and on the man belaying him. And Schoening, tied to the axe so precariously planted behind the frozen-in rock, held them all. The resilient nylon stretched and creaked, but it did not break. Three hundred feet below on the ice-wall dazed men began to lift bloodstained faces, to look about them, to scrape a cautious footing on the frozen wall. No one had been killed. But all five were injured in various ways, and their positions were precarious in the extreme. Bates, hanging upside down on his rope, was the first to recover, having nothing worse than severe bruises and cuts. Beside him Molenaar was climbing to the same projecting rock with blood streaming down his face; he had a deep cut in his thigh and a cracked rib. Sixty feet below, George Bell, whose gloves had been ripped off in the fall, was dragging himself up over the lower lip of the ice-wall, below which he had been suspended above the gale-swept void. Streather, the least badly injured, was higher up the slope trying to haul in the tangled ropes. Thirty feet below Bates, Houston lay unconscious on a tiny bracket of rock projecting over space. Bates secured Molenaar and with great difficulty climbed down to Houston; as he bent to touch him the fallen leader's eyes opened. "What are we doing here?" he mumbled. A frightful blow on the head had given him concussion and temporarily deprived him of memory and the power of reasoning, so that he was unwilling to move. Bates's explanation, yelled above the continuous screaming of the icy wind, meant nothing to him. He would not move. All of them had passed the normal limits of endurance long ago; there was no hope at all of hauling the bemused man up the ice. Bates put his mouth close to Houston's ear and shouted the names of his wife and daughter. "Charlie!" he bellowed desperately. "If you ever want to see them again, climb up there *right now!*" This got home to the darkened, groping mind. With

Molenaar taking in the rope above, Houston climbed up. "What are we doing here?" he kept asking Molenaar dazedly.

In fact, they were all still struggling for life. Up on his cliff, half-hidden by the blinding snowstorm, Schoening was fast losing his ability to hold Gilkey suspended; his hands were freezing. Craig had heard his urgent shouts and had left the ice-ledge to traverse, unroped, across the ice to Gilkey. He drove two ice-axes as deeply as he could and anchored the helpless man to them, thus allowing Schoening to detach the frozen ropes from the belay and climb down himself.

It was imperative that the other hurt and shaken men should somehow be got into shelter. Some sleeping-bags and other equipment had been lost in the fall, flying down into the depths below, but they still had the little bivouac tent with them and there was another small tent cached on the ice-ledge. The first essential—if it could be managed—was to erect both tents and help the casualties into them. Gilkey understood this. He forced a faint smile to his frozen lips as Craig explained that it might be half an hour before they could return and begin the long and exceedingly difficult task of edging him across the ice-wall to the ledge. They left him hanging there and crept back to help in the chipping-out of a wider ledge.

The exertion required of shocked and exhausted men at that height of 24,700 feet was very nearly beyond them, but nerve and will drove them on. Sheets of wind-blown powder snow poured over them as they toiled; the thunderous hiss of small avalanches tearing down the ice-wall beside them was lost in the louder roaring of the storm. The cutting of a ledge in the ice was the least difficult part of the task, for when they started to erect the tents the wind threatened to hurl tents and men off into space. "It was like working in the slipstream behind an airplane," Bates says. Houston was still dazed and unable to help, while Bell's hands and feet were so badly frostbitten that he could do little with them, but they got the tents up. There was the bivouac tent they had left on the ledge—a two-man tent—and the even smaller tent they had carried down with them. Into these tiny shelters eight men had to get. Both tents overhung the outer edge of the shelf and were likely to slide off into space if anyone pushed incautiously against the fabric on that side. Houston was got into shelter, and then the severely frostbitten Bell. The instant this had been accomplished Streather, Craig, and Bates roped up and set out across the ice-wall to get Gilkey. They were the only three now able to move. Schoening had attempted to start with them, but had nearly collapsed and had to crawl back. Molenaar's gashed thigh was too stiff for movement.

The place where Gilkey had been left hanging was out of sight from the ice-ledge behind a fold of the sheer wall. Through the flailing snow the three men clawed and balanced their way across to the fold, and looked into the shallow trough beyond it. The trough bore the deep groove made by an ice avalanche. Otherwise it was empty. Gilkey had been swept down to his death.

To men as near death as the seven survivors the shock of Arthur Gilkey's fate was dulled. There were three gravely injured men to get down now, and the worst of the descent was yet to come. The radio set was lost with one of the loads that had been torn off in the fall and they were completely cut off from the world below; their doctor, Houston, was unable to help them. Perhaps Streather and Bates and Craig had a chance, one chance in a thousand, of getting down alive by themselves. That thought did not enter their minds as they struggled back across the ice-wall with their tragic news. They knew that the seven of them would stick together, and that they would die. Molenaar and Bell and Schoening, helpless and in pain, knew it too. But Houston did not know it, for his senses had deserted him.

All that dreadful night, while they crouched on top of each other beneath the straining fabric of the tiny tents, Houston was in a kind of delirium. He tried continually to burst out of the tent where he huddled with Bates and Molenaar and Bell, crying out that he was suffocating.

127 The upper wall of K 2

28. Dent Blanche   *H. N. Collinson*

Fortunately he was so weak that he could be held down, but he persisted in his delusion that their salvation depended on getting out of the tent at once. At times he would slump over unconscious, reviving in a less violent mood. "I *know* about these things," he would argue piteously then. "I've studied them. We'll all be dead in three minutes if you don't let me cut a hole in the tent."

In a way the men who had to deal continually with Houston's obsession were lucky; it kept their thoughts from dwelling on the impossibility of getting down alive. Even to think of starting down was to think of impossibility. Bell's hands and feet were swollen with great frostbite blisters and he could not get his boots on, let alone walk. Molenaar had bandaged his wounded leg but could not move it. Craig and Schoening were both badly frostbitten and Schoening had developed a lung sickness that kept him gasping and coughing alternately. And there was Houston, whose semi-madness was likely to prevent him from making one sensible step when it came to getting across the ice-wall. With these sick and crippled men, how could they dream of getting down the frightfully loose ridge to Camp VI, or the iced rock of the Black Pyramid, or the verticality of House's Chimney? These were climbing problems severe enough to turn back a fit and expert mountaineer in any but the finest weather. But—"there was no question about the next move," writes Robert Bates. "We had to go down." He knew, all the same, that another miracle would be needed before they could so much as leave the ice-ledge.

And again the miracle happened. This time it was no single incredible chance but a multiple miracle of the human will. When the morning dawned, grey but less stormy, Molenaar declared that he could walk. Bell slit his boots with a knife; it invited possibly fatal frostbite, but it allowed him to get them on. Schoening's cough was still bad, but he was ready to start, and Craig's frostbitten feet would just enable him to shuffle along. Houston was the chief worry. He could do nothing for himself and seemed unable to realise what was happening. Schoening and Craig took him between them on the rope and started across the slope, uncertain whether he would drag them all down by some wild movement. He had no axe and had to be nursed very carefully across the ice, but though he would halt every so often to stare about him in a puzzled way he went steadily and there was no mishap. The others followed. Great gusts of driven snow lashed the ice-wall, but the wind was mercifully tempered to their weakness. Bell, who had also lost his axe, was without his glasses, broken in the fall; to him the white wall on which exact placing of the feet was vitally necessary was only a blur, and he had to grope for the nicks where his clumsy, agonisingly painful feet must go. Two hundred feet down the slope they found Houston's axe sticking in the snow, and with this Bell was able to move more safely.

The ice-wall was passed. The dreaded ridge down to Camp VI heeled over below them. The wind was rising savagely, but now hope was reviving in them all and its warmth fired their spirits for the ordeal. Foot by foot they clung down the seemingly endless steeps, with night advancing grimly through the whirling snow. The slip of one of them—and never was a slip more likely—must have meant the end of their long struggle. But no one slipped, and suddenly they were stepping down off the rock almost on to the half-buried tents of Camp VI. Sleeping-bags; food in plenty, drink in plenty, stoves and fuel to heat it. These things meant Life instead of Death.

That night they slept warm. And in the morning Houston had regained his senses. "If we can only get below House's Chimney," someone said, "it'll take mighty bad weather to stop us after that!" The worst was over.

Three days later they reached Camp II and found three Hunzas waiting for them. Houston, with an injured chest and right eye but back in full command again, had insisted on being the last man down House's Chimney, the final severe obstacle. Gilkey was dead; but seven men had come down alive—seven who had beaten Death in the grimmest battle ever fought on a mountain.

A year later, in 1954, Professor Ardito Desio's team of Italian climbers reached the summit of K2. The terrible weather of "the Savage Mountain" hampered them severely, but the expedition, organised

128 Rey, Lacedelli and Viotto of the Italian K 2 Expedition

and conducted with that minute attention to detail which characterised Hunt's Everest assault, reached its objective with the loss of one
Italian climber. The Americans had earned the right to think of K2
as their own mountain. But it was appropriate that the Second Highest
should have been climbed finally by fellow-countrymen of the great
mountaineer who was the first to attempt the Abruzzi Ridge.

129 Kangchenjunga from the foothills

11 The Five Treasures of the Snow

"FELICITY. 20 feet. Very Severe.

  Strenuous. The middle of the main overhang is split by a thin crack . . . Start from the platform below the crack and move out under the overhang with hands gripping the left edge of the crack and feet braced against the right wall . . ."

This is a rock-climb. The description is quoted from the third volume of *Climbs on Gritstone*, which contains descriptions of more than 600 such climbs, the great majority of them less than 100 feet in length and the product of the great upsurge of interest in rock-climbing which took place immediately after the Second World War. The gritstone out-crops that occur over a wide area of northern England attracted many hundreds of young men, and a lesser number of girls, to their short near-vertical walls and delicate balance-moves. The prime interest of these routes, as in the longer ones on Welsh and Cumbrian crags, lies in the exercise of a skill not unlike that of the chess-player; the moves on the upright board of the rock-face are the result of prior mental calcula-tion, the "pieces" are the various tensions that can be applied by a human body to the unique arrangement of cracks and rugosities—the opponent's "pieces"—of each route. On these and larger precipices the technique of pure rock-climbing progressed beyond the balance-climbing that had seemed the highest form of the craft. Expert leaders now began to tackle not merely verticalities but actual overhangs. Muscular strength, for jamming fingers or clenched fist in an over-hanging crack, again became an asset to the advanced rock-climber. Places that had been dismissed as completely impossible by the star climbers of the thirties now became possible and were ascended by the few leaders with the build and expertise to do so.

The difference between "Felicity, 20 feet", and Kangchenjunga, 28,146 feet, is obvious enough. An expert might climb the former in ten seconds; the latter took ten weeks to climb, after years of assault and failure and exploration had found a way. Yet both are mediums for the climber's expression of his peculiar urge. And they are linked by a figure who more than any other has stood for the re-uniting of the divergent trends of pure rock-climbing and greater mountaineering in our modern area of climbing.

About the time when Felicity was first climbed a north-country lad, fifteen or sixteen years old, appeared among the weekend groups at the gritstone faces within motor-cycle distance of Liverpool. This boy would look long and earnestly at some unclimbed problem which had baffled three generations of ambitious leaders; he would then climb it, having "appeared to experience very little difficulty". Rumours of this phenomenon spread through the widening circles of the climbing fraternity, which now numbered many thousands. But before the legend had grown he disappeared to do his National Service in the Far East, and it was not until 1951 that he turned up again in North Wales to attempt, and conquer, one after another of the "un-climbable" problems on Clogwyn du'r Arddu and the Three Cliffs of Llanberis. Only one or two of the most expert climbers were able even to follow where he led. Before long, to have climbed a Joe Brown route was the surest way of achieving a great reputation in the climbing world.

Joe Brown is short, stockily built yet light, possessed of great strength in fingers and arms. Modest and slow of speech, he is a builder by trade and a mountaineer by predilection. To see him at work high on some sheer and apparently quite holdless precipice, quietly and confidently finger-jamming his way up a two-inch crack angled out over 500 feet of empty air, is to broaden suddenly one's preconception of human capabilities. Before the advent of Joe Brown it had been accepted that fitness and perfection of technique made it possible for any climber, of any height or build, to overcome the hardest rock routes. Now it began to be said that certain of Joe Brown's climbs could only be tackled by a

130 Joe Brown

131 The West Face of the Dru

132 Climbing the ''90-metre dierdre'', West Face of the Dru

man of the same build, weight, and reach as Brown. In 1965 it still remains to be seen whether this theory is correct.

In the 'fifties the huge unclimbed faces of the continental mountains were being conquered one by one by the finest climbers of France and Germany and Italy. Bonatti and Ghigo of Turin had climbed the east face of the Grand Capucin, the final 1,000 feet of which is one enormous overhang. A French party in 1952 succeeded in ascending the terrific west face of the Aiguille du Dru (*Plates 131* and *132*), described as "an enormous vertiginous plaque, without holds, without fissures". The ascent took them seven days. Joe Brown and his climbing-partner Don Whillans went out to the Alps in search of virgin cliffs to conquer, and after polishing off a couple of the lesser "impossibilities" repeated the Dru west face in only two days. There was ground for the assertion, made at that time, that Brown was the greatest cragsman in the world. The Alpine climbs gave him the additional experience of snow and ice work. It was not so incongruous as many mountaineers seemed to think, that when a British expedition was organised for the ascent of Kangchenjunga Joe Brown should be invited to join it.

"There is no doubt," Sir John Hunt wrote, "that those who first climb Kangchenjunga will achieve the greatest feat of mountaineering, for it is a mountain which combines in its defences not only severe handicaps of wind, weather, and very high altitude, but technical climbing problems and objective dangers of an order even higher than we found on Everest."

It is the third highest mountain in the world, its summit only a hundred feet lower than that of the second highest, K2. Its name means "The Five Treasures of the Snow", and refers to the fact that its immense mass contains four subsidiary summits in addition to the crowning peak. To see the other Himalayan giants such as Everest and Nanda Devi a man must make a long and difficult journey on foot into the mazy recesses of the Himalayan gorges; he can gaze at this one without walking a yard. Thousands reaching Darjeeling by train or car have seen, fifty miles away beyond the hot foothills of Sikkim, a vast and glittering wall of white culminating in a noble peak. Vertical flutings on the white wall, discernible only as faint shadow-lines, are in fact the huge troughs carved by avalanches of ice or snow. Even at fifty miles' distance that gleaming citadel looks singularly lofty and inaccessible. This is Kangchenjunga.

Frank Smythe, one of the great climbers who took part in the early assaults, calls Kangchenjunga "an independent mountain". It rises on the frontier between Sikkim and Nepal about 100 miles south-east of Mount Everest, and is neither part of a continuous range nor the culminating point of a high plateau; the 500 square miles of glacier,

237

rock slope, tropical forest, and river valley that surround it are all dependencies of this mighty monarch. Its four ridges and their faces are built of red granite, but all are loaded and plastered with ice and snow. For Kangchenjunga, more than any other Himalayan peak, is the barrier between the snow-laden monsoon winds and the mountains farther north, receiving the first and heaviest discharges and shouldering them off down its flanks in avalanche and hanging glacier and tumbled ice fall. The avalanches of Kangchenjunga are the chief of those "objective dangers" noted by Sir John Hunt. To find a climbing route that avoided their constant threat was the aim of the first expedition that attempted the ascent.

A mountain so high and prominent, throwing out so obvious a challenge to mountaineers, was bound to receive early attention. In 1899 Douglas Freshfield's party made a complete circuit round Kangchenjunga. In 1907 Dr Kellas tried, and failed, to reach a gap on the great north ridge of the mountain. Their explorations confirmed the opinion that Kangchenjunga was both dangerous and unclimbable; though Freshfield thought the only possible route—ignoring the ever-present avalanche threat—might be found on the south-west side, starting from the Yalung Glacier (see *Diagram 12*).

In 1905 a small expedition took up the challenge hinted at by Freshfield. Three competent Swiss climbers and one Italian—Guillarmod, Reymond, Pache, and De Righi—chose as their leader an

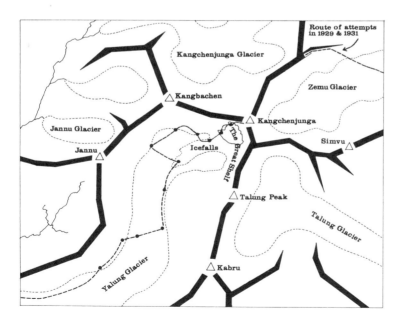

Diagram 12
The Kangchenjunga Massif, showing route followed on first ascent.

238

Englishman, a skilled mountaineer named Aleister Crowley. Crowley was perhaps the most extraordinary character who ever took to the mountain sport. He was ostentatiously careless and inhuman in all he did, styled himself "the Great Beast of the Apocalypse", and practiced Black Magic and Satanism. The party advanced up the Yalung Glacier and reached a height of 20,400 feet on the face below the main peak and to the west of it; and here, at Camp VII, the Swiss called a conference at which Crowley was formally deposed from leadership because of his sadistically cruel treatment of the porters. Crowley refused to accept this. The expedition was then called off and all except Crowley started down for the lower camps. There was a slip which set off an avalanche. All of them were swept down and buried under the snow. Guillarmod succeeded in freeing himself and digging out De Righi, while Reymond (who had escaped the worst of the fall) came to his aid. Together they dug feverishly to try and rescue the deeply buried Pache and the three porters who were engulfed with him, at intervals shouting up to Crowley to come and help them. But Pache was dead, and the porters too.

Crowley had heard the frantic calls for help but had not troubled to come out of his tent. That evening he wrote a letter, later printed in an English newspaper, commenting that he "was not over-anxious in the circumstances to render help. A mountain 'accident' of this kind is one of the things for which I have no sympathy whatever." Next morning he climbed down, keeping well clear of his late companions who were toiling to recover the bodies, and proceeded to Darjeeling by himself. As a Satanist, it seems, he was doing rather well.

After this shameful and tragic incident Kangchenjunga was left alone for nearly a quarter of a century, until a lone American climber, E. F. Farmer of New York, made in 1929 an attempt to reach the Talung Saddle on the south ridge. He had with him three ex-Everest Sherpas, none of whom were equipped with crampons. High on the great snowslopes Farmer, who was wearing crampons, ordered the Sherpas to halt while he went on alone. They did their best to dissuade him, but he vanished in the upper mists and never returned.

In the same year as Farmer's fatal attempt Paul Bauer's German expedition tried to climb the mountain by the north-east spur and the north ridge. The approaches from the Zemu Glacier were swept by avalanches, but they gained the crest of the spur safely—only to find its whole length crowned with towers of ice and overhanging masses of snow. How, for four weeks, they tunnelled and hewed a way up the spur to 22,500 feet, sleeping in caves carved out of the ice, is one of the epic passages in mountaineering history; that they retreated down that fantastically difficult route without losing a man is one of its miracles. The following year an international expedition led by Professor Dyhrenfurth (and including Frank Smythe) tried a new route approaching from the Kangchenjunga Glacier on the north-west. It was a dangerous route and they did not get far. When one of the many ice-avalanches had narrowly escaped killing the whole party and had swept a porter, Chettan, to his death, the attempt was called off. Next year Bauer was back again with a strong party for another try at the north-east spur. This time it took them twenty-three days to carve and burrow their way through the ice-towers from Camp VIII, at 21,000 feet, to Camp XI, a hole in the ice at 24,150 feet. They had to retreat before they had reached the junction of the north-east spur with the north ridge. One of the Germans, Schaller, and a Sherpa porter were killed by a fall early in the attack.

The north ridge route had been proved impossible. At least equally difficult were the very long east ridge and the west ridge which climbed over the 25,000-foot Kangbachen peak. The mountain had claimed seven victims. For the next eighteen years Kangchenjunga was left alone.

It was in 1953 that John Kempe, of the Hyderabad Public School, took a close look at the upper Yalung Glacier and the south-western flanks of Kangchenjunga—the way taken by Aleister Crowley's ill-fated expedition forty-eight years before. Kempe was an experienced climber, and thought the possibility of a strong party climbing the mountain by this side so good that he led a reconnaissance expedition to it in the next year. From the head of the Yalung Glacier they looked up at a gigantic cirque of rock and snow and ice whose walls were 10,000 feet high. On their left front precipices of reddish granite alternated with white avalanche slopes under the crest of Kangchenjunga's west ridge; on their right a mighty staircase of broken ice led up an opening beneath the south summit; straight in front was an even mightier staircase, a tremendous and evidently extremely difficult ice-fall leading to a great shelf of ice running across the mountain's face some 4,000 feet below its summit. The task of this six-man party was to find a practicable route, and for a month they climbed and retreated, probing for a way that would avoid that formidable icefall; for it was clear that if the Great Shelf could be reached, a way to the summit—hard and possibly dangerous—could be made. But the icefall proved to be the only way. By a steep rib of rock that contained the shattered ice on one side they at last gained the halfway snow-ledge that divided the icefall into Upper and Lower sections. Their time was now up, and an alarming avalanche that narrowly missed carrying down three Sherpas hastened their retreat. The rock rib (subsequently named Kempe's Buttress) was very steep and difficult but they had carried a camp up it; there seemed little doubt that the Upper Icefall could be climbed by a strong and well-equipped party and the Great Shelf gained. The way had been found.

Charles Evans, a Liverpool surgeon, had been one of the two men who first stood on Everest's South Summit in 1953. He was thirty-six in 1955 when he led to Kangchenjunga a strong expedition sponsored by a committee of the Alpine Club and the Royal Geographical Society, with Sir John Hunt as chairman. There was the big Scotsman Tom MacKinnon, Tony Streather who had survived the American adventure on K2, a tough New Zealander named Norman Hardie, John Jackson (now warden of the Snowdonia National Park Recreation Centre) whose brother Ron had found the route up Kempe's Buttress; Neil Mather was a first-rate mountaineer who liked walking seventy miles at a stretch, Dr John Clegg another who could supplement his medical duties with a fund of good songs; tall, spectacled George Band was a fine rock-climber, though not quite up to the standard of the youngest member of the party, Joe Brown.

Evans used all the advantages he could get and used them well. He took ample supplies of oxygen and three different kinds of oxygen sets—open-circuit, closed-circuit, and special sets for use while sleeping. Aerial photographs helped out those taken on the reconnaissance. Twenty-eight Sherpas were taken, twelve of them for high-altitude climbing and the others for ferrying loads up to the lower camps. Three hundred coolies carried the expedition's equipment and food to Base

133 Charles Evans

Camp on the moraine of the Yalung Glacier. Walkie-talkie radio would keep the various camps in touch with each other, and the experience gained on Everest had been used to improve even further the boots and tents and stoves that would be used high up on the mountain. Given the right weather, this expedition would surely put two men on the summit of Kangchenjunga. And yet those two men, if they succeeded in climbing to the summit, were to leave it untrodden, a virgin summit still.

The people of Sikkim, on the eastern side of Kangchenjunga, reverence the great mountain as a god and protector, whose wrath may be aroused by the desecration of its topmost sanctuary. Charles Evans had promised the Maharajah of Sikkim· that the climbers would leave the summit untouched, and would go no farther up the mountain than was necessary to assure them that the top was within easy reach. Kangchenjunga was to remain what Evans later called it: the Untrodden Peak.

To assume that the expedition would get within easy reach of the top was to assume a very great deal. For all the careful organisation and the optimism, the ascent of Kangchenjunga was very far indeed from being a foregone conclusion. The mountain was less than a thousand feet lower than Everest and no one had as yet reached a point within three days' climb of the summit. Six thousand feet of unknown precipice remained to be explored above the place reached by the reconnaissance party, and it was an even chance that some impassable obstacle, or a passage exposed to continual avalanches, would defeat Charles Evans and his men. There was also that unpredictable factor—the weather. And the weather showed its "pattern" long before the expedition reached its Base Camp. At the camp near the snout of the Yalung Glacier, where the 300 coolies dumped their loads and were paid off, snow buried everything during the afternoon; in the morning clear sunlight dispersed the snow, but cloud built up at noon into another snowfall. For many weeks, until they got high on the mountain, this was the rough timetable by which their advance had to be made.

It took them a month to ferry loads and camps step by step up the difficult Yalung Glacier and establish a Base Camp in the cwm below the ice-falls of the west face. The laborious route up the great stream of ice, now over stony moraines and blue-green clefts, winding between fantastic white pinnacles, was to some extent dictated by the avalanches that roared down from the mountain walls on either hand. Since great Himalayan peaks are in a continual state of disintegration, it was no surprise to find that though Kempe's Buttress could be climbed it was now quite impossible to reach the halfway plateau above the Lower Icefall from its top. After several days of hard climbing on rock and ice the route had to be abandoned and another one sought.

134 Ice pinnacles on the Yalung Glacier

This period of the expedition, says Evans, was the most trying of all. Base Camp was in danger from avalanches falling from the Great Shelf of ice 5,000 feet overhead. Nothing serious had fallen yet, but the reconnaissance party had seen one such avalanche fall, and photographed it (*Plate 135*). In this picture the summit of Kangchenjunga is seen top left; the Great Shelf, its edge of ice about 600 feet thick, slants slightly downward to the right from beneath the summit. The rising cloud of ice particles at the foot of the wall, the result of a mass of ice the size of a cathedral falling from the shelf, is travelling towards the camera at about sixty miles an hour. On this occasion the camp was well over a mile distant from the area covered by the debris, but the terrific blast of air had all but hurled their tents down and covered everything with two inches of powdered ice. The re-siting of the Base Camp after the failure to get up by Kempe's Buttress was a relief to the 1955 party.

It was impossible to go up the Lower Icefall, impossible to reach the higher face by the buttress on its right. There remained a very steep and long snowslope on the left of the Lower Icefall, and by this, eventually, they climbed, to traverse rightward across a great shoulder known as the Hump and thus gain, at long last, the plateau between

135 Avalanche on Kangchenjunga

29. Path towards Obergabelhorn   *H. N. Collinson*

136 Retreat from the icefall

137 In the lower icefall

138 From Camp II

the Lower and Upper Icefalls. Here Camp II was placed at 20,400 feet (*Plate 138*). It had taken them more than six weeks of mountaineering to get there, but in those six weeks the climbers had become acclimatised and fit for the high-altitude work that was to come. With their Base Camp on the glacier reasonably safe from avalanches, the first major obstacle overcome, and the Sherpas busily moving loads up the prepared and marked route between camps, they pushed the route slowly upward through the creaking ice-towers of the Upper Icefall. The distances between the camps marked on *Plate 139* hints at the difficulty of the route, which included the ascent of a fifty-foot vertical wall of ice and the crossing of several tremendous crevasses; but on May 5th, a week after the establishment of Camp II, Camp V was pitched at 25,300 feet on the higher end of the Great Shelf.

All through this long period of ascent there had been mixed weather, blizzards and temperatures below zero alternating with hot sunshine. Every night heavy snow covered the tents and the trail. John Jackson had been badly hit by snowblindness (in spite of which he insisted on carrying on with a heavy load) and one of the Sherpas, Pemi Dorje, was seriously ill at Base Camp. But now the summit was only 3,000 feet above and the climbing party were itching to get at it. And they

139 Camps on the upper and lower icefalls

were enjoying themselves. Discomfort and the hardest of hard work, the "ten steps and a rest, ten steps and a rest" that was their life for hours on the endless walls of snow, could not blunt the mountaineers' delight in the beauty and intricacy of their mountain.

> We were falling in love with our route: the smooth steepness west of the Hump; the intricate corner at the top of the Lower Icefall; the complexity of the Upper Icefall, its blues and whites and long shapely lines; beyond, the broad recess of the Shelf, under the red rocks of the summit ridges. Beautiful from far away, the mountain was beautiful also from here.
>
> *Kangchenjunga*, by Charles Evans, 1956.

So writes Charles Evans of their arrival at Camp V. This was something different from the grim and cheerless struggle that had characterised the attempts on other Himalayan giants. Instead of desperate strife with a hateful monster which held death in its icy claws there was here a cheerful acceptance of difficulty and beauty alike—a flash-back to the Golden Age of Alpine climbing, when triumph on a summit was an insignificant matter beside the sheer joy of mountaineering. Streather and Mather, MacKinnon and Jackson, who more than once climbed to the Great Shelf without oxygen, reported "that they had had some of the most enjoyable climbing of their lives".

It may well be that Charles Evans's Kangchenjunga expedition will be remembered, by the mountaineers of the future, not so much for its material achievement as for its timely reminder that mountains are there to be enjoyed, not "conquered".

But now the structure of the upper mountain rose immediately above Camp V on the Great Shelf. *Plate 140* shows this final 3,000 feet as seen from the slopes of Talung Peak, three miles away. The lowest arrow points the way on the Upper Icefall. Just to the right of a crescent of dark cliffs (known as the Sickle) at the higher end of the Great Shelf a second arrow marks the Gangway, a long and steep incline of snow ending just under the summit ridge which runs up to the right to the top of Kangchenjunga, plumed with cloud. The original plan had been to gain the ridge at its lowest point and climb along it to the summit, but a snag had cropped up: the aerial photographs had shown that the last part of the west ridge was certain to be exceedingly difficult; it was a jagged, knife-edged crest corniced with snow and supporting several "gendarmes" or rock towers. The photographs seemed to suggest that the upper half of the ridge might be climbable, and that this could be reached by traversing out from the Gangway across the rock-ribs and ice-gullies of the south-west face. Joe Brown and George Band, who had now been chosen as the first summit pair, planned a route on these lines as well as they could from below. All that was needed now was a spell of fine weather. It was May 20th. If the weather forecasts from Darjeeling were to be trusted, they had perhaps eleven

140 The route on the last 3,000 feet

days in which to make the summit attempt and get off the mountain before the coming of the monsoon made climbing impossible.

The weather broke. Blizzards and furious gales swept the high camps, obliterating the laboriously cut steps and burying tents and equipment deep in soft snow. An avalanche swept away a dump of stores. Their plan to try for the summit on May 23rd had to be revised, and it was May 24th before the men at Camp V could move. Camp VI, the final camp before the assault, had to be carried high up the Gangway, and all depended on whether the Gangway was of hard unclimbable ice or of snow. Evans, Mather, Band, and Brown, with four Sherpas, started up in windy but clearer weather and found the Gangway just climbable. A little more than halfway up its 2,000 feet they put the little tent on a ledge scraped out of the snow. Then six of them descended, leaving the summit two alone up there.

The outer edge of the tent sagged over the ledge, overhanging the great white wall below. Joe Brown broke a matchstick and they drew, long or short, for who should occupy the outer berth. George Band lost. Both of them felt so precariously perched that they tied on to the climbing-rope and belayed it to a spike of rock on the steep right-hand wall of the Gangway before getting into their sleeping-bags. If the tent slipped from its narrow shelf in the night, or was blown off, they would remain tied on to the mountain.

At 8.15 of a clear, sunny morning they left the tent and set off for the summit. Masked and goggled, with their open-circuit oxygen sets on their backs, they looked more like spacemen than climbers; and indeed the thin, cold, unbreathable air around them was like the aether of outer space. The snow was hard. Band led, making each step with two slashes of his axe. Through the nozzles of their oxygen tubes the life-giving gas flowed at the rate of three litres a minute. Above them the dazzling white incline of the Gangway rose up and up to its rim against the dark-blue sky, while on their right the red granite walls and columns glowed warmly beyond parallel couloirs of green ice. Joe Brown looked longingly at those rocks. Afterwards, when an admiring friend requested a description of the Kangchenjunga adventure, Joe considered for a moment and then said "It was a long troodge." In fact, he was to get on steeper rocks before long.

A false start to the right from the upper Gangway brought them across ice to the foot of a sheer red wall 200 feet high. "VS stuff," said Joe briefly, meaning that any route up that wall would be of Very Severe standard and therefore unclimbable at 27,000 feet. They retraced their steps to the Gangway and went farther up it. A line of snow patches and broken rocks led out to the right again, and these they followed, cutting steps in the snow-ice. A forty-foot buttress of rough, red-brown rock barred the way, and to climb this they took off their crampons. Their bootsoles gripped bare rock for the first time since leaving Base Camp. Some way above this Brown climbed an ice-filled chimney and then traversed to the right across a great slab where the space below his feet ended only on the Great Shelf, now nearly 2,000 feet down—"a really nice position," he called it. It led to the foot of an ice-gully 120 feet long, so steep that as Brown cut his way up it he could rest one thigh against the slope. George Band wanted to take over the lead here, but he was not going so well as his companion; moreover, his fingers had been frostbitten and blistered for some days. A more easily angled snowslope lay above. They cut up it—and found themselves on the knife-edge of the main west ridge, with the summit in plain view beyond the rising crest of rock and snow. Here they rested for ten minutes.

"Two o'clock," said Band, "and we've two hours' supply of oxygen left. We must turn back at three or spend the night out."

"In that case," said Joe Brown, "we've got to be *there* by three."

They climbed on along the narrow crest with the enormous precipice of the north flank under their toes. It was easy scrambling now—"like Crib Goch," Brown says—but it didn't last for long. The way was blocked by a gendarme, a sixty-foot tower of brown and grey rock. They traversed below it on the south flank of the ridge and found themselves beneath a sheer rock-wall with a crack running up the back of a recess in it. It was a rock-climbing problem which Joe Brown could have solved with ease on a British crag, but here at 28,000 feet above the sea a tenfold effort was required. All the same, it was "right up his street". He fixed running belays and jammed his way up, round a bulge made by some overhanging rocks.

Below him, watching anxiously and belaying with the rope, George Band saw him reach the top of the rock-wall and halt, motionless. Then Brown turned his head to shout down.

"George, we're there!"

A few minutes later Band stood beside him on a platform of grey slabs. Twenty feet away rose a shapely cone of snow a few feet higher than their platform. It was the summit of Kangchenjunga.

Next day, in equally good weather, Norman Hardie and Tony Streather reached the same slab platform. None of the four went farther. According to their promise, they left the summit snow undespoiled.

Many people have asked Joe Brown whether there wasn't a great temptation to go those last few feet. His answer is always the same: "No. For one thing, I was too tired to want to take another step. But apart from that I'm glad we left no footmark on the top." Nor, incidentally, did they hoist any national flags, symbols of a fleeting epoch, on a noble summit that will stand unmoved above the world long after the nations have passed from it for ever.

141 Cho Oyu, 26,750 feet

12 The New Golden Age

FAR from marking the end of the greatest epoch in mountaineering history, the ascent of Everest in 1953 was like the lighting of a beacon to illuminate the future. The light spread across a prospect of mountains and mountain adventure that seemed illimitable. It was as if the climbing of the mountain that *had* to be conquered released a new army of young mountaineers and made them free of the world's treasury of peaks, from the Antarctic to Alaska and from the Caucasus to the Andes. Only the Communist-controlled nations of northern Asia, by an odd contradiction of Communist theory, withheld their mountains from this most international of sports; elsewhere hundreds upon hundreds of unclimbed peaks awaited the happy warriors of a new Golden Age.

In Britain the 'fifties were the era of the small private expedition. From universities and climbing clubs, from schools and other organisations, well-equipped parties set forth to Arctic Norway or Spitsbergen or Greenland to survey and climb in the unexplored areas. They asked and received little or no publicity. Often the only record was an article in the club journal—and a small but valuable addition to the map of the world. Many a young man entered a job and worked hard at it for twelve months in order to save money for a cherished exploit of mountaineering or exploration, thereafter vanishing for half a year into the wilderness with a few chosen friends. Little was known of these modern adventurers outside their own circle, and as the opportunity for pioneer surveys and first ascents narrowed they tended more and more to keep their plans secret. The adventures and achievements of this nameless band, if they could be collected in a book (it would have many volumes) would make heartening reading for those who deplore the decadence of modern youth.

In the Himalaya the unsponsored, unpublicised expedition of three or four mountaineers became a common event. They sought one of the unnumbered peaks between 20,000 and 24,000 feet, where they could manage without oxygen or a multitude of expensive tents. Their climbs and explorations were recorded in the journals of the Himalayan Club and the Royal Geographical Society. But the great climbers still made for the great peaks.

Kangchenjunga was the seventh of the fourteen *Achttausenders* to be ascended; seven remained unclimbed in 1956. The ascent of Makalu, the fifth highest in the world, by a French party in the same year as Kangchenjunga passed almost unnoticed by the general public. "Like happy people, ascents that go off well have no history," wrote Jean Franco, leader of this expedition, and dubbed Makalu "the happy mountain". Tragedy and narrow escapes from death may be the essence of mountain adventure for the reader in his armchair, but for the mountaineer they are evidences of bad mountaineering; for him the adventure is something far deeper and quite inexpressible, a personal matter between himself and his mountain. Cho Oyu, 26,750 feet, was climbed by three Austrians and a few Sherpas in this spirit. "The world around me showed a kindly benevolence such as I had never before experienced," wrote Herbert Tichy, the leader, of his arrival on the summit. "Snow, sky, the wind and myself were an indivisible and divine whole. It was a mystical experience, a nearness to the divine and the essential, never felt before." A hundred years before him Alfred Wills, on the summit of the Wetterhorn, had had this same "mystical experience". The golden link broken by the materialists of the summit-or-death school was being mended.

Names from the list of Himalayan climbers in the years before Everest recur in the story of the last *Achttausenders*. Raymond Lambert, who with Tenzing had gained the South Col of Everest in the year before the British success, made a gallant but unsuccessful attempt on Cho Oyu; with him was Madame Claude Kogan, a brilliant woman climber, who had climbed Nun (23,410 feet) in the Punjab Himalaya. Ernst Reiss, who had been with Lambert on the second Swiss Everest Expedition, reached with Fritz Luchsinger the summit of Lhotse, the fourth highest mountain in the world. And this Swiss Expedition of 1956 not only climbed Lhotse but also gained, six days later, the summit the Swiss of 1952 had deserved to gain—Everest itself. Far off in Peru, that year, George Band of Kangchenjunga and Michael Westmacott of Everest were climbing the much lower but very difficult peak of Huagaruncho, 18,850 feet; Band, with a party from Cambridge University, had made a resolute attempt on the unclimbed giant Dhaulagiri, the sixth highest, in 1954. Manaslu (26,658 feet) was also climbed in 1956, by a mighty Japanese expedition which included twelve climbers, twenty Sherpas, and nearly 500 coolies (fifteen of whom were needed to carry the money for paying the rest) and which began its assault "on the Emperor's birthday". In this same crowded year an Austrian expedition climbed Gasherbrum II, thirteenth on the *Achttausender* list. Of the fourteen great ones only four now remained unclimbed: Dhaulagiri, Gosainthan, Broad Peak, and Gasherbrum I. Among the members of the Austrian party that climbed Broad Peak in 1957 was a man whose outstanding, always near-tragic figure has appeared more than once before in this history: Hermann Buhl.

Buhl of the lone climbs on the Watzmann and the Piz Badile; Buhl of the fierce struggle against the storm-swept Eigerwand in 1952; Buhl of the solitary ascent and night out on Nanga Parbat in 1953. He was now thirty-three years old, a legendary figure in the climbing world and leader of the climbing-party on Broad Peak. But the superhuman effort on Nanga Parbat had cost him dear; the loss of two toes due to frostbite, and the consequent lessening of his resistance to cold, had weakened the physique which, allied to an iron will, had performed such wonders of climbing. There is an unforgettable picture of him— one of the last—in Kurt Diemberger's account of the climb to the summit of Broad Peak.

Diemberger and Buhl were the second assault pair. It was a fine clear day, with the black rock and dazzling snows of the Karakoram giants sinking lower and lower as they climbed the final ridge. But it was pitilessly cold. Buhl's injured feet were giving him agonising pain and he was moving ever more slowly. At last, when they were a little above 25,000 feet, he sank down in the snow, gasping out that he could go no farther. Diemberger asked if he might go on by himself and Buhl agreed. When he had climbed a few steps Diemberger looked back, and saw Buhl sitting upright, staring with strange intensity at a huge and solitary peak far away in the west. It was Nanga Parbat.

Diemberger went on, very slowly because of the great altitude, and reached the summit late in the day. The sun was setting as he started down, wondering if he could reach the tent before dark. At six-thirty he saw Hermann Buhl—coming up. He shouted, and got no reply. "Hermann kept coming up, slowly, step by step, his face drawn, his eyes set straight ahead." Diemberger turned without a word and followed, making for the top a second time, trusting in "Buhl's luck". Darkness fell as they stood on the summit, 26,414 feet above the sea. The iron will had conquered the crippled body; and the luck held for that 3,000-foot descent through the Himalayan night. They were back at their tent, safe but utterly exhausted, half an hour after midnight.

A few weeks later the successful Broad Peak party turned its attention to the neighbouring peak of Chogolisa, 25,110 feet, a great snow-summit with a magnificent but heavily corniced south-east ridge. Again Diemberger and Hermann Buhl climbed together. After some days of bad weather, a glittering morning induced them to start for the summit from their camp at 22,000 feet. Above them the enormous ridge rose for 3,000 feet in a knife-blade structure, vast snow-cornices hanging far out over the north face on the right, a sheer precipice on the left. They mounted slowly up this, having some difficulty in keeping off the dangerous cornices because of the steepness of the slope above the precipice. At about half past ten, when the summit was in sight 1,500 feet above, a violent storm smote without warning at Chogolisa. In a few moments the air was filled with driving clouds of ice-particles and blown snow. They fought their way onward, upward, for another 500 feet before Buhl gave the word to turn back.

Already they had pressed on too far for safety. When Diemberger, who had been following Buhl, turned to descend he could see nothing of the white knife-blade that fell away from his feet. The thick veil of flying snow hid everything—had even filled and drifted over the steps they had kicked up the ridge. The only things distinguishable in the white blankness were the small deep holes where they had thrust in their ice-axes. These alone marked the frightfully narrow path between snow and space, between life and death.

Peering for the vital marks, Diemberger edged slowly down with Buhl following a dozen paces behind. They had unroped lower down in order to climb more swiftly, and Buhl did not suggest roping-up again in this perilous situation. Diemberger, a younger man and an ardent admirer of Buhl, did not venture to make the suggestion himself. It was impossible to make out the edge where the giant cornices over-hung, though he knew this could only be a few feet away on his left. There was a sudden muffled *Crack!* and the snow seemed to sink under his feet. Instinctively he made a frantic leap to the right, seeing as he did so the jagged edge of snow beneath him and the fragments falling into the void. He landed safely. He had actually been walking on the overhanging cornice! What would Hermann have to say when Diemberger told him of his escape?

He stared back through the thinning drift of snow. Buhl seemed to have fallen farther behind him. He waited, and still Buhl didn't come. He shouted, and there was no reply. Fear gripped at Diemberger suddenly. He clawed his way up to the edge. He saw now that many yards of cornice had peeled off from the crest. He saw Hermann Buhl's footprints on the very edge of the break. Beyond was only the blackness of the depths.

One of the first expeditions of the years following the ascent of Everest was the *Daily Mail* Expedition of 1954 which went to the Himalaya to solve the mystery of the *Yeti* or Abominable Snowman. The mystery is still unsolved.

As early as 1921 the first Everest Expedition came upon some odd footprints, resembling the prints of a naked human foot, on the snows at 21,000 feet where no man had trodden. One of the native porters suggested that these were made by "a wild man of the snows". At intervals during succeding years other explorers, in other districts of

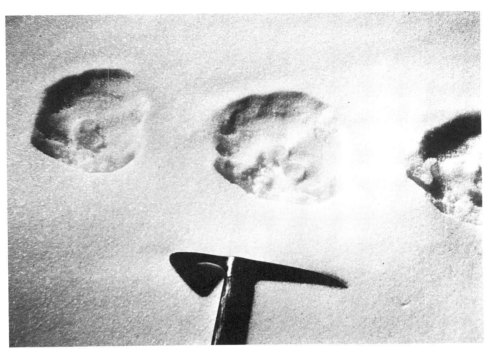

142 "Yeti" footprints at 17,500 feet

the Himalaya, saw similar prints; and one of them was told they belonged to a creature described in Tibetan as *metch kangmi*, which he translated freely as "Abominable Snowman". Frank Smythe photographed some of these prints in 1937. *Plate 142*, taken by John Jackson of the 1955 Kangchenjunga Expedition, shows two clear "yeti" prints with the head of an ice-axe—10½ inches across—for comparison of size. The three front toes and the fainter impression of two hinder toes are characteristic, as is also the placing of the prints exactly behind each other which makes it certain that the creature is either two-legged or a four-legged animal walking erect on the two hind legs. The Sherpas believe that these are the prints of the terrible *Yeti*. Modern scientists incline to the belief that they are the prints of a rare species of bear. Who is right?

The *Yeti* is a figure in Buddhist mythology, a fearsome earth-spirit resembling an ape-man and capable of such diverse feats as biting off the head of a yak and walking with his feet turned backwards. Since demons as well as gods are sacred to the Buddhist, any evidence the Himalayan monasteries may possess is kept secret from unbelievers; which is why the tenuous clues followed by Ralph Izzard of the *Daily Mail* Expedition ended in frustration. Izzard did indeed find some curious excrement, containing the fur of rabbit-sized rodents as well as vegetable matter, but this could have been the excrement of eagles or

257

panthers. The relation of the mysterious footprints to the *Yeti* has no foundation except superstition, though it is not hard to find Himalayan natives who claim to have seen the monster.

A Russian scientist, Professor Pronin, reported that in 1958 he saw a number of simian-looking creatures running away to vanish in the high snows of the Pamirs. In subsequent years three Soviet expeditions went there to search, but found no sign of any such creature. Edouard Wyss-Dunant, of the 1952 Swiss Everest Expedition, found the three-toed tracks in the snows of the Khumbu Basin. At one point a great rock blocked the way across the snow, and the creature had crossed it. Wyss-Dunant examined the snow on the other side of the rock and found that the landing had been made "on all fours". From this he deduced that the animal was very probably a bear; one capable of living in conditions of intense cold and given to walking erect, as some bears are known to do. There is such a bear, *Selenarcios tibetanus*, which had been seen and identified in Eastern Tibet by a German scientist-explorer. But in spite of all the footprints, it has never been seen by a European in the Himalaya.

So there is a mystery still, and the Abominable Snowman, close kin to that "Missing Link" of our grandfathers' day, may be waiting some-where in the Himalaya for some fast-moving expedition of the future to catch him unawares.

In 1958 an American Expedition climbed Gasherbrum I, known as the Hidden Peak. It included Pete Schoening, the man whose astonishing feat of belaying on K2 in 1953 saved the lives of five men. Dhaulagiri was climbed in 1960, and Gosainthan, last and least of the fourteen great ones, in 1964. The "musts" of exceptional height had been cleared off the board and mountaineers could get back (as Dr Tom Longstaff had phrased it) to the real enjoyment of their sport.

The rising tide of mountaineering had not waited for the finishing-off of the *Achttausenders*. From all over the world, now, came climbers eager for adventure on the great mountains. Indians and Pakistanis, Australians and New Zealanders, Argentinians and Japanese, joined the ranks of mountaineers from Europe and the United States. Two years after Everest an all-Indian expedition climbed Kamet (25,447 feet), which had only been climbed once before; one point about this ascent gave particular pleasure to all Himalayan mountaineers—the successful party on the summit included four Sherpas. The often-attempted Rakaposhi (25,550 feet) was climbed in 1958 by a British-Pakistani Forces' expedition. There was an expedition from the Argentine climbing in the Himalaya while two British parties were climbing in the Andes of Peru and Bolivia—a prime hunting-ground for beautiful unclimbed peaks—and a French expedition led by the

143 Kamet (25,447 feet) on the Tibetan border

144 Rakaposhi, 25,550 feet

145 The Towers of Paine from Lake Pehoe

famous Chamonix guide Lionel Terray made new ascents on the fantastic Towers of Paine in Tierra del Fuego (*Plate 145*).

One of the results of motor-racing is the improvement of performance in less specialised cars. In the same way the triumphs on the giant peaks raised the standards of mountaineering so that climbers could attempt some of the lower summits whose ascent had previously been thought impossible. Of Ama Dablam, the huge fang that stands sentinel on the approaches to Everest, Sir John Hunt wrote: "This mountain . . . rises to 22,700 feet and appears utterly inaccessible." Yet it was climbed by a British party who finished the ascent up the sheer ice-wall seen immediately below the summit in *Plate 146*. In 1957 Machapu-chare, the spectacular Fish's Tail, was climbed to within 150 feet of its blue-ice summit pinnacle 22,958 feet above the sea. One of the party was Wilfred Noyce, who had made the route to the South Col of Everest in 1953 and was killed in 1962 on Peak Garmo during the British-Soviet Expedition to the Caucasus. "Machapuchare," wrote Noyce after that climb, "fits into the growing pattern of Himalayan mountaineering. The highest peaks have been climbed, chiefly be-cause experience has increased and men know progressively that they can do better than has been done before." The ascent of the Mustagh Tower in the Karakoram, another "inaccessible", clinched the matter. The obsession with mere height has passed from Himalayan climbing, as the obsession with mere danger passed from the Alps of Europe. Once again mountaineers are choosing their mountain because it has some attraction other than great altitude or a reputation for danger.

"No end is visible or even conceivable to this kingdom of adventure," Mallory wrote of the Himalaya. It is just as true today. Hundreds of peaks higher than 20,000 feet await the first climbers. Thousands of summits higher than any in Europe stand above the lovely valleys of Nepal and Kumaon, Hunza and Ladakh, Kulu and Spiti, all un-climbed. For the man or woman whose eyes (in Rickmers' phrase) have feet, this is surely the dawn of a new Golden Age.

260

31. Summit of Gran Paradiso   *H. N. Collinson*

146 The face by which Ama Dablam was climbed

147 A Canadian rockface

Epilogue

To express his highest sensation of well-being, his feeling of complete satisfaction with life, Man has no apter phrase than *to feel on top of the world*. It contains the germ of the reason why mountains are climbed.

The expression of a climber's attitude to mountains, or to climbing, is hardly possible in words. Many mountaineers and many writers of books about mountains have made the attempt and failed. Sir Leslie Stephen, great Alpine climber and essayist, implied that there was no way of explaining, to a non-climber, why men climbed mountains; it was a matter of personal taste, and *de gustibus non disputandum*. "No more argument is possible than if I were to say that I liked eating olives, and someone asserted that I really eat them only out of affectation. My reply would be simply to go on eating olives; and I hope the reply of mountaineers will be to go on climbing Alps." This is not much help to the inquiring person who—not himself hearing the voice that calls the mountaineer—wants to know what sort of voice it is. Mallory's answer when he was asked why he wanted to climb Everest—"Because it is there"—is no more helpful. His questioner knew already that it was there; what he wanted to know was why anyone should want to do more than let it stay there.

One thing at least is clear: there is no material gain in climbing a mountain. The thing is useless, like poetry, and dangerous, like love-making. To some people—only a very small percentage of people—mountaineering appears to be as essential and satisfactory as poetry or love-making are to some others. What, then, is the root and germ of this essentiality, this satisfaction? The stories in the brief survey of mountaineering history which this book has aimed at have used, for lack of better terms, words like *achievement*, *conquest*, *success* and *triumph*; but all these have connotations removed from the real meaning of a mountain ascent. The climbers themselves, the characters in the stories, have shown themselves widely varying in their apparent reasons for doing what they did. Men rarely do anything from a single reason. A multitude of causes, inseparable even by the most skilled of psycho-analysts, make up the effect of a human action; and when the central cause is indefinable in words it is easier to explain the action in terms of the others. Thus one may say that he climbs for physical exercise,

263

148 Ama Dablam from the Dudh Kosi

another for the view from the top, another because he likes the thrill of the thing. They will be telling the truth, but only part of the truth; these are extraneous reasons, and the central reason is still unexpressed because it is as inexpressible in words as an orchestral passage from a Brahms symphony. Indeed, perhaps music will one day convey the real nature of the mountaineer's passion, though so far no great musician has been a great mountaineer. But even then—it would need a mountaineer-musician to understand the music.

To the man who thinks mountaineering and rock-climbing foolish and inexplicable pastimes, then, no comprehensible explanation of their attraction can be given. But perhaps the nub of the matter may be approached a little closer by recalling that mountaineering as a sport grew with the growing complexity and stress of life. It is an escapist occupation, filling an increasing need felt by an increasing number of people. To these it gives a simplification of being that is like a revelation, stripping away the vast unnecessary load of cares and tensions forced upon them by the modern way of life. Existence is reduced to getting up and not falling off; there is no room for anything else on the great bare slabs and the clean sheer snowslopes. And when the thing is done, when by a man's own skill and nerve he has worked out the difference between life and death, he experiences an uplift of the spirit that has little to do with conquest or triumph. Somehow he has linked himself—for a moment only—with something far greater than himself; as Herbert Tichy sensed on Cho Oyu, when he felt that he was a part of everything around him.

264

149 "Greenland's icy mountains"

This feeling, or something like it, comes to all who climb. It may be on the first ascent of a mighty peak, on a much-climbed British hill, or after climbing *"Felicity. 20 feet. Very Severe."* A modern rock-climber, dangling from a steel piton driven into a crack below an overhang, might deny with indignation that his sport produces any such mystical result; and indeed it can be buried beneath the mere human satisfaction of technical achievement. But he would be the first to maintain that there is something more to his rock-climbing than the pleasure of banging in metal pegs and hauling himself up by them. This "something more" is the indefinable reason why men climb.

In Britain today there are nearly 200 climbing clubs, and many who climb regularly are not members of clubs. The Central Council for Physical Recreation, the Outward Bound schools, the Boy Scouts Association and a great number of other organisations both educational and industrial are every year giving thousands of youngsters the chance of mountaineering. In the United States thousands more are learning the craft on courses like the rock-climbing seminars held in the Rocky Mountain National Park. Of these thousands it may be only a hundred or even less that will hear the clear call of the great hills and become the mountaineers of the future. For them there is no narrowing of the mountain horizon, though so many summits have been attained since Whymper climbed the Matterhorn a hundred years ago. If the inexhaustible treasury of the Himalaya is too far afield there are the great ranges of Greenland, with summits more than 12,000 feet high; there are new ascents to be made in the mountains of Persia and

Turkey; and in British and American hills new routes are being "put up" every weekend on their profusion of rock-faces.

But it does not take a first ascent to put you on top of the world. The few who get the chance of attempting the "inaccessible" Changabang above the Rishi Gorge, or mighty Himalayan peaks still virgin like Taweche and Balakun, will not be specially privileged in this respect. You may climb the Matterhorn or Snowdon a score of times and find it a different mountain on each occasion, and your own first ascent of any peak is—for you—the climb into the unknown, though thousands have made it before you. For mountains are both changeless and ever changing. Symbols of eternity, they yet (like men) suffer the black storms and the scars of time; and their heads, too, turn white with winter. But beneath the sparkle of the new snow and the drifting clouds they are always the same, holding steadfastly in their sanctuaries that same undying flame which Man finds within himself, when he climbs to their summits.

150 In the Sat Dag mountains of Turkey

266

Unclimbed Peaks:
151 Taweche   152 Balakun

153 Changabang and Kalanka

154 Cornish sea-cliffs: Ochre Slab

32. Gabelhorn, Trifthorn and Triftglescher from Sunnega   *A. Kirkham*

55 "Artificial" climbing

156 Shrike route, Clogwyn du'r Arddu

157 The Adang Kamin, Dolomites

Index